ALL OUT OF LEEDS

A DI ADAMS MYSTERY

KIM M. WATT

For further information contact www.kmwatt.com

Cover design: Monika McFarland, www.ampersandbookcovers.com

Editor: Lynda Dietz, www.easyreaderediting.com

ISBN ebook: 978-1-067011-60-4

ISBN Ingrams paperback: 978-1-067011-62-8

ISBN KDP paperback: 978-1-067011-61-1

First Edition May 2024

10 9 8 7 6 5 4 3 2 1

To everyone who
knows the power of
ducks and chocolate.
Thank you for being here.

A NOTE BEFORE WE BEGIN

Lovely people, thank you so much for joining me on yet another foray into the strange and secretive wilds of Yorkshire. Here be dragons, and treachery, and ducks …

But, a warning! If you are ambling over from Toot Hansell, you may find that tea breaks are in short supply (coffee is plentiful however, due to the needs of stressed DIs and invisible dogs), and there is a distinct dearth of cake. Although DI Adams will already be known to you, these tales are a little darker and toothier than the Beaufort stories, so I want to let you know that right from the start (although they are still my stories. There will be ducks and absurdity).

In the event that you're already familiar with Toot Hansell, this tale picks up after the events of *A Manor of Life & Death,* where Adams encountered Dandy properly for the first time. She has yet to make the move to Skipton, although the dragons and the redoubtable ladies of the Toot Hansell Women's Institute have already taken up quite a lot of her time.

And finally, regarding those ducks … if you have yet to read the DI Adams prequel, *What Happened in London,* I would recommend starting there in order to fully understand the relevance of ducks and chocolate bars (and also Adams' horror of bridges). But it's not vital to this story, and you won't be lost without it.

Suffice it to say: in case of monsters, always keep your duck handy.

Have you got yours?

Then let's begin …

1

AN UNPROMISING CASE

DI ADAMS WENT UP AND OVER THE HIGH WOODEN FENCE WITH rather less grace than she would have liked, following a shout of alarm on the other side. She snagged a trouser leg on the top and stumbled as she landed, dropping into a crouch and catching herself on her hands. The garden was empty, the ground a slick expanse of mud interspersed with weedy, dandelion-strewn patches, and there was a network of puddles in the centre reflecting the sky serenely, even though it hadn't rained in at least two weeks. Yorkshire was putting on an uncharacteristically dry start to the summer, but going by the wetness on her knee where it had hit the ground, the drought hadn't hit here yet.

Adams launched herself up again, ready to sprint to the fence on the opposite side, where muddy footprints on the wood indicated her quarry had already made their escape. As she did so, three large dogs that were evidently the cause of the alarmed shout spun toward her, and she stopped short. They were making the sort of furious noise her head immediately classed as baying rather than barking, and showing an alarming array of teeth. They shot toward her, chains rattling after them, and while Adams assumed they were attached somewhere, she wasn't waiting around to make sure. She spun back to the fence, jumping to grab the top, already kicking her boots into the slats to help herself up, and a grey, dog-like form appeared at the top. It launched itself easily into the garden, dreadlocks flying gracefully and allowing a mercifully brief glimpse of red eyes, luminous as LEDs. The dogs stopped so hard one of them somersaulted twice, wrapping itself up in its chain and howling piteously, while the other two beat a tail-tucked retreat toward the house, yelping in terror. The dreadlocked creature stopped at the edge of a puddle and watched them go curiously.

"Good boy," Adams hissed, dropping back to the ground, then sprinted across the garden, slipping in the mud but not slowing.

Up and over a fence that swayed alarmingly, not used to such rough treatment, and she was into another scruffy backyard, this one a bit less muddy, made up of bare dirt with thin grass patches growing here and there, everything worn thin by neglect and indifference, and full of the ubiquitous discarded buckets and fallen bricks that seem to breed in unattended gardens everywhere. Ahead of her, a slight form in an oversized red hoody was just vanishing over a brick wall that marked the end of the row of houses, and she shouted, "West Yorkshire Police! *Stop!*"

Of course they didn't stop, but as the kid vanished she heard a yelp from beyond the wall. She looked down at her mud-encrusted boots, sighed quietly, and jogged across the garden to heft herself up just enough to hook her elbows over the top of the wall. She peered down at DC James Hamilton, who was pinning Hoody to the ground almost casually, not looking even slightly out of breath.

"Nice one, James," she said.

"Yep," he replied, and, to his credit, he didn't look too

smug. A little, maybe, but she supposed that was fair. Her trousers were only marginally less muddy than her boots, sweat was sticking her shirt to her shoulders, and she'd scraped her hand at some point, blood beading the graze. He, on the other hand, looked barely more pink-cheeked than normal, and his well-groomed blond hair was behaving with the sort of obedience Adams found mystifying. He hauled Hoody to his feet, not ungently. He really was just a kid, probably still in his teens, with a spattering of facial hair trying to establish a little bit of authority somewhere on his chin.

The kid glared at them both. "Police brutality," he spat. "Just bloody racial profiling, this."

Adams cleared her throat, raising her eyebrows at him.

"You're the worst sort," Hoody said. "Acting like some bloody white oppressor. Traitor. I'll have you both for harassment."

James looked at Adams. "You are pretty oppressive," he said. "I think it's the coffee habit."

"I think it's my superior rank and experience," Adams said. "I'll be around in a minute." She dropped back to the ground and went to find a gate, heading down a narrow passageway between the old red brick of the house and the wall, smelling damp and disrepair, and feeling eyes on her. It was the sort of place where everything was observed, but no one saw anything. Not officially, anyway. The dreadlocked dog was investigating the corners of the garden still, but she didn't worry about him too much. He seemed to have his own way of navigating walls, doors, gates, and everything else for that matter.

She dragged the gate closed behind her, the wood scraping on the broken concrete of the path, then headed around the corner to where James was cuffing the boy, ignoring him demanding a lawyer, a civil rights activist, and his mum.

The kid glared at Adams as she joined them. "Fascists," he said, and then added after a moment's thought, "Down with the system."

Adams picked his backpack up and checked the side pockets, then unzipped it to peer inside. "Where were you off to in such a hurry, then?" she asked.

"Visiting my grandmother," he replied and grinned at her.

She raised her eyebrows at his red hoodie, then went back to the bag. "That so?" she asked, and pulled a pouch out of the main compartment. It looked like a slightly oversized pencil case, but it didn't feel like pens inside. She showed it to James, then unzipped it, revealing a nest of small Ziploc bags. She tweezed one out between her fingers, holding it up in front of them so the four pills inside were visible. "How big do your grandma's eyes get on this, then?"

The kid barely looked at the pouch, just lifted his chin and glared at her. "That's not mine. You planted it. Bloody pigs."

Adams looked from the bag to the detective constable, and said, "What do you think, James? Do you reckon we planted this?"

"I'd say it's two against one. Don't think he's going to get too far with that."

The kid scowled at them both. "Pigs. All as corrupt as each other."

"He's got the patter down, at least," James said, and started propelling the kid toward the car. "May as well take him in. It's something, isn't it?"

Adams made a non-committal sound. It might be something, but only in the sense of it being an arrest on the books. The kid was nothing but a courier. The likelihood of him knowing anything beyond the next very small fish in the chain was minimal – he'd be at least a couple of contacts removed from anyone who mattered, and no one was going to be stepping in to help him. Odds were, all an arrest record would do was take away another option in a life already pretty short on them. She'd much rather have just channelled her mum to put the frights on him, then let him go. But on the other hand, it *was* an arrest, and they'd been pulled onto this case to get a few people off the streets and make it look good in the local news, nothing else. No one was expecting them to make any breakthroughs. So she supposed James was right, it was something. There was even the possibility that they might get him to talk, but she doubted it. It wouldn't be worth the kid's while.

THEY GOT HIM INTO ADAMS' car and headed back to the station, while the dreadlocked almost-dog panted over James's seat, making him jerk his head away a few times then twist around to glare at the kid.

"Stop it," he said.

"What?" Hoody asked.

"Blowing on my ear."

"Don't flatter yourself, mate," the kid said, leaning back in the seat with a look of absolute disgust on his face. "I'm adding sexual harassment to the list, like."

Adams looked in the rear-view mirror at the dreadlocked creature, his tongue lolling out of his mouth in something that was far too like a grin to be accidental. She was sure the kid would be including menacing with a hairy animal to his complaints if he could see Dandy, but he couldn't. As far as Adams could tell, only she could. Or her and some other … individuals. Non-human individuals, which she didn't like thinking about too much. Plus one journalist, which was even worse than the non-humans. She directed a very small shake of her head at the rear-view mirror, but Dandy just leaned forward so his jaw was almost touching James's shoulder, making the detective constable growl and look at the kid again.

"*Stop it.*"

"I'm not *doing* anything!"

Adams decided to ignore them, navigating the snarl of afternoon traffic that curled around Leeds, glittering in the flood of sunlight and turning the green spaces luminous and unfamiliar, full of a strange and half-seen magic.

At the station, she found herself back at her desk while James got the kid processed and shut in a cell to percolate a while. With nothing else requiring her attention she poked at her computer, knowing she had reports to write and really wishing there was something much more interesting to do, although preferably not involving fences or dogs other than Dandy. He'd given up on harassing James and was drifting around the room like a heavily matted, Labrador-sized shadow, investigating everyone's empty coffee cups. She tried to click her fingers at him unobtrusively, but he ignored her. He seemed mainly motivated by caffeine, which she related to strongly, and seemed far too fitting for comfort.

Adams wasn't entirely sure that he might not be a figment of her own imagination, except for the fact that he was surprisingly effective at destroying her coffee mugs. Well, not destroying them, but emptying them and also getting into the bin after the coffee grounds. Which weren't the worst things in the world, really. If one was going to have a dog, an invisible, possibly not quite real dog was a pretty convenient option. Her landlord could hardly complain about him, and he didn't seem to need an awful lot of care. She'd tried buying him dog food and worming tablets, figuring they were sort of universally required pet things, but he'd gagged at the first and vanished for three days at the sight of the second.

She'd decided the easiest way to deal with him was to guard her coffee and not ask too many questions. He came and went as he pleased, fended for himself, and mostly seemed interested in just following her around. She had yet to decide whether it was simply for her coffee or if he was actually going to make himself useful at some point, but the company was surprisingly nice. She'd never needed a lot of companionship, but Leeds was a long way from London. A long way from Sunday lunch at her mum's, and the annoying, permanent presence of her brothers, and her father's gentle inquisitiveness, and simply the feel of a city that had been part of her all her life. It hadn't left a gap, exactly, but maybe there was an *absence*, and the silent, ghostly presence of the sort-of dog filled it in a way she couldn't quite explain.

Adams opened one of the lingering reports in which she'd put *carjacker arrested, no injuries,* which apparently was not sufficiently detailed for government working. She looked at the flashing cursor for a bit, thinking that it really did cover everything, and that she wasn't a novelist, and maybe if she just added *rude carjacker promptly arrested, no injuries sustained* it might do the trick, and also that another coffee might not help, but it certainly wouldn't hurt. She'd reached the conclusion that coffee was certainly an answer of sorts when someone loomed over the desk, and she looked up at DCI Temple, also known as the Temper, who looked to be living up to his name at the moment.

"Busy enough, Adams?" he asked.

"Just catching up on some paperwork," she said. "We brought in a kid, one of the runners. Never know, we might get something out of him after he's been sitting for a bit."

Temple grunted, giving the impression that he had about

as much hope of that as she did. He tapped his mobile phone on the desk lightly. "Just sent you a new case," he said.

"Okay," Adams said. "I thought we were all-in on this whole drug thing." There had been a distinctly castigating write up in the national papers regarding Leeds being a complete den of iniquity – the birthplace of all crime in the north, rife with countywide drug runners, fraudsters, and thieves, and probably not wiping its feet before it came indoors, either. Adams didn't think it was any worse than most places, but the mayor was not happy, and was making his opinion felt.

Temper made a noise that was alarmingly close to a growl. "Bloody PR campaign, more like. We can't all be on it just because some sodding politician's got his knickers in a knot, like he's not sneaking to the bathroom every five minutes himself. We do have other cases, you know." He gave Adams a glare that suggested he thought she was disagreeing with him.

"Sure," she said. "What is it?"

He tapped the phone on the desk again. "Check your inbox. I think this one fits your skill set."

Adams tried not to look sceptical as she clicked over to her inbox and pulled the case up. "Harassment?" she said. "Really? That hardly seems like our department."

Temple raised his eyebrows. "I don't know about London, Adams, but up here the DCI decides what cases are ours, and the DIs get on with their bloody job."

"Of course, boss. Just … harassment?"

"The complainant, Scott Samuels, is the proprietor of a jewellery shop. Apparently one Gladys Hudson dropped some family heirloom necklace off to get repaired, and now keeps going back asking them where it is, even though they've already returned it to her. They're worried she's going to turn it into some big thing, ruin their reputation."

"Right," Adams said. "Surely there's CCTV or ..."

Temper waved impatiently. "You can sort all that out. Just get yourself on this. Take James with you. The old dears always love him."

Adams grimaced, trying not to let it show too much, and Temper scowled at her.

"Problem, Adams?"

She hesitated, then said, "I get that we don't need to all be on the drugs thing, but this seems really straightforward. Does it really need two of us?"

"Well, it's still a potential jewellery theft, and around here you take the cases you're given. Plus you've been hanging out with all those oldies in Toot Hansell. You seem pretty good with that demographic, so it makes sense for you to keep working with them."

Adams didn't answer straight away. She wasn't quite sure how to without sounding either difficult or like a soft southerner, which was apparently a thing, as was being a whinger, although she wasn't sure if that had any geographical basis. There was also being a big city cop with a chip on her shoulder. She wasn't sure if the north just really didn't like Londoners, or if it was her specifically. And that was before she even got into the official reason she moved up from London, which was attributed to a traumatic case that had caused her to have a mental health break. That reason was only half-true, although she did wonder about the other half sometimes, especially when she was wrestling stolen deli meats off an invisible dog. Or dealing with the little village of Toot Hansell and its bizarre cast of inhabitants, not all of whom were human. She supposed she should just be happy that she was getting any cases to herself at all and not being constantly supervised.

So she just said, "Right, boss. I'll grab James and we'll get on it."

"Good," he said. "Try not to upset anyone."

She nodded slightly and watched him walk away. Dandy trailed after him, his nose twitching hopefully, and Adams looked through the file a bit more carefully, but there was nothing more to it. It was essentially a *he said, she said, they said* situation, which should get sorted out pretty quickly through the CCTV.

She texted James then got up, grabbing her jacket from the back of the chair, not that she really needed it with the oddly warm weather they had going on at the moment. She headed for the door, almost bumping into a slim, compact woman with sleek blonde hair curled into a ferociously neat bun.

"Adams," the woman said, smiling at her. "Saw you and James brought a courier in."

Adams nodded. DI Lindsay Marks was one of those people she felt she should dislike at least a little for being so effortlessly efficient and permanently well-groomed, but she couldn't seem to. She was immediately aware of her muddy trousers again, though. "Just a runner. Doubt we'll get anything from him."

"Hey, it's something," Lindsay said, raising a water bottle at her in a salute. "I appreciate you two jumping on this. You heading out again?"

"Temper's given us something else. Shouldn't take much to sort out."

"Oh? Let me know if you need anything. Local knowledge and that. Sooner you're back helping me, the better." Lindsay sighed, and added in a lower voice, "Plus it's such a bloody boys' club around here. I need you, Adams. Otherwise I'm going to be in spitting contests with the lot of them by the end of the week. And I will *not* lose."

Adams snorted. Lindsay both looked like she'd never spat in her life, and also like she absolutely would win if she put her mind to it. "I believe you," she said. "Catch you soon."

She headed for the parking garage, Dandy loping ahead of her down the stairs. By the time she got out onto the pavement James was already waiting for her, a tall, skinny lad who looked like he hadn't really grown into his limbs yet. He was a decent sort, and he'd be a decent detective too, given a bit of time, but she still felt the urge to ask him if he'd remembered his lunch money every time she saw him.

"What've we got?" he asked. "Have they given us something more on the drug case?"

"No," she said, beeping the car open. "Possible jewellery theft."

"Oh, interesting. Armed?"

"No."

"Safe-cracking?"

"No."

"Complicated heist involving misdirection and devious disguises?"

"No. Just sounds like a disagreement, to be honest," she said, climbing into the car.

He sighed, his shoulders slumping. "We're being fobbed off again, aren't we?"

"Sorry," Adams said, "I think that's what you get for hanging out with the southerner."

James snorted, folding his long legs into the passenger side of the VW Golf. "Yeah, I don't think so. I'd've probably been on this one anyway."

He didn't elaborate and she didn't ask. James had never asked her about her supposed mental health break. He seemed quite happy to trust her, so she returned the favour. Sometimes that was the way the best work relationships functioned. Mutual acceptance without too much personal stuff getting in the way.

2

COFFEE AND COMPLICATIONS

ADAMS DECIDED TO GET THE OLD DEARS PART OF THE equation out of the way first, since, in her experience, it was quite likely to be the most challenging, and apparently no one had even bothered to take a statement so far. From the notes, the desk sergeant who'd taken the complaint hadn't questioned Scott Samuels's depiction of Gladys Hudson as *getting on a bit and quite, shall we say, eccentric*. Adams didn't particularly think that meant much, and definitely didn't think it had any bearing on the potential missing necklace, but there was only one way to find out.

Gladys lived in a rambling two-storey, or possibly three-storey (it was hard to tell through the jumble of old leaning trees and exuberant bushes that surrounded it) house on the tangled streets that encircled Roundhay Park and rambled somewhat indecisively through shady green slopes and properties that ran the scale from rundown terraces to gloriously renovated old Victorian beasts. Gladys's house was more closely related to the latter, set on a corner plot and surrounded by a high wrought iron fence with matching gates, hiding its secrets behind a heavy skirt of greenery. Just the upper storey peered out above the trees, a confusion of gables and small, high windows.

Adams parked by the kerb and got out, climbing a couple of old stone steps to the gate and staring through the smooth-worn metal bars at the house while Dandy stood on the pavement panting at her, and James examined the garden.

"Nice roses," he said.

Adams looked at the profusion of red and dusky pink blooms, and made an agreeing noise. They were about the only plants she could identify, but now they had a better view of the inside she could see it was stuffed with crowded flowerbeds in vibrant colours, everything growing at a different height and doing the sort of thing one saw in flower shows and magazine shoots. It almost seemed at odds with the building's more formal edges, a well-preserved old place of the sort that had sprung up when all the money had been in textiles and mines in the north. Even now, wearing a coverlet of ivy over its old, stained grey stone, there was something of the genteel old lady to it. One almost expected it to be sipping gin from a cut-crystal glass.

Adams checked the gate, but there was nothing as modern as a call button on it, so she pushed it open and led the way up a well-kept gravel path. A koi pond slumbered off to the right, the flat, spreading leaves of lilies pocking it and the surface dimpled with movement below, and little paths and patches of grass ran everywhere, forming neatly trimmed sections of lawn that seemed to beg for croquet and garden parties. The hum of traffic was muffled, even though the street outside was a reasonably busy one. It was as if the house held itself in a cocoon, turning its back on the world outside and creating its own pocket in reality, suspended in sunlight and silence like luminous amber. It was both peaceful and oddly *heavy,* and Adams looked around for

Dandy, but he'd evidently decided he had better things to do than make house calls. There was only James to accompany her, which made her more uneasy than it should have.

Adams knocked briskly on the old wooden door, spotting softly peeling paint on the sills of the closest windows, and a scuffed base to the door. Nothing truly damaged, just age showing around the edges. Everything about the place had the sense of being maintained just well enough to keep going but nothing more, no upgrades to triple-glazed windows, or well-insulated PVC doors. It felt as if the years had got away on the house and it was yet to arrive in the twenty-first century, but was perfectly happy with itself nonetheless, self-contained and timeless.

The door was opened by a stocky man who looked to be a little younger than Adams, probably in his early thirties, with soft ginger hair and a teal blue polo shirt with *Home Angels* embroidered over his chest. He smiled at them, exposing slightly yellowed but neat teeth. "Can I help you?"

"DI Adams and DC Hamilton," Adams said, pointing at each of them. "We're here to talk to Ms Hudson about a missing necklace."

"Ah," the man said, giving a resigned nod and stepping back from the door. "I thought that might happen. She's just in the parlour. Come on through."

He turned and led the way into the shadows of the house. James and Adams looked at each other.

Parlour, James mouthed, his eyebrows raised.

Adams smiled slightly. She wasn't sure she'd ever heard anyone actually use the term in real life before either.

They followed the young man through a hall, past stairs scaling the wall on one side, and down a broad, darkly carpeted corridor. Panels of complex, multi-hued wallpaper were framed with varnished wood, sconces leaning over them and flushing the design with colour. It looked almost as if it had been done by hand, delicate birds and curling foliage dancing across the old paper. The wood was dark and smooth, and everything smelled softly of polish and lemons and old roses crumbling to dust in the corners.

The young man showed them into a sitting room full of chubby armchairs and overstuffed sofas, a cacophony of clashing fabrics and designs that mingled modern pink furs and sequins with faded paisleys and tartans, and said, "I'll just let Gladys know you're here."

"What was your name?" Adams asked.

"Olly," he said. "Well, Oliver. Oliver Davidson."

"And you're her home help? Or carer?"

"Home help," he said. "I come in a few times a week. Gladys doesn't need an awful lot doing, though. She's pretty independent. I mostly just do the heavier lifting – clean the windows and scrub under the fridge, that kind of thing."

"Anyone else work here?" Adams asked.

"Someone comes in to do the garden a couple of times a month, I think," he said.

"Same company as you?"

He shook his head. "No, I don't know who they are."

"You've not seen a van or anything?"

He scratched his chin, a soft coating of rust-coloured stubble scraping beneath his fingertips. "No, I've never actually met them. I guess our schedules don't overlap."

"Alright," Adams said, and nodded at the door. "If you can tell her we're here that'd be great."

Olly wandered off, hands in his pockets, and Adams and James looked at each other.

"Big house for one person," James said.

"I guess it's what you're used to," Adams said, examining the room. There was an electronic drum kit in one corner, and an old record player hooked up to flashy speakers. She wondered if Gladys had grandkids or something who came in to play with this sort of stuff, as it seemed to bear zero relation to the mash-up of colours and textures going on in the room. She thought it might be giving her a headache.

Movement in the hall pulled her attention away from fascinated contemplation of an eye-wateringly bright purple sheepskin draped over a rocking horse that looked like it cost more than her car. She wasn't quite sure what she expected from Gladys Hudson. Given the house, a pale and fine-boned old spinster with an accent that could shatter glass, sporting a tweed twin set and pearls, perhaps.

Instead, the woman who walked in, while pale and fine boned, appeared to be wearing about three different floral sundresses, going by the multiple colours and floating layers. They were all sleeveless, exposing creased but startlingly well-muscled arms, and her white hair was piled on her head in a careless bun, skewered with a hairpin and a rose. Giant plastic pineapple earrings dangled from her ears, and she was barefoot on the old carpet, her toenails painted luminous orange.

"Hello, detectives," she said, smiling at them, and her accent was broad Yorkshire. "I've just asked Olly to make us a pot of tea. Can I get you anything else? Is tea alright? Would you prefer coffee?"

"If it's going," Adams said, trying not to stare at Gladys's hands. *Salt* and *Pink* were tattooed across the knuckles, and she couldn't work out what the connection was. Pink Himalayan salt?

"Ooh, yes, I've got the loveliest machine," Gladys said, clapping her hands together. "It's *so* fancy. And fun! I'll do it!" She rushed back out again, almost running on the balls of her feet, and Adams and James exchanged uncertain looks.

A moment later, Olly reappeared. "Apparently my coffee machine skills aren't good enough for guests," he said. "How does everyone want their drinks?"

"Um – tea, two sugars, milk," James said.

"Just black coffee," Adams said.

"Right. Back soon." He vanished again, leaving them looking around the room at the big, heavily framed oil paintings and the huge bay windows that opened onto the garden. Somehow, despite the wildly overgrown nature of it, plenty of light still poured into the room and it was almost uncomfortably warm. Adams plucked at the front of her shirt, glad she'd left her jacket in the car. The heat wasn't the only thing making her uncomfortable, though. She thought she'd have been more comfortable with some supercilious posh heiress, rather than Gladys. There was something uneasily Toot Hansell about those tattoos.

It wasn't long before Gladys came rushing back in, clutching a plate of biscuits, trailed rather more sedately by Olly with a pot of tea, cups, a small jug of milk in the shape of a cow, and a very old and very expensive-looking sugar bowl with silver tongs in it. He also had a cup of coffee that was strong enough Adams could smell it from across the room. He handed it to her then set about putting the tea out on a low coffee table cluttered with travel magazines and a half-played game of Solitaire.

Gladys descended into a chair like a tropical bird coming in to roost, skirts fluttering around her, and accepted a large mug topped with a swirl of frothy milk and an overabundance of cinnamon from Olly. "Thank you, love." She sniffed deeply at the cinnamon, then wrinkled her nose and rubbed it, snorting.

"Every time," Olly said, barely looking at her as he swirled the tea in the pot.

"So rude," Gladys said, without any heat, then looked at Adams. "Now, Olly tells me you're here about my necklace. Have you found it?"

"Well, we're just starting," Adams said, trying the coffee. It was alarmingly strong, even for her, but smooth and rich at the same time. "Can you run us through what happened?"

Gladys sipped her cappuccino, then wiped froth off her top lip. "Are you sure you don't want milk with yours? The frother's quite exceptional."

"I prefer without."

"And it's delicious with some cinnamon. Do you like cinnamon?"

"I do," Adams said, "but not in my coffee."

"Oh well," Gladys said. "Each to their own. More cinnamon for me." She had another sip, squeezing her eyes shut in pleasure.

"The necklace," Adams suggested, as Olly handed a little plate of Jammie Dodgers around.

Gladys patted his arm. "Thank you, Olly. He's very good," she added to the detectives. "Such a wonderful help to me."

"You don't even need my help, Gladys," he said. "You just like my company."

"That too," she agreed, and he smiled at her, setting the plate back down.

"I'll leave you to it. Let me know if you need anything." He wandered off, taking a cloth from his pocket as he went and wiping a couple of shelves on the way out.

Adams looked at James, but he already had his notebook out on his lap. He'd been all about notes on his phone when they first met, but she thought she might be starting to rub off on him. "So … the necklace," she repeated.

"Yes," Gladys said. "The necklace. I take it the shop has come to you with their ridiculous accusations?"

"They seem to feel you're harassing them."

"*Harassing* them. They lost my necklace!"

"They claim you collected it," Adams said.

"Of course they do. Covering themselves, is all."

"I see." Adams took another sip of coffee. It was proper,

barista-grade stuff, and she wondered what sort of machine Gladys had. "Why didn't *you* report it, then?"

She sighed, and set her mug down, clasping her tattooed hands in front of her as she leaned forward to examine Adams. "One of the unfortunate things about becoming a woman of a certain age is that one is rarely taken seriously. I was hoping the shop would come to their senses and return it, rather than my having to make it official and end up with police looking at me as you are." She shifted her gaze from Adams to James as she spoke, and he stared back at her in alarm.

"I'm not—" he started, and Gladys cut him off with a wave.

"It's your job to be sceptical. But I'd rather you had a better reason for it than my age."

Adams tried to arrange her expression in the least sceptical manner she could and said, "Tell us your side of things, then."

Gladys examined her for a moment, and Adams had the fleeting thought that the cut-glass aristocrat she'd imagined might've been easier to deal with.

Then Gladys nodded and said, "It's a very old family heirloom. I don't wear it often, but when I took it out the other day I found the clasp had broken. Hardly a large job, so I didn't think it needed specialist care. Just somewhere that does little repairs and so on."

"Of course," Adams said. "Very straightforward."

"Yes, exactly." Gladys nodded vigorously. "But when I went back to collect it on the agreed day, someone had already picked it up, according to them. Me, in fact, which is blatantly impossible. I'm sure they've taken it for themselves. There's no other explanation."

"It was quite valuable?" Adams asked.

"Well, it was very valuable to me. For sentimental reasons,

you know." Gladys thought about it. "But I suppose it is gold, so I imagine it would be quite valuable to some unscrupulous monster."

"Was it insured?"

"No," Gladys said. "One doesn't think of these things."

Adams thought that she for one had certainly never thought of such things, but then she'd never owned a gold necklace or anything else that might have required insuring. Or expected to come into any family heirlooms for that matter. Unless her mother was planning to pass down her knitting needles or something like that.

"Alright," she said aloud. "Do you have any photos of it?"

"No, nothing like that. Why would I have a photo? I can look at it any time I want."

"Any pictures where maybe you're wearing it?" Adams suggested.

"Oh." Gladys tapped her fingers on her mug thoughtfully. "I might be able to find some. I'll see what I can do."

"That's a really good start. Otherwise, if you write down a really detailed description of it, we can maybe get someone to draw up a picture from that. Just so we know what we're looking for, and can use it as a reference when we're asking about it."

"Oh," Gladys said. "Yes, that's a very good idea. Well done, you!" She smiled brightly, and James took a hurried sip of his tea, not quite quickly enough to hide his grin.

"Thanks," Adams said.

"Of course. What else? What can I do to help?"

"Can you walk us through what happened at the jewellery shop?"

"Oh, yes. I went in and I explained what I needed. And a very nice young lady behind the counter gave me these forms and I signed them all. I have a receipt. I'll show you." She jumped up so quickly that James and Adams both grabbed for her mug where it balanced on the edge of the coffee table, and she gave them a quizzical look.

Adams waved her back down. "It's alright, you can show us that later."

"No, no. I'll forget. I'll get Olly to get it now." Gladys said.

Adams started to say something, but was drowned out by Gladys heaving a great breath of air and screaming, *"Olly!"*

Adams barely managed to stop herself from covering her ears, and there was a moment's ringing pause before Olly ambled through the door with his cloth still in his hand.

"You called," he said, smiling at her.

"Can you get the invoice from my desk for the jewellery shop?"

"Of course." He wandered off again, without any great sense of urgency. Adams had a feeling that he was probably quite used to his boss's excitability.

"So the young woman gave you this invoice," she said aloud.

"Yes. I had to bring it back in order to collect the necklace, you see. Which again proves I didn't pick it up, since I still have the form."

"Could anyone have taken the form without you knowing?" James asked. "Copied it, perhaps?"

Gladys shook her head. "I brought it straight home, and it's only me and Olly here. Besides, that young woman said it was *me* who came in. How could it have been? I didn't go back at all!"

"So what happened when you did go back?" Adams asked.

"Well, they hadn't called to update me on anything, but they'd said a week, so I just popped in. That's when they said I'd already collected it and ..." She trailed off, then shook her head firmly. "They must have stolen it themselves. It's the only possible explanation."

Adams wondered if Gladys could have gone back to

collect it and simply forgotten. But while she did seem *odd*, she didn't give the impression of any sort of loss of capacity. So she just drained her mug and said, "Thanks for the coffee. We'll take it from here. If you can find a picture or do that description, though, that would be a huge help."

"Oh, of course," Gladys said, clasping her hands together. "It's wonderful to have such helpful police around the place. Absolutely marvellous."

Movement drew Adams' attention to the door, and she looked around, expecting Olly. Instead a little robot vacuum cleaner came battling across the carpet toward them, a feather duster stuck upright to its top like a palm tree and googly eyes bouncing below.

"Oh, hello, Daffy," Gladys said.

"Daffy?" James said.

"Yes. I just love technology, don't you?" Gladys smiled happily at the vacuum, and Adams got up before it could run into her foot.

"We'll just have a word with Olly before we go."

"Of course." Gladys jumped up. "Where is he with that invoice, anyway?" She rushed out, still armed with her coffee cup, and James and Adams looked at each other without speaking. They didn't have to wait long before Olly appeared, a piece of paper in hand.

"Here we go," he said.

Adams took the invoice, examining it. It didn't tell her much, simply listed one (1) necklace for clasp replacement, along with the date. She handed it to James. "Take a photo of that, can you?" While he shuffled his notebook and phone she looked back at Olly. "Is Gladys—"

Olly raised his hand, interrupting her. "She's really fine. If she says she didn't go in and pick up the necklace, she didn't go in and pick up the necklace. I know she looks like this dotty old lady, but she's not. Not really. Eccentric? Yes. Dotty? No."

Adams nodded. "That was kind of my impression. I just thought I'd check."

"Everyone always does, just because she's a bit weird," Olly said. "I think she's always been like that, though. Just different. Mentally, though, she's absolutely fine."

"Alright," Adams said. "Thanks for your help."

Olly showed them back through the warm, rose-scented hall and out into the garden, and Adams couldn't escape the feeling that the house was leaning over them as they left, vaguely threatening and defensive. Through the gate she glimpsed Dandy waiting by the car, panting in the heat, and she wondered why he hadn't come into the house with her. Normally he'd be anywhere there was a chance of coffee.

"Shop, then?" James asked cheerfully as she pushed through the gate, the noise of the city descending on them along with the scents of exhaust smoke and burning rubber, and Adams didn't answer straight away. She felt as if she were coming up from deep water, everything too loud and too harsh, and part of her wanted to dive back to the safety of the house at the same time as its regard prickled the hair on her neck.

"Adams?" James asked. "You alright?"

"Sure," she said, rubbing her arms. "Just thinking."

About ducks and bridges and the long, slow Thames, hungry and endless and raw.

3

A NECKLACE IS JUST A NECKLACE

THE EARLY AFTERNOON TRAFFIC STOPPED AND STARTED, slowing and snarling into knots of heat and frustration and aggression as people rushed from one side of the city to the other, buried deep in their own thoughts and fears and lives. Adams slipped the car back toward the heart of Leeds without talking, her mind still on the uneasy feel of the house, on Dandy's reluctance and Gladys's wild decor. She was being paranoid. Just because Gladys reminded her of someone from Toot Hansell, where the old, magic bones of the land lay rich and wild, close to the surface and barely concealed, didn't mean it had anything at all to do with such things. It was just a missing necklace. Nothing else. She was seeing ghosts where there were none.

The jewellery shop was just outside the pedestrianised centre, fancy enough to be hanging on the edges of the city's regeneration, but not quite enough to be rubbing shoulders with Harvey Nicks and the big high street chains. The display windows were draped with carefully arranged silver and gold chains, embellished with little pendants or initials, price tags subtle and almost hidden, the lighting rich and imbuing everything with a warm lustre. Heavy watches and finely made ones, slim wedding bands and bling-y engagement rings, hefty signet rings and a bewildering array of earrings filled the remaining space, and one entire section was given over to a collection of strange little crystal animals that looked a little sheepish, as if they hadn't asked for this sort of attention and would rather be languishing under the dust in someone's gran's dining room display cabinet. Adams tried not to jump when Dandy's dreadlocked head appeared in the glass on the inside, cocked as he stared out at her.

They had to be buzzed in, Adams peering through the door and trying to look unthreatening, which James informed her she wasn't very good at. The door clicked open, though, and she raised her eyebrows at him.

"It's because I'm with you," he said. "I'm very approachable."

"Good for you," she said. "See how far that gets you in a riot." Then she pushed the door open before he could ask her if she'd been in many riots in London (not one, as it happened, unless she counted the brawls with her brothers, but three kids probably didn't constitute a riot, no matter what her mum said).

A thin young woman with painfully straight hair smiled at them from behind a counter full of bracelets and delicate chains. "Can I help you?" she asked as the door swung shut behind them, cocooning them into a quiet little haven full of the sound of lift music.

Adams introduced them, and the young woman's face paled even further than it was already. "Are you Meredith Williams?" Adams asked.

"Um, yes," the young woman said, her voice so low it was almost a whisper.

"Great. So you were the one who dealt with Ms Hudson?"

Adams tried to keep her voice as friendly as possible, since Meredith looked like she was about to either keel over or throw up on the spot.

"Yes," she said again, her voice even smaller. "Do you want to talk to my boss?"

"I want to talk to you," Adams said. "You're the one who handled the necklace, right?"

Now Meredith looked like she might cry instead, her nose turning an alarming shade of red against her white cheeks. "I really think you should talk to Scott. Mr Samuels, I mean. My boss?" She was twisting her fingers together so tightly that Adams winced in sympathy, waiting for her knuckles to crack – or something to dislocate. She wondered what was making the young woman quite so nervous, if it was a guilty conscience or some threat her boss was holding over her. She was unlikely to make employee of the month if she'd lost a necklace.

Adams opened her mouth to insist that they wanted to ask Meredith their questions first, then realised both that James was smirking and that the shop was still open. If Temper was worried about press coverage, then reducing a witness to tears in a public place wasn't going to make her any more popular.

"Fine," she said aloud. "We'll talk to him first."

Meredith almost lunged for a phone below the counter, poking the buttons with a shaking hand and whispering into it urgently, half turned away from the detectives. A moment later a lean, palely tanned man wearing a crisp white shirt and well-cut trousers came through a door in the corner of the room, showing too many teeth when he smiled.

"Can I help you, detectives?" he asked.

"Just a few questions on this missing necklace," Adams said.

"The harassment, you mean," the man said, extending a

hand for her to shake. It was dry and long-fingered, the grip firm. "Scott Samuels. I take it you've talked to Ms Hudson, and she's still keeping up this ludicrous story. The necklace isn't *missing*, or if it is, it's nothing to do with us. Meredith did exactly what she was expected to, and Ms Hudson signed for the necklace when she left. I don't know what else to tell you, other than that she really needs to stop. I'll have to take out a restraining order on her otherwise."

"Interesting," Adams said, and pulled her phone out, finding the photo James had sent her. She turned the picture of the invoice to Scott. "This is the invoice Ms Hudson was meant to bring back, and which should've been signed by your shop to prove collection. Ms Hudson's still got it, and it's not signed."

Scott sighed. "A small and regrettable error on Meredith's part. But it doesn't change the fact that Ms Hudson did collect her necklace. She signed *our* copy of the invoice."

Adams frowned. "She signed for it?"

He nodded. "Come into the office and I'll show you. I've got all the paperwork handy."

Adams and James followed in his wake as he headed through the door into a small, sterile passageway, all fluorescent lighting and scarred linoleum flooring. A door opened off to the right, giving onto a tiny little staff room with a two-person table and a cramped sink area, complete with kettle and tiny fridge. Dandy padded in, presumably to investigate the coffee supplies, while they bypassed it and headed to the next door along. It opened into a crowded office, a large safe taking up a good proportion of the floor space and much of the rest given over to stacked file boxes. There was no window, but a small desktop fan laboured on top of the safe. Somehow a desk that barely allowed enough room for Scott to squeeze around the end to sit behind it had been wedged in, and two sturdy wooden chairs faced it. Scott waved at them to sit down as he sank into his own chair and picked a file up from next to a chunky computer monitor.

"I've put it all together for you," he said, offering it to Adams. "I knew this was going to be an issue."

"Stolen goods tend to be," Adams said, and he made a scoffing noise.

"Nothing's been stolen. And I'm sure Ms Hudson is a very nice woman, but …" He trailed off, making a sympathetic face. "I imagine it's her age."

"You think she's lying?"

"I think she's confused. She came in here making a fuss after she'd already collected the necklace. All I can think is that she's misplaced it, or left it on the bus or something, and then decided she must not have picked it up."

"That seems like a stretch," Adams said, watching him. His face was a little pinker than necessary, but it was hot in here.

"I see why you might think that, but the idea that we'd steal a necklace which was entrusted to us is just ridiculous. I mean, simply the *rumour* could ruin our business. The fuss that she's kicking up certainly could, which is why I brought it to your attention."

It was a fair point, and one that had already occurred to her. But it was also just the sort of thing that provided if not an alibi, at least a reasonable doubt for their defence. "Why does Ms Hudson still have her copy of the invoice, unsigned by you, then?"

"Yes, well. That is a problem," Scott admitted. "She didn't have it on her, and Meredith should have insisted that she come back with it, but … Well. She's an elderly lady. Meredith used her judgement, and in this case she got it a little wrong."

Adams opened the file, which contained just two sheets of

paper. One was a work order, detailing the repairs, with *Charles Worthington, Silversmith* printed on the header. The other was an identical invoice to the one Gladys had shown her, signed on one line to show it had been dropped off. On this one, though, there was another signature further down the page next to a date and printed text that read *Collected by*. It had the shop's stamp next to it, and another signature that must be Meredith's. Adams rubbed her forehead as she looked between the two signatures that should be Gladys's, her vision swimming momentarily. It really was too hot in here, despite the fan.

Scott leaned over to tap the invoice. "And there you have it. What she did with the necklace after she left, if she lost it, misplaced it, if she's had a memory lapse and doesn't remember what she did, that is not our responsibility."

Adams blinked to clear her vision, then examined both signatures, comparing the one on paper to the one on her phone. She wasn't an expert, but as far as she could tell, they looked identical. She handed the file to James so he could check it.

"Interesting," she said again. "CCTV then. I assume you have it."

"Yes," Scott said, with rather less enthusiasm than she would've imagined, considering it could potentially exonerate him instantly.

"Yes, but?" she asked.

"Yes, but it malfunctioned on that day."

"How inconvenient."

He frowned. "It is, actually."

"How exactly did it malfunction?"

"There was some sort of interference, and the picture's all scrambled. We've never had a problem before and honestly, we wouldn't even have realised except that we tried to run the recording back to Gladys when she came in, to prove she'd collected the piece."

"We'll need that recording," Adams said.

"Of course. I can email it to you." He was already tapping away at his computer, peering at it hopefully.

"Is there anything else you can tell us?"

"Only that Meredith is very shaken up. Terribly upset about the whole thing, really. She feels she's done something wrong, which, of course, she hasn't." He gave Adams an admonishing look. "I hope you won't upset her further."

"Hopefully not," she said. "We do need a word, though. Can you perhaps send her in here to talk?"

"Of course," he said, pushing back from the desk. "I'll get her straight away."

There was a moment of awkwardness as he squeezed himself out from behind the desk, and James had to wedge his chair almost on top of Adams' to give the jeweller room to get past, but then he was hurrying out the door, leaving them in the stuffy silence of the office, broken only by the whimpering fan.

"Thoughts?" Adams asked.

"I mean, he's got a point," James said. "Stealing from their own customers is a bit short-sighted. Be interesting to see the CCTV."

"Gladys didn't strike me as that easily confused."

"No," he agreed. "There is that."

They fell silent as heels clicked down the hall toward them, and a moment later Meredith slipped into the room, looking even slighter and paler than she had in the shop, Dandy following after her. She looked from Adams to James, and he gave her an encouraging smile. She swallowed hard and said, "I did give her the necklace. I really did."

"Of course," Adams said. "But your boss has filed an official complaint, so we need to go over everything, alright?"

"Alright." She edged around the desk and sat down in the seat Scott had vacated, her fingers twisting together again on her lap, not quite looking at either of them.

"Just talk us through what happened," Adams said.

Meredith started to speak, but her voice caught in her throat. She swallowed audibly and started again. "Ms Hudson brought the necklace in and asked for the clasp to be replaced. We don't do repairs on site, but we send them to a silversmith in York. She said that was fine, so I did all the paperwork. She signed the deposit form to show she'd dropped it off, and I signed to show I'd received it – we're very careful," she added, shooting a look at James for reassurance, and he gave her a smile that appeared to be the facial equivalent of a soothing pat on the hand.

Adams managed not to roll her eyes and indicated to Meredith to keep going.

Meredith took a breath. "It's payment on collection, so I packed the necklace up and put it aside for Charles – he's the silversmith – to pick up on the Wednesday, which is when he comes by. And that was it." Meredith shrugged, still not quite looking at Adams, her gaze mostly on her hands. "And then … Then I just don't understand."

"Good start," Adams said, as encouragingly as she could, which didn't seem to be as effective as James's smile. "All the forms done, necklace dispatched, so far so good. What happened when she came back?"

"When she came back …" Meredith touched her forehead, a light little tap. "It's a bit blurry, to be honest. I had a headache. I don't normally get them, but … I mean, I didn't have it all day, but when she came in my head was hurting terribly. It made me feel quite sick. But she … She'd forgotten the invoice, and I didn't want to make her go home for it. It didn't seem fair, you know? And she signed our form, so I thought that would be fine." She was rubbing her temples with the fingers of both hands now, eyes closed against the light. “My head just hurt so *horribly.*”

Adams watched her. For some reason, she could taste the Thames again, feel that terrible shift in her vision, her own headache pressing at her temples the way it had under the bridge, the way it had in Toot Hansell last summer. Her mouth was full of salt and copper, and she jumped when James cleared his throat. She bit the inside of her cheek lightly.

This wasn’t London. It wasn’t even Toot Hansell. This was just a bloody dispute over a missing necklace, and figuring these things out was what she did. When she didn’t have an *actual* case to be working on, anyway.

“You’re doing well, Meredith,” she said aloud. “Just a couple more questions. Did you notice anything unusual about Gladys? Did she seem particularly confused? Or under duress?”

“I don’t … I don’t remember,” Meredith said, her eyes still closed. “I don’t think so. I think I would have noticed. But … *Oh.*” She pressed her fingers harder into her forehead. “I’m getting a headache again. I *never* get headaches.”

“It’s probably stress,” James said, his voice gentle.

“Or a migraine?” Adams suggested.

“I don’t think so,” Meredith said. “I’ve never had one before, I mean. Although, I really did feel awful the other day, after Gladys came in. Scott made me go home.”

Adams leaned over to James and looked at the invoice again, squinting at the signatures, swallowing hard. There it was again. Old metal and deep, hungry shores, cold indifferent water and high distant stars. The scent of mud, thick and cloying at the back of the throat. A warning throb swelled behind her eyes, and she said, “The migraine started while Gladys was here?”

“I suppose. Or just before. I didn’t really notice it until she arrived," Meredith said. She was still rubbing her temples with both hands, and now she pressed her palms over her eyes. "But I *did* give her the necklace. And she signed our invoice. You can see that."

"I can, yes," Adams said, not looking at the invoice again. "What happened after she left?"

"I had to sit down behind the counter for a bit, because I felt quite sick. Then Scott said I should go home, and I did. That's all." She fell silent, and they listened to the fan for a moment.

Finally James leaned forward. "Don't take this the wrong way. But were you drinking the night before at all?"

"No," she said, peeking at him. "I don't really drink much at all, and definitely not before workdays."

Adams thought she actually looked like it might not be a lie. Meredith had the air of someone more inclined to tea parties than club nights.

James looked at Adams, then back at Meredith. "Do you take any other substances?"

She opened her eyes properly. "No. Never. I don't even like paracetamol, although I had to take some for the headache."

"Alright," he said. "We just have to check these things."

"Of course," she replied, but she was definitely looking slightly less charmed by James and his approachable smile.

After a moment, Adams realised James was sneaking sideways glances at her, and she shook herself. Headaches were just headaches. "Alright, Meredith," she said, taking a card from her pocket and handing it to the young woman. "That's it for now, but we may be back in touch. If you think of anything else, though, just give me a call. Even the smallest thing."

"Of course," Meredith said, setting the card on the desk in

front of her. "Do you get migraines? You seemed to recognise it."

"Sometimes," Adams said.

"Is it to do with age, then?"

James barely contained a snort as Adams got up. "Check with your GP," she said, and headed for the door.

Scott was behind the counter, and she handed him a card, repeating the request for him to call her, not that anyone usually did. She collected a card for the silversmith in return, then headed back out onto the pavement, pausing as the door swung shut behind them, breathing in the overly warm, city-scented air, and squeezing the bridge of her nose.

"Alright, Adams?" James asked.

"Sure. I think her headaches must be catching or something."

"Maybe," James said, looking up and down the street with a slow, thoughtful gaze. "I felt a bit weird too. Not as bad as you apparently, but yeah. Off."

Adams dropped her hand and looked at him. "Was it too hot in there?"

He grimaced. "Maybe. Or … I don't know. Some sort of fumes from cleaning supplies or something." He shoved his notebook back in his pocket. "What's next?"

"Get the CCTV to Isha, then start poking around and see what stolen goods are popping up," Adams said, stretching her neck to one side then the other. Her head was clearing now she was out of the shop.

"I could really go with some food," James said, patting his flat belly.

"Ooh, veggie sausage roll," Adams suggested, and he shook his head.

"Ever think your diet is to blame for your migraines?"

"I barely get them," she replied. "Anyway, veggie sausage rolls are basically a health food."

"Tell your cholesterol that."

She ignored him, heading for the nearest bakery as Dandy appeared out of a side alley, loping toward her. Something was off. She didn't want to think about it too much, though. Not right now. That way lay deep dark rivers and long night shadows and bridges that spanned the hungry Thames.

She didn't want to think about bridges.

4

AN INDESCRIBABLE THEFT

BACK AT THE STATION, ADAMS FOUND A LINK TO THE CCTV files from the jewellery shop already waiting in her email. There were four – Scott had evidently just made the ones around the time the necklace was dropped off and picked up available, one from each date taken by a camera that showed the inside of the shop, proportions slightly distorted by the wide-angle lens, and the other two from a camera that covered the door and gave a view each way down the street. She started with the interior on drop-off day, skipping forward until she found the time that approximated what was written on the invoice.

Adams didn't recognise Gladys at first. She'd been expecting some multicoloured apparition such as had greeted them at the house, but instead a woman in a well-tailored suit, her back resolutely straight and her hair elegantly coiffed, stepped through the door and strode straight to the counter. Adams paused and zoomed in where she could see the woman's face better. As far as she could tell, it was definitely Gladys. Evidently her outdoor outfits were the polar opposite of her indoor ones.

She hit play again and let the recording run forward until Gladys reached into a cavernous (and, Adams was certain, despite her only interest in such things being their vulnerability to theft and likely resale value, high-end designer) handbag and produced a soft cloth bag. She didn't pull the necklace out of it entirely, just enough to show the clasp to Meredith, who examined it, then made a gesture evidently indicating she'd like to see the whole thing. There was a pause, then Gladys lifted the necklace from the bag and set it on the counter. Adams hit pause, leaning in to the screen and squinting at it. She thought she could make out the dull heaviness of old gold, wrought into an intricate, descending pattern that encircled at its lowest point a black smudge which must have been a stone of some sort. The detail wasn't good enough to tell a lot, though, everything pixelated and bit *off,* and she fiddled with the contrasts, hoping she didn't irrevocably send the display skew-whiff and have to get IT to fix it, like she had last time.

"Didn't your mum tell you you'll ruin your eyes being so close to the screen?" someone asked, and Adams jumped, spinning her chair to see Lindsay grinning at her, a bottle of unsettlingly greenish-brown juice in one hand.

"She also told me that eating carrots would give me good night vision, so I'm not sure I should be going to her for my optometry needs."

Lindsay laughed and pointed at the screen. "What's Temper got you on, then? Stolen goods?"

"Something like that. Harassment over a missing necklace."

Lindsay leaned over Adams to peer at the image. "Looks fancy. You getting anywhere with it?"

"Just started." What could she say, *our best lead so far is a mysterious migraine and a house that gives me the creeps? A* ***feel-***

ing? Being accused of being a soft southerner would be the least of her worries.

"Bloody Temper. You're wasted on stuff like this. Let me know if you need some help to get through it a bit quicker." Lindsay turned to go, sipping from a metal straw stuck in the bottle. Of course she brought her own straw.

"Hang about," Adams said. "You know anyone who might move stuff like this? Seems pretty high-end. I'm thinking most pawn shops won't touch it."

Lindsay turned back, taking another look at the screen. "If that's all real gold – and depending what the stone is – then yeah. You could be right." She leaned over Adams again, clicking the keyboard to zoom in. She smelled of soap and some soft, fresh citrus scent, and Adams was uncomfortably aware that she'd been sweating all bloody day, and still had veggie sausage roll on her breath. "I know someone who works art theft cases. I'll see what he says. Get a still of this and I'll send it through to him too, ask him to keep an eye out."

"Thanks," Adams said, as Lindsay straightened up.

"Sure. Girl power, right?" Lindsay winked at her then headed off, and Adams made a mental note to remember to bring a spare shirt in tomorrow. She normally had one, but she'd had to use it when a very posh, very drunk man in his seventies had vomited on her shoulder while complaining about the standards of today's youth.

Adams wasn't about to try to get a still off the video herself. The only way she knew how to do it was by screenshot, and it wasn't going to be anywhere near as clear as what Isha would get with her tech magic. Instead she hit play and watched Gladys finish up in the shop. Nothing seemed untoward or out of place. Papers were signed, the necklace was handed over in its bag and placed in a large Ziploc with more papers inside it, then Meredith waved at Gladys as she left. As soon as she was gone the young woman took the bag through the door at the back of the shop, presumably to put it in the safe, and that was it. Adams swapped to the outside camera, watched Gladys arrive and leave, striding purposefully down the pavement, then closed the file with a sigh. There was nothing to be learned there.

The second interior file was dated for when the necklace had been picked up, and Adams skipped through a few moments of Meredith polishing bracelets before the young woman looked up, smiling toward the door, and set the tray of jewellery aside. The door swung open on the edge of the screen, and then everything distorted. Adams blinked at the screen, barely resisting the urge to hit the side of the monitor, like her gran used to do when the picture would start rolling on her old TV. It had always worked, too, which Adams put down to even technology being too scared of her gran to misbehave, but she doubted that was the problem here. The change had been instantaneous, from clear enough to see the bracelets Meredith was working on, to swirling, complicated patterns that made the picture look as if it was burning at the edges. She could barely make out anything through it. There was a figure, but she couldn't even make out the colours of what it was wearing, or anything more than the most vague and general shape. It could have been anything human-shaped. Any*one* human-shaped. Not any*thing*. Why would it be any*thing?* She pushed the thought down, feeling the warning throb of a migraine again. Any*one*. That was what she'd meant.

"Great footage, that," James said, making her jump. "Where'd they get their security from, a Christmas cracker?

The coffee machine's bust again," he added, handing her a takeaway mug of coffee.

"Of course it's bust. No one ever puts any water in the damn thing, so it shorts out. It's going to burn out permanently unless people learn how to actually look after it properly."

"Alright," James said. "Not that you feel strongly about it or anything."

"I feel very strongly about anything caffeine-related," Adams replied, taking a sip of coffee. It was better than the station machine even when it was working, anyway. The many instances of running dry had left a permanent burnt taste to anything that came out of it.

"I had noticed," he said. "So what's with the mucky picture?"

"It happened as soon as whoever it was came to the shop." She scrolled back and played it again, showing the picture collapsing, and then kept it running forward. There was no way to tell what was going on underneath the interference, but a few minutes later it lifted again. Meredith was alone in the shop. She had both elbows on the counter, her fingertips pushed into her hairline. She straightened up, slumped back down again, then finally managed to straighten up properly, one hand pressed to her forehead like a fainting maiden in some eighteenth-century novel. Adams could almost feel the throb of the headache from here.

"Doesn't look like she was lying about the migraine," James said.

"Doesn't look like it, no." Adams pulled up the file for outside the shop, but it was the same problem there. Just before the person entered the frame, the whole picture was swallowed by twisting colours and static, allowing only glimpses of forms passing, disembodied and indeterminate. It cleared once whoever it was had gone inside, only to start up again around the time they must have left, then lasted long enough that, by the time it cleared, there was no way of telling even what way they might have gone.

"That's really weird," James said. "You think it was like some sort of scrambler?"

Adams looked at him. "Is that actually a thing? Sounds like something out of James Bond."

"Well, yeah," James said. "But I'm pretty sure it's a real thing, too. It *sounds* like a real thing."

"Huh." Adams picked up her phone, pulled up a number, and hit dial. She didn't have to wait long.

"Adams," a woman said.

"Hi, Isha. I need a little bit of expertise."

"*No.* And here I thought it was a social call. For my sparkling repartee, like."

Adams snorted. "Call it a mark of professional respect. I wouldn't waste your time on a social call."

"Most people don't think being social is a waste of time, Adams. What is it?"

"I've got a lot of weird interference on a recording. Can you take a look at it?"

"Sure, pop it over." The line went dead.

James sipped his coffee, looking at Adams. "You're making a lot of progress there. I reckon she'll be inviting you around for a besties sleepover soon."

She frowned at him and said, "It's *work.*"

"Yeah, most people at least try to make work friends. You know, let them use their first name, that sort of thing."

"Don't insult your superiors." No one used Adams' first name, other than her mum, and her brothers when they really wanted to wind her up. It was Jeanette, which wasn't a *bad* name. It just didn't feel like hers, and these days any time someone used it she automatically thought she was going to be told off for coming into the house with her shoes on.

"Oh, I'm not insulting you," James said. "That was an observation of fact."

Adams shook her head, trying not to laugh, and waved him off. "Whatever. Off you go, then, tech boy."

"Go where?"

"Find out about scramblers and things. See if anything can actually do this."

"What are you going to do?" he asked.

"Start canvassing some of our dodgier pawn shops. I think it's too fancy a piece for them to touch, but it's worth checking."

"I'm coming, then."

"You don't need to come. You need to find out about fancy tech."

"We can just ask Isha about that," he pointed out. "She'll know more offhand than I'll find out in an afternoon online. Besides, poking around dodgy pawn shops asking questions on your own sounds like *Things Not to Do as a Detective 101.*"

Adams sighed. "Fine. What we do need though is a picture of the necklace. Have we had anything from Gladys?"

"No, nothing."

"Alright, I'll ask Isha to do that first off." She picked up the phone again, and James said, "Pleasantries, Adams. *Pleasantries.*"

She scowled at him, and took a pointed sip of her coffee as she turned away.

Isha pulled the still off the video easily enough, although the picture still wasn't great. She enhanced it as much as she could then blew it up until they could see the detail. It was much as Adams had thought from her initial examination of the video – an ornate necklace with nothing delicate about it.

Heavy, curved gold bands descended from the neck and would have lain across the décolletage, and there were no stones in it other than the one at the very bottom of the bands, heavy and dark as a monster's eye.

"What is that?" Adams asked Isha, leaning over her desk to look at the big screen the other woman had half turned toward her. "I can't see the colour properly."

"It's not coming up," Isha said. "I don't know why – there's some distortion on everything, and all the pixelation isn't helping. Bloody off-brand, budget eBay cameras, probably. That's as good as I can get it."

"Weird," James said. "Looks like a miniature black hole or something."

Or the Thames at midnight, Adams thought, but aloud she just said, "Well, it's good enough. Print off half a dozen of those for us, will you?"

"Your wish is my command," Isha said, not looking up from the screen. A moment later the printer in the corner started spewing out copies.

"Thank you," Adams said.

Isha had shut the file and was investigating the corrupted ones. "Get me a coffee next time you go. Bloody machine's broken again."

"Because no one puts any water in it," Adams said.

Isha finally looked up at her, dark eyes serious and licked with purple shadow. "I hope you're not accusing me of anything."

"No," Adams said. "No, absolutely not." The last thing she needed was for anyone in the tech department to be angry at her. She'd been in that situation in London once, and it had wound up taking months to get the simplest request through.

Isha stared at her expressionlessly for a moment, then grinned. "Yeah, I know," she said. "You're quite funny when you squirm though."

ARMED WITH THE PHOTOS, they headed for Adams' car, and she swung them back onto the streets, joining the after-school and early-finishing work traffic that was swelling to choke the intersections. Their list of places to visit was pretty short. It wasn't like they could go to every pawn shop in Leeds, after all. There were more of them than there were chemists, same as in pretty much any city. Pawn shops and betting shops, legit or not, were the two places that always flourished when all else faded. *Especially* when all else faded. When the rent's due and the shelves are empty, wages tight or non-existent, there always needs to be somewhere people can go. Somewhere for when things get desperate, somewhere that both preyed upon them and saved them for this month, this week, this day, giving them just enough to keep going. To keep scraping, even as it pushed them deeper into the chasms that gaped within society. They didn't offer hope, even when it seemed that they did, but they did offer survival. And sometimes that felt like the same thing.

But the necklace was high-end. It wasn't the sort of thing that could be taken down to the local cash converters. The places that dealt with things like this were, at best, only borderline legal. Which meant they were never super happy to talk to the cops, but on the other hand, borderline legal places also needed to make sure they didn't give cops any excuses to be poking around. So sometimes a little bit of pressure and a tiny bit of persuasion could produce quite a lot.

The first shop had two small display windows protected by chain link shutters on the outside. Through them, Adams could see some dull bracelets and a handful of dusty digital watches that were too new to be vintage and too old to be desirable, plus a couple of scratched MP3 players. Not that it'd be all the shop offered, of course. All the good stuff would be inside, and a lot of it wouldn't even be on display. It was the sort of place that sold pretty much anything that was needed, as long as the customer didn't mind paying the price.

They were buzzed in by a sharp-eyed woman with bleached blonde hair that hung in Dolly Parton curls to her shoulders. She watched them enter without moving from her spot, one hand resting below the counter. Adams was entirely certain there would be a cricket bat down there, if not something a little more lethal and a lot more illegal.

The woman examined them, then placed both hands on the counter, not quite relaxing, but evidently deciding she wouldn't be needing whatever weapon she had stashed. "Oh, aye," she said. "What have the coppers lost now?"

"A necklace," Adams said, sliding the photo across the counter to her.

The woman picked it up and examined it. She smelled of cigarette smoke and a dusky, floral perfume, and her nails were perfectly shaped, long and red, with little daisies at the end of each one. She set the photo down on the counter and pushed it back toward them. "Not seen it," she said. "Nice piece though."

"Think you can keep an eye out for it?" Adams suggested.

She shrugged. "Maybe. Got to protect the privacy of our clients, though. Can't have them thinking I run to the cops every time I see something pretty. Bad for business, that."

"I imagine," Adams said, looking at James.

"Did we come here with that thing last month?" he asked her.

"Last month?" Adams said.

"Oh, it wasn't you," he said. "I was working with Rajesh. Whole collection of Ming vases got stolen from some country house out Harewood way. Never did track down the entire lot. Only got about five of them back." He looked at the shelf above the counter, and Adams followed his gaze. A collection of vases stood shoulder to shoulder, milky green porcelain and old cut glass, probably nothing more than car boot tat. "I don't think we checked here," James added. "Probably should've."

The woman scowled at him. "I run a legitimate business," she said. "And I don't like what you're insinuating."

"I imagine not," James said, smiling.

Adams tapped the photo. "We need to find this," she said. "Do we have to turn your shop over?"

"You can't do that without a warrant."

"Well, we're still looking for those Ming vases," James said, nodding at the shelf. "I mean, that looks like one to me, doesn't it? Don't you think, Adams?"

"Absolutely," she said. "My trained eye says it almost definitely could be a Ming vase."

The woman sighed. "You know I don't have any Ming vases. Do I look like I have Ming vases? Do I look like I *even know* what a Ming vase is?"

"Yes to the last one. To the rest, I guess the warrant will tell us."

The woman shook her head. "Look, no one's come in here trying to sell a necklace like that. But I'll take your bloody photo and let you know if anyone does. Happy?"

"Happy," Adams said, and put her card on the counter with the picture.

"What colour's the stone?" the woman asked, peering at the picture again.

"We don't know," Adams said.

"Well, that's not much bloody help, is it?"

"I don't think there's many necklaces out there that look like that. I imagine you'll be alright." She smiled at the woman, who just scowled and muttered something about filthy pigs.

Back out into the street, James looked at Adams as she unlocked the car. "She really hadn't seen it."

"No," Adams said. "But it could still come in. They might not have gotten to the stage of selling it yet."

"Don't you think it's more likely something like that's been stolen to order?"

"Could be," Adams agreed. "And we still can't discount the possibility that Gladys either really did mislay it, or is saying she did. Insurance scam, perhaps. We only have her word it wasn't insured."

"True. But what about the interference on the CCTV? That was weird."

"If your scrambler idea has legs, she could've done it herself. She had more tech in her home than I've got in mine," Adams said, and James made a non-committal noise that indicated he didn't think that was saying much. "Alright, more than *most people.*"

"The vid makes it seem more like it could be the shop. Meredith, or Scott, or both of them. She was jumpy enough."

"Entirely possible." And both possibilities made much more sense than that sliding, twisting feeling that had crept up on her in the shop, and the strange dislocation of Gladys's house. Adams liked the idea of it being an insurance scam, or a robbery. She liked the idea of arresting someone. She didn't like thinking of the Thames, or the throb of a migraine, or the deep dark gap of the stone in the necklace. Didn't like thinking this case was something *other.*

And she didn't need to. James still insisted scramblers existed, even if Isha had looked at him like he was five, and thieves were everywhere, and it was just a necklace. Everything else was simply Adams' knowledge of the other world clouding her judgement, making her paranoid.

Surely.

5

WISHING FOR TOASTIES

THE DAY HAD WOUND ON ENOUGH THAT THEIR VISITS TO THE handful of other pawn shops that might deal with items as high-ticket and questionable as the necklace were very much after-hours affairs. But then again, shops that did the sort of deals that might involve such things hardly had nine-to-five schedules. As expected, no one had seen the necklace, but all of them, with a little persuasion, took a copy of the photo and reluctantly agreed to call if anyone came around trying to flog it. Adams didn't go so far as to think that any of them would be rushing to share any relevant info they came across, but it was enough that if it turned up in their shop, there was at least a passing chance they'd call it in.

She drove James back to the station and said, "We may as well call it a day. Tomorrow we'll look into Scott and Meredith some more, see what we can turn up about Gladys."

He looked at his watch and stretched his long limbs out as much as he could in the front seat. "Awesome. I've got football tonight."

"Don't break anything," Adams said, trying not to feel

guilty about the fact that she hadn't been running for about three days. If she went home now, she supposed she'd have time to get one in.

"Yes, Mum," he said, grinning brilliantly. "See you in the morning."

She waved him off and he clambered out, shutting the door behind him and jogging across the parking garage to the stairs. She sat there in the car for a moment, wondering if she should go up and continue with her looming backlog of reports. In the end, though, she turned the car and headed back out of the garage. It wasn't like they were *urgent.* Not really.

Her flat was on the canal, which she wasn't particularly keen about. When she agreed to transfer up to Leeds, after that dark, strange Christmas, she hadn't thought there'd be any bridges. She hadn't thought there'd be any *water*. The city was in the middle of the bloody country, after all. She hadn't accounted for the River Aire. But at least it wasn't a big river, and there weren't big bridges. Just big enough for canal boats to drift through and walkers to amble across and take photos. Not big enough for anything to hide underneath. Or not anything big enough to concern her.

Although she still remembered the way that proportions had drifted and distorted on the bridges in London. Or under one particular bridge, anyway. She tried not to think about it too much. That just filled her mouth with the taste of the Thames, setting her coughing. Salt and copper, salt and copper over and over again, keeping her awake and colouring the edges of her days with insomnia and caffeine, until it almost made her wish that she'd taken one of the toasties.

She hadn't, though. She hadn't even made one at home since, even though she knew on a logical level that the toasties she had been offered in London hadn't been anything like normal sandwiches. They'd been laced with forgetfulness, or blindness, or, worse, indifference. They were a way of turning one's back on the hidden world, of closing out an aspect of reality that still seemed somewhat shaky to Adams, but which nevertheless impacted the reality she knew. Impacted it, bled into it, and sometimes preyed on it. So … no. She never *really* wished she'd had the toasties. Not entirely. Although the whole thing where it had put her off them was kind of a shame because she really liked toasties.

SHE PARKED and headed up to her flat, where she'd stacked all the still-unpacked boxes against one wall in the living room and was trying to ignore them. It was hot and a little stuffy when she let herself in, and she opened the sliding door that led out onto the balcony, giving the canal below a warning glance, then turned to look at Dandy. He was sprawled on the sofa, his belly up to the ceiling, his tail thudding softly on the cushions as he watched her. She put her hands on her hips and scowled at him.

"Useless," she said. "What happened to you?" She hadn't seen him since they'd left the jewellery shop.

He rolled over and jumped off the sofa, coming to push his head into her hands and lick her fingers.

She sighed and scrubbed the back of his head. "I suppose. Not really my dog, are you? You might ask where I go, too."

He whined at her and looked hopefully at the little kitchen, which took up a corner of the main living area. She went around the breakfast bar to discover that he'd evidently been up on the worktop and had got into the cupboard where she kept her coffee. The fresh bag she'd bought just the other day was on the floor, covered in tooth marks and slobber. There were no coffee grounds left to speak of, though. It had been licked entirely clean, as had the floor.

She stared at it for a moment. "You didn't even leave me enough for breakfast," she said. "What am I going to have to do? Buy a coffee safe?"

He huffed, and nudged the bag toward her.

"What sort of dog lives on caffeine? And no wonder you don't hang around the station—" She stopped, narrowing her eyes as a horrible realisation hit her. "Do you keep drinking the coffee from the machine? Is that why it's empty all the time?"

He tipped his head at her, and she couldn't tell if he thought the question was beneath him, or if he was mocking her for not figuring it out earlier. Then again, he was just a dog, albeit of a strange variety. She shouldn't be anthropomorphising him. She'd be buying him joke T-shirts and non-ironic bandanas if she kept this up. She dropped the coffee bag in the bin and checked the fridge with unwarranted optimism. The fridge fairy hadn't been, so there was nothing inside but half a very old and disturbingly tan-coloured lettuce, plus some tomatoes that were setting up a new civilisation. She was going to have to go shopping. If it wasn't for the coffee, she'd have just ordered takeaway and hoped her mum didn't have her *kids eating badly* sixth sense on, but the prospect of having no coffee was even more intolerable than the idea of shopping.

Dandy did not make the shopping experience easier. Having spent the afternoon snoozing, he had apparently decided he needed to accompany her in all other activities. He toppled a pineapple display by chasing a rogue sparrow up it, licked the icing off all the cupcakes in the bakery section, and when he deftly removed two pork chops from a bench where the butcher was dressing them Adams decided to ignore him. It was bad enough being a police officer with an invisible dog. Having a delinquent, criminal one seemed needlessly ill-fitting.

She finished the shopping as quickly as she could, both for her own sanity and for the sake of the store's health and safety certificate, and once home shoved some vegetables that were more aspirational than practical into her fridge, then quickly changed into running gear. A few minutes later, she was back outside again, the long summer days of the north ensuring she had plenty of light left. She jogged at first, Dandy ranging alongside her while she kept an eye on the shifting waters of the canal. Sometimes she saw movement beneath them, something that was more than pike or minnows or whatever the hell the people kept in canals. It could've been her imagination, of course, or shadows, or actual fish, but she didn't think so. And as much as she didn't like it, she'd had to reluctantly accept that her perception had forever been changed by the bridge. That she saw things she hadn't before, even though they'd always been there – a thought that was somehow worse than the seeing itself. And just because she wished it wasn't part of her world didn't make it unreal.

It was the same with the people she saw, the ones that weren't quite human. The ones that had eyes that weren't quite *right,* too wide-set or too narrow, too many or two few or the pupils the wrong shape. The ones with the shadows of wings on their shoulders, or horns on the heads, or tails that swung with the cockiness of cats. She saw them, but she tried not to notice them too much. Noticing gets you noticed. She knew that from the human world, and it held true in this one, too. And she wasn't ready for that yet. She hadn't been ready for what happened in London, and when she'd moved north she hadn't been ready for the village of Toot bloody Hansell, with its ridiculous name and dragons and sprites and talking cats and, even worse, the Women's Institute (even though, admittedly, they were entirely human). She hadn't been ready for whatever the hell the weird little things in the manor house had been that spring, or for Dandy, and certainly not for the goblins that had been running across the fells last Christmas.

She hadn't been ready for any of it, but she'd dealt with it. And as long as those things stayed out in the countryside and well behind her in London, she could almost imagine that's where they belonged. That as long as she was in this city, everything still made sense. That Leeds was just humans and their hungers and their desires, their grievances and grudges and hatreds. All those things that she didn't like but she understood. All those things that made sense.

So no. She didn't want to notice anything here, and she definitely didn't want to be noticed back. So she tried not to look too closely at any of the things she saw in the city. Only the things that affected her job.

But this case was making her uneasy. That strange house in its whispering garden. Meredith's migraine and the scrambled recordings. The way the taste of the Thames kept coming back to her, more reminder than memory. Everything was floating too close to the surface, and even the catch of breath in her throat and the burn of her thighs as she pushed herself harder, the pound of her feet on the pavement, none of it was drowning things out like they should. Everything was too raw, too sharp, like an HD screen when she'd been used to watching her gran's ancient telly. It was too much to ignore.

So when she ran past three lads sitting on one of the benches that faced the canal, sharing a two litre bottle of cider that was beaded with condensation, she couldn't help but notice that one of them had horns and hooves. Another was too pale, his fingers too long and his eyes too large. The third looked fairly human but there were sharp edges to him that most humans didn't have, as if he were just a little more in focus than most people. Adams recognised it. That sharpness seemed to belong to people who lived on the edges of the human world, never as deeply attached to it as others, with their soft edges and muted colours. Not everyone who had been pushed to the outskirts of society had that clarity, of course, but she'd never seen anyone firmly anchored in the human world who did. And what she hated was that sometimes she looked in the mirror and she saw those same sharp edges on herself.

But she couldn't exactly be surprised. She had a bloody invisible dog. Which was a whole other thing. She had no idea where the hell Dandy had come from. She'd encountered him in the manor house in the spring, where he'd stolen a leg of lamb and had sent the chef into a meltdown, but otherwise hadn't done much of anything. Then he'd just turned up in Leeds and moved in, and now he was sometimes there and sometimes not. He did seem to be around more and more often now, though. Stealing her coffee and thieving from the deli.

She pushed up to a sprint, Dandy breaking into a lope next to her as she tried to lose herself in the rhythm of her breath. In-two-three, out-two-three. In-two-three, out-two-three. The world settling, all the sharp and jagged edges starting to even out. Dandy matched his pace to hers, running into the long rich shadows of the endless afternoon, his grey dreadlocks flying, and she felt people noticing as they passed, her if not him. Not humans noticing. Others. Folk, as the dragons called them, and she supposed that's what she had to call them now as well. Since there was no getting away from any of it.

Adams cobbled together a passable stir fry from the fresh veggies and half a bottle of black bean sauce that had been in the fridge for longer than was probably advisable, but didn't seem to have anything growing on it. She even cooked off a bit of brown rice and ate while sitting cross-legged on the sofa, feeling virtuous and craving some noodles in peanut sauce, preferably with deep-fried tofu. Dandy sniffed her bowl, gagged pointedly, then fell asleep next to her, his hind legs jammed against her thigh and his head pillowed comfortably on the cushions. She supposed he'd already eaten plenty with what he'd stolen from the butchers.

She still wasn't sure if he was the same dog she'd seen in London. He'd never come close enough for her to see him properly back then. But the way this world worked, she thought he probably was. *This world.* She hated that, as if she'd fallen through a crack in reality and ended up somewhere else entirely, an older and less well-dressed Alice in Wonderland. This was still her world, but somehow everything had changed. It had all started changing in London, and after a little lull when she'd first arrived in Leeds it had just kept changing. Accelerating, even. She exhaled slightly and put the TV on, looking for something suitably mindless. She couldn't think about this every minute. It was too much.

The next morning rose with a sleepless flush to the sky, a heat haze hanging everywhere. It made Adams uneasy, as if it were trapping all the strangeness into the city. And heat was like the full moon, in a way. Everyone knew it didn't *really* make a difference, but it did. Maybe the heat even more than the moon, because everyone was frazzled, and everything felt too complicated and fraught. Tempers broke over nothing, and disagreements escalated with the heat like kerosene to a fire. She could feel it as she stepped outside, walking up to the police station. The day had a raging weight to it.

There were broken bottles scattered across the pedestrianised area by the canal, and as she left it she heard screeching brakes and then shouts rising, words indistinguishable, just exclamation marks of fury. She slowed, listening until she was sure it didn't sound like it was going to degenerate into anything that really threatened bodily harm, then kept going. She passed the market on the way, a clunky old building with an outside area encircled by a high wall. Inside the wall she could hear the shouts of the fruit and veg vendors.

"Strawberries two pounds a punnet! Five pounds for three! Lovely fresh strawberries!"

And someone else shouting even louder, trying to drown them out. "Watermelons! Watermelons from Spain! Get your watermelons here! Four pounds each! Four pounds each! Six pounds for a large!"

More people were yelling about potatoes, or tomatoes, each louder and fiercer than the first, adding to the heat and haze of the morning. Adams pushed her fingers into the tightness of the hair at the base of her skull. It was just a bit too tight and a bit too uncomfortable, but she had an idea that was the heat as well. The seams of her shirt were scratching her sides, and she was sweating already. It was going to be one of those days.

The station was just down the block from the market, a stolid building in red brick. Someone had thrown up on the steps, which was a brave move, and Adams skirted the mess, stepping into the over-warm interior and diving into the warren of rooms beyond, heading for Isha's office.

Isha was already in, the window cracked open and a fan going, and she was misting a collection of plants that lined a full set of shelves on one wall when DI Adams walked in. Isha turned around with the spray bottle held out like a weapon, a tall, strong-looking woman with a thick tangle of dark hair and a gold ring in her nose. Adams placed a gluten-free raspberry and chia muffin she'd bought at the shop the night before (not one that Dandy had licked) on the desk.

"I haven't been for coffee yet," Adams said, then set a to-go mug from her collection next to the muffin. "My home machine's pretty good, though."

"It's too hot for coffee. Needs to be iced in this weather." Isha set the spray bottle down and tried a sip of coffee anyway. "*Hmm.* Not bad, though."

"I'll put some ice cubes in it next time."

"That'll do it." Isha sat down, jiggling the mouse to wake her screen up.

"What've you got for me?" Adams asked.

"Nothing."

Adams frowned. "Nothing?"

"Nothing. I farmed it out to a few people to see what they come back with, but honestly, if I can't get anything off it, I don't think anyone can." She didn't say it with any sort of cockiness, just as a statement of fact, and given what Adams had heard about her, she didn't doubt it.

"But I don't understand how there can be nothing," Adams said. "I mean, it was just a bit of interference, right?"

"Pretty serious interference," Isha said. "The whole file's corrupt. I can't clean it up or pull anything off it. But, like I said, I've asked a few people. They'll get some of their algorithms on it or whatever, but I don't reckon we're getting anything from it."

Adams tipped her head back, looking up the ceiling, then looked back in time to slap Dandy's snout away from the muffin. She hadn't even seen him come in. Isha gave her a curious look, and she just said, "Bollocks. Any idea what could have caused it?"

"Virus," Isha suggested.

"What about James and his scrambler? Did you look into

that, or has he just been watching too much *Mission Impossible?*"

"I've not heard of anything that can do that. Stuff that screws with facial recognition, sure, but not the whole file. I can look into it, though. New tech comes in all the time. But whatever did it, it doesn't change the fact that we can't get anything off the recording."

"Nothing at all?"

"Not a sausage," Isha said, and leaned back in her seat, watching Adams and sipping on her coffee.

Adams looked back at her and took a mouthful of her own coffee. "Tell me," she said, and Isha grinned.

"It's not the only one."

"What?"

"It's not the only file like this."

Adams stared at her. "What, so someone's going around injecting viruses into CCTVs?"

"You know it's not an actual virus, right? It doesn't need injecting."

"You know what I mean."

Isha shrugged. "Could be."

"How would they do that? Are all the cameras from the same company?" Adams was feeling distinctly out of her depth.

"No, they could hack in," Isha said. "Most of them aren't usually that secure, so someone could do it pretty easily."

"Where are the other places?" Adams asked.

"Calm your trot. Only one so far. Apple Store."

"Apple Store?"

"Yep. Just came in yesterday. Hadn't actually had a chance to look at it when you gave me your stuff. But then once I had a look at yours and sent it off to a few people, I opened the Apple one, and there it is. Exactly the same – the footage's completely fried. Every single camera has a meltdown, then five minutes later, all fine."

"Huh. Why were the tapes brought in?" Adams asked.

"*Tapes.* I do like you, Adams." Isha tapped a couple of keys, then read off the screen. "Theft. Top of the line MacBook, newest, most high spec phone, and a matching watch to boot, plus a couple of iPads."

"Just one each of the really flash stuff," Adams asked.

"Just one of each."

"That's really weird," Adams said. "Sounds like personal use rather than resale."

"Personal use, stolen to order, something like that." Isha clicked a few more keys. "I've sent you the file notes."

"You're a star," Adams said.

"I am. And I'll take a chocolate muffin next time. Plus ice, milk, and a bit of caramel syrup for the coffee."

"Noted," Adams said. She was still smiling as she left. After all, what were the odds of someone magic robbing an Apple Store? This was looking more and more like regular, common, or garden variety thievery, and she couldn't have been happier. She didn't even stop Dandy when he vanished into the staff room. Although that was also because she didn't want to know if he was responsible for the slow destruction of the coffee machine. She had enough to deal with without trying to figure out how to train an invisible dog.

6

HARD QUESTIONS ARE HARD

James was sitting at her desk, and he jumped up as she came through the door. "I've been looking into Scott Samuels," he said.

"Nice one. Come up with anything?"

"Two kids, recently divorced, sports car on a payment plan that got repossessed last month."

"Interesting," Adams said, sitting down in the seat he'd vacated. "Don't imagine rent on the shop is cheap, either."

"No. His home address is out in Pudsey, and I did a street search on it. Not a great area – think he's hurting a bit financially."

"And Meredith?"

"Lives with her parents, no car, no debts that jump out. Haven't found out much else about her so far."

"Alright," Adams said. "Well, we can re-interview both of them a bit more formally, see what pops up. Meantime, we may have something else. That same video thing has been going on in other places."

"Seriously? Where?"

"Well, one other place so far, anyway. Apple Store in

town. Bunch of stuff got swiped, and the recordings were sent to Isha to take a look at. She thinks it's the same as the jewellery shop one."

"So we're going to check it out?" James looked like he was ready to run for the door already.

Adams hesitated. It was exactly what they should be doing, of course, but Gladys and her tech was still niggling at her. Robot vacuums weren't unusual, but combine it with the drum kit and the unseen but evidently high-quality coffee machine, and even her statement about loving technology … A flash watch and a fancy phone seemed like they might tie in nicely with everything else. And the video had scrambled when Gladys picked the necklace up, if the signatures were to be believed. That was where it all fell down, though. There were easier ways to stage a robbery if one was just after the insurance money, and she hadn't even reported it to the cops. The shop had.

But something was going on with Gladys and the necklace. Adams could feel it, an itch she couldn't scratch, Thames fever on her skin. The way the necklace was so hard to see in the vids, the edges blurring much the way the signature on the invoice in the shop had. Meredith's migraine, and the creeping edge of her own, familiar from when she tried to see things that didn't want to be seen. She wondered if it was possible that the necklace wasn't just the stolen piece, but the method of theft somehow, which would mean whoever had hit the Apple Store might still have it.

Aloud, she said, "Check in with Isha and see if there are any other recordings that've come in over the past few days. Take a look at them if there are. We might have a bigger pattern here."

James made a slight face. "Is that really the most important thing right now?"

"Yes," she said. "I'm going to go and talk to Gladys again."

"On your own?"

"I'm pretty sure I can handle Gladys." And she also didn't want James with her, just in case there really was something *off* about all this. She needed to be able to ask the questions she needed to, without feeling she was being evaluated for her next mental health break at the same time.

"You know the meaning of *partner* and *team,* right? Also *backup?*"

"And do you know the meaning of *small budgets* and *stretched resources?* Or Detective *Inspector,* for that matter, Detective Constable?"

James gave her an unimpressed look. "You're setting a very bad example for impressionable young constables."

"Then you can do better once you're promoted. Take Isha an iced coffee, triple shot with caramel syrup."

"Fine." James still looked put out as he headed toward the stairs. Adams didn't blame him. She knew she wasn't being terribly fair to him, or exactly following best practices, but if he didn't know that was the world's situation normal by now, it was about time he worked it out.

She went downstairs to find the uniformed sergeant who had answered the call at the Apple Store and written up the report Isha had given her. It was, she had to admit, rather more fluent and detailed than her own reports ever were, but also seriously long and, at least from a quick scan, maddeningly lacking in information. No one had seen who took the gear, and it had happened while one of the sales assistants – sorry, *associates* – was being seen to by paramedics for a sudden medical issue. The officer had evidently assumed the camera would answer most of the questions, as the report concluded with a note saying he was handing the files over to the tech department.

The sergeant was no more helpful in person, when Adams tracked him down. When she said the case might be related and she wanted to look into it, he just waved at her vaguely. "Sure, whatever. Those Apple things are probably more your style anyway."

Adams frowned slightly, looking at her own phone, clutched in her hand. It was a mysterious brand she'd found on eBay, and had probably been cobbled together from the cannibalised remains of half a dozen more well-known models. One corner of the screen was cracked, and there wasn't a scrap of the case free of scuff marks. She looked from it to the officer, eyebrows raised.

"Well, I mean, London, you know? You're all into that fancy rubbish, aren't you?"

Adams thought he was probably trying to make a joke of it, and she couldn't be bothered being offended even if he wasn't. So she just smiled at him, or at least showed her teeth, and left, hurrying down the hall to the stairs.

Dandy overtook her, licking his chops, and she heard someone that sounded very like the sergeant shout, "Who nicked my bacon butty?"

She waited until they were alone in the stairwell to scowl at Dandy. "Stop stealing food. It's getting embarrassing. And I can feed you, you know."

He huffed, evidently indicating that he didn't have all that much confidence in her, considering she ate greenery.

She scratched him behind the ears instead. "Brat." She clattered down the stairs with him ghosting behind her, and before long they were hurrying back past the market and toward her apartment building.

Once she was in the car, it didn't take long to drive back out to Gladys's, the mid-morning streets quiet and the houses slumbering in the heat. Adams pulled into the kerb in the same place she'd parked yesterday, wondering if Gladys had a car. There was no garage, so it'd be parked out here if she did. Beyond the iron fence, the trees cast rich, heavy shadows across the house and the garden, and when Adams climbed out of the VW, birdsong rose around her in a chaotic chorus, accompanied by the oddly nostalgic smell of fresh-cut grass.

Adams let herself through the gate, seized again by that same sense of the world falling away, not just muted by the trees but cut off, as if a barrier had been dropped behind her. The quiet should have been peaceful, but instead it raised the hair on her arms and the back of her neck, an instinctive little shudder running over her. She looked around for Dandy, but he was still standing on the pavement, his nose up and twitching as he caught scents.

"What is it?" she whispered to him, telling herself she was only keeping her voice low because she didn't want to be seen talking to an invisible dog, not because of the sense of unease permeating the garden.

He whined and took a step back.

"Don't be silly. Come here." She patted her leg, suddenly certain she didn't want to be separated from him, as if he were an anchor to the world beyond the gates.

Dandy hesitated, then slunk up the steps and came to join her. He seemed smaller. She'd have said that was impossible, but invisible dog and all that. He was usually around the size of a golden retriever, but now he peered up at her, giving her a glimpse of the LED-red eyes, and he seemed more the size of a spaniel. Adams didn't quite dare risk crouching down to scratch him behind the ears, considering they were right by the house and anyone could be looking out the window, but she nudged him with her foot and muttered, "Good boy," then set off up the gravel path toward the house, Dandy trailing behind her.

She knocked briskly, and before long she heard hurrying footsteps inside. Gladys opened the door, her hair loose and tumbling softly over her shoulders. She was barefoot again, this time in blue denim dungarees with stars embroidered on them.

"Inspector Adams," she said, smiling brightly up at her. "Wonderful to see you! Have you found my necklace?"

"Not yet," Adams said. "I just had a few more questions for you."

"Oh, well. Anything I can do to help. It's imperative that I get it back."

She didn't move from the doorway, still smiling happily at Adams. Adams raised her eyebrows, and they looked at each other for a moment longer, the birdsong swelling wildly around them. There was a splash from the koi pond, and Adams resisted looking around to see if Dandy had fallen in. She was sure he'd be able to defend himself against some overgrown goldfish, anyway.

Finally Gladys gasped and said, "Oh! Do come in. Sorry, completely forgot myself there." She turned and headed inside, and Adams followed her into the dim hallway, wondering if Gladys was as entirely together as she'd thought.

Gladys led her into the kitchen this time, where a wall had been knocked down and a conservatory had been built onto the side of the house. Its doors were open into the garden beyond, and the glass walls and ceiling flooded the entire room with light. A set of wicker chairs with big, soft-looking cushions filled the space, framing a matching table with a glass top. There were palms in the corners, and the whole thing had an oddly colonial feel to it. Adams had to stop herself looking around in case a tiger was sprawled in the corner, soaking up the sun. But the only thing she spotted was a very large and very fancy coffee machine taking up half the worktop in the kitchen, which gave her a momentary stab of jealousy – and also confirmed her theory on just how high-tech and expensive it likely was.

"Oh, it's wonderful," Gladys said, following her gaze. "I've worked out how to make *the best* iced coffee, too. Would you like one?"

"No, but a regular one would be lovely," Adams said, watching as Gladys set about fussing around with the machine. It was some sort of computerised beast which ground the coffee to order, heated milk, had two different handles for different sized shots, and, as far as Adams could tell, probably sourced beans directly from the growers at the touch of a button. She put it on her mental list of *things I shall never own but would really like to.*

Gladys produced a mug of black coffee with impressive efficiency, placing it in front of Adams, then fished a large, fluted glass out of the cupboard. She put two scoops of ice cream in it, and proceeded to top it off with more black coffee, cold milk, and a generous helping from a can of squirty cream. She settled down with it into one of the chairs, waving Adams to join her.

"Now do tell me what else I can help you with," she said. "I'm getting most anxious about my necklace."

"Things are progressing," Adams said, not entirely honestly. "The CCTV at the shop appears to have had a malfunction at the time that whoever it was picked up your necklace."

Gladys grimaced. "Yes, that seems likely," she said, almost to herself.

Adams frowned at her. "Why does that seem likely?"

Gladys looked at her, still sipping from her straw, and finally said, "Oh, you know, it just seems to make sense, doesn't it?"

"In what way?"

Gladys gave her a large, winning smile. "Well, anyone who went to such an effort as to steal my necklace is hardly going to leave anything to chance, are they? Of course they made sure the CCTV didn't work."

"It's very curious," Adams said. "Because it was working perfectly fine afterward. And there's also the question of Meredith being quite certain it was you who came in."

Gladys waved vaguely. "She was a very nice young lady, but at her age all old people look alike."

That was actually a decent point, but Adams added, "The signature from the pick up looks pretty much identical to yours."

"You're obviously dealing with a very clever thief," Gladys said, and Adams examined her, looking for a twitch in her mouth, a tension in her shoulders, anything that might give her away. But she just sat there, tucked into the chair with one leg folded underneath her.

"What did you do before you retired?" Adams asked. "Were you an artist?"

"Not professionally," Gladys said. "I was a companion."

"A companion?"

"Yes, to the woman who owned this house. I started when I was sixteen, doing a bit of cleaning and cooking and so on, but mostly just being company. Helping her keep up to date with the news, and music, and fashion trends. Oh, I did like that bit. We used to shop an awful lot." Gladys smiled, tucking a heavy lock of hair behind one ear, her pale gaze distant. "And we travelled. It was a wonderful job, really."

Adams wondered for a moment if she'd just been transported back a couple of centuries, but the coffee machine seemed to argue against it. "Right. And she's …?"

"She passed on a few years ago," Gladys said. "I had a lot of trouble coming to terms with it. It took Olly coming in and showing me there was still so much life to be had before I could start to find myself again." She looked around, as if seeing the room for the first time. "Verity had no family, so I inherited the house and everything in it. Including the necklace, which is why it's so precious to me."

Adams nodded. "I thought it was a family heirloom."

"It is," Gladys said. "It belonged in Verity's family, and now it belongs in my family, and when I die, I will pass it on to someone else, and then it will belong in their family."

Adams smiled slightly. "Do you know who you might pass it on to?"

Gladys made a little *hmm* sound. "Probably to Olly," she said. "He really is quite wonderful, and I think he'll care for it very well."

"Doesn't really look like the sort of thing that Olly might wear," Adams said.

"One never knows," Gladys replied. "But we have to get it back first. Do you have a plan?" She raised her eyebrows as she went back to her straw, reminding Adams uncomfortably of a maths teacher she'd had at school.

"We're following up on the CCTV," she said. "There appear to have been other incidents, so we're looking into those at the moment."

"Other incidents?" Gladys said, lowering her glass. "What other incidents? More jewellery shop robberies?"

"No, not jewellery, but at least one other theft in which the recordings were affected the same way."

Gladys frowned at her. "Well, that's no good at all," she said. "That's quite a problem, in fact."

"Well, yes," Adams said. "I don't suppose you have anything you could add to what you've already told us? Anyone who's been here and maybe seen the necklace? Anything else missing?"

"No. But you must find it as a matter of urgency, you know. Especially with these other incidents."

"Why especially with those?"

Gladys didn't answer right away, but finally, with her eyes

on her coffee, she said, "It just indicates that it's quite a sophisticated gang, don't you think? And the longer they have my necklace, the more likely it is I'm not going to get it back. And I must, *I must* have that necklace back. Do you understand me?" There was a note of imperiousness in her voice, and Adams leaned back in her chair.

"We're doing everything we can," she said. "But we need all available information in order to make progress. So if there's anything else you can tell us – such as, say, why you weren't surprised about the CCTV not working – that could really make a difference."

Gladys shook her head. "It just made sense, that was all," she said. "They wouldn't take any chances."

Adams sighed. "Alright. But obviously the necklace was targeted."

"Well, surely the shop are the most likely culprits."

"They're the ones who reported you for harassing them about it. I hardly think they'd want to draw the attention of the police if they took it, do you?"

Gladys wrinkled her nose. "Maybe it's just to mislead the investigation."

"That seems unlikely," Adams said, although it wasn't impossible. "Who knew you were taking it to the jewellers?"

Gladys thought about it. "Only myself and Olly."

"Is he in today?"

"No, it's his day off. But he wouldn't have done anything."

Adams nodded. "Just eliminating possibilities. Do you have an address for him?"

"For his agency."

"Can you get it for me?" Adams said. "I want a quick word with him."

"Of course, but he won't have had anything to do with it," Gladys insisted. "He's a good boy."

"I'm sure he is," Adams replied. "But he may have inadvertently mentioned it to someone else, in which case that could give us another lead."

Gladys scrunched her face up dubiously, but she got up and padded over to the big, American-style fridge that loomed in the corner of the kitchen, incongruous against the old-fashioned wooden cabinets and broad, dozing AGA cooker, and took a card from under a magnet off the front. She brought it back to Adams. "There you go," she said. "He won't have anything to tell you, though."

Adams pocketed the card. "I'm sure you're right," she said. "Thanks for your time."

"Not at all," Gladys replied. "Do come back if you need anything further. But please hurry. I can't lose the necklace. I just *can't.*"

"Of course," Adams said, and let herself be escorted back to the front door. She could feel Gladys's gaze on her until she let herself out of the gates, and paused there for a moment, staring up at the empty windows of the house. Gladys knew *something,* that was for sure. And maybe she should have asked different questions, but what? *Hey, was your Verity some sort of witch? Is the necklace magical? What the hell is a companion, anyway?* No, the last thing she needed was to be kicked off the case for freaking out the complainant. It was bad enough she was being put on low-profile jewellery cases. She'd never see anything above traffic stops if she kept this up.

She beeped the car open, and Dandy bounded around the corner, dreadlocks flying and tail wagging, leaping past her and into the car as heat swelled out of the open door.

"You were helpful," she said to him.

He just panted at her.

7

MAGICAL BLOODY CONCLUSIONS

Once Adams was back in the car, Dandy panting over her shoulder and the engine running to get the air con going, she called James. He answered on the second ring.

"Got anything?" she asked him.

"Haven't found anything else so far, but Isha says she's ninety per cent sure the issue with the Apple Store footage is the same deal as the jewellery shop."

"Alright. I'll be back soon. Have a poke into Olly, see if you can come up with any debts or wild purchases or anything like that. Then we'll head to the Apple Store."

"Where're you going now?" he asked.

"To have a word with Olly."

"You think he took the necklace? Surely there'd be a better time to steal it than from the shop."

"Not if he's the only one other than her who has access to the house."

"Still, he couldn't exactly impersonate Gladys." James sounded doubtful, and she couldn't blame him. "It's not like they have the same build, is it?"

"I don't know," she said. "See if you can find any connections between him and Scott or Meredith, too, just in case they're working together somehow. But if nothing else, Olly might talk a bit more freely away from the house. About her mental state and so on."

"Fair enough," James said. "Alright, I'll report back."

Adams hung up, then plugged the number from the card Gladys had given her into the phone. It rang a few times before it was picked up by a crisp-sounding woman, her tones so precise and efficient that Adams straightened her shirt, as if her already wilting outfit was on display.

"Home Angels," the woman said. "How may I direct your call?"

"Detective Inspector Adams, West Yorkshire Police," Adams said. "I'm looking for Olly Davidson."

"He's off today," the woman said. "Can I perhaps help you?"

"No. I need to talk to him in connection with a case. He's not in any trouble, but he may have witnessed something that would be of assistance. Can you give me his contact details?"

"*Hmm,*" the woman said, and Adams could almost hear her debating with herself. She was wondering if she had to repeat *police* a bit more loudly when the woman said, "He hasn't been involved in anything untoward that might reflect badly on our company?"

So much for loyalty to your employees. "No. We just need a statement from him."

"Of course. I'll send the contact card through now. This phone number?"

"Yes," Adams said, and the phone binged in her ear, alarmingly efficient. "Thanks. How long has Olly worked for you?"

More tapping on the keyboard, loud in her ear. "Six years now."

"And with Gladys Hudson?"

"A little over a year." There was a note of disapproval in the woman's voice.

"And no problems?"

"Not at all. Mrs Hudson has been very happy with Olly. They seem to get on very well. He's very likeable."

"Always good to know," Adams said. "Any problems previously?"

"No, none at all."

"Does he have any other houses that he works at as well?"

"Yes, he's only at Gladys's two days a week. Has three other houses that he also attends, and also covers for other team members when necessary."

"Sounds busy," Adams said.

"Does seem to enjoy his work," the woman replied.

"Alright," Adams said. "Can you send me through the details of the clients he works with? Just so I can confirm a few things."

That hesitation again, the woman obviously deciding between privacy and not wanting any undue attention from the police. Finally she said, "Alright, I'll send them through."

Adams thanked her and hung up, then clicked Olly's address on her phone.

Olly lived on the edge of Bradford, in the middle of a row of terraced houses which had been sliced up into flats, all of them ragged around the edges and worn down by years. There was rubbish collected in the front garden, and the downstairs flat had a broken window patched by a piece of wood. A corner shop across the road had graffitied steel shutters pulled permanently down over its windows, advertising cheap off-brand whisky and frozen pizzas. It looked a lot like the neighbourhood Adams had lived in when she first moved out of home.

It hadn't taken long to get there, the morning traffic city-heavy but steady, and by the time she arrived, Adams had already talked to four of Olly's other clients. The general consensus seemed to be that he really was very likeable, and she got the impression that at least one woman wanted to adopt him, and another seemed to harbour hopes he was interested in a more mature demographic. The one man she spoke to just kept saying, "Well, 'e's my mate, innit?" Certainly no one seemed to harbour any suspicions he might be thieving about the place, but being exceptionally likeable was a good trait for a thief.

Adams found a parking spot between a skip that looked like it hadn't moved for about thirty years, its contents sprouting grass and a couple of aspiring shrubs, and a low-slung boy racer that would definitely have lights underneath it. She ambled back to the terraced row with Dandy walking along the low stone wall that separated the properties from the pavement next to her, and hit the buzzer. It didn't take long until Olly answered, his voice wary.

"DI Adams," Adams said. "We spoke yesterday at Gladys's."

"Yes, I heard you were coming," he said, the door buzzing open. "Top floor." So there was a little bit of loyalty to employees there, then. Or else the efficient-sounding woman had called to make sure Olly wasn't going to say anything to get the company in trouble.

Adams shoved the door open, the bottom catching on the scarred wooden floor, then forced it closed again behind her. She headed for the stairs, wrinkling her nose against the scent of damp and boiled cabbage that always seemed to hang around these sort of houses. It seemed to be baked into their very nature.

Olly was standing in the doorway of his flat waiting for her when she arrived on the landing. He was wearing a faded but clean T-shirt and sunlight washed around him, turning his red hair fiery on the tips. He had a cleaning cloth in one hand, and Adams glanced at it as she stopped at the door. "Taking your work home with you?"

He followed her gaze and smiled slightly. "I haven't got anyone to clean my place," he said. "It's this or drown in dust."

Adams made an agreeing noise, thinking guiltily that she hadn't dusted since she moved in. The kitchen and bathroom were clean, though. What more did she need?

Olly stepped away from the door, revealing a small box of a room, a little sink area and some cabinets taking up one corner, with a small oven sitting on top of an equally small fridge. There was a sofa bed neatly tidied away against one wall, and a door that she assumed led to the bathroom. Light poured in through two big old sash windows that looked like they'd leak both rain and wind in the winter.

"Do you want a cup of tea?" he asked. "I don't have any coffee, I'm afraid."

"No thanks. I don't want to take up your day off. I just want to talk to you a little more about Gladys."

He nodded, running the cloth through his fingers absently. "Sure, but there's nothing more to tell. Mentally, she's in better shape than some people my age. There's no way she picked up the necklace and forgot about it."

"Right," Adams said. "Thing is, we're struggling to make the facts fit. The young woman at the shop is entirely sure it was Gladys who came in."

"Meredith," Olly said, and Adams tilted her head slightly, then immediately stopped when she realised Dandy was looking up at Olly with his head at the identical angle.

"Do you know her?" she asked.

"Not really. I went in there when Gladys told me about the missing necklace. I wanted to see if Meredith might talk to me. People usually seem pretty comfortable with me, you know?"

Adams nodded, although she wasn't at all familiar with that experience. "And?"

"She just got really upset." He frowned as he spoke, twisting the cloth in his hands. "It's *such* a terrible thing to do to Gladys, though. That necklace was precious to her. Not just valuable."

"You really should have left the interviewing to us, you know."

"I know. But Gladys didn't want to call the police. She wanted to handle it herself, in case ... well, she just did. And I went along with that, but when the shop just wouldn't budge I told her we needed to report it. She wouldn't, though, and now they've got this ridiculous harassment thing going on."

"Not entirely ridiculous if you and Gladys have both been in there."

"I suppose."

"And in case of what?"

"What?"

"You said Gladys wanted to handle it herself, in case ...?"

"Nothing. I mean, just, she didn't want anyone thinking she was dotty, I imagine." The cloth looked at risk of being torn apart in his hands, and Adams let the silence lie between them until she was sure he wasn't going to add anything.

Finally she said, "Do you know if Gladys had any sort of financial difficulties? Might she have been in need of insurance money?"

He shook his head. "I don't think so. And I'd be kind of surprised if she has anything insured at all, to be honest."

"Not even all those paintings in the house? They look pretty valuable."

"I have no idea. I think they were her friend's. Verity's."

"What about the new stuff? The coffee machine and so on? They're not cheap."

"It's just not really her style. She thinks things like that are fun, but she's not worried about what they cost or anything."

Adams thought that must be a nice position to be in, but aloud she just said, "Has she ever indicated that she might leave you something in her will?"

Olly made a face. "Not as such, but it's possible."

"You don't seem surprised by the idea."

He sighed, looking at her directly for the first time since she'd arrived. He had surprisingly dark blue eyes, and a scattering of freckles across his nose. "I've been doing this job since I left school, for different agencies. Most of the people I work with leave me a little something. It's not anything I ask for or want, though, especially as some far-flung relative who hasn't seen them for thirty years is sure to turn up at the funeral and dispute a bloody china shepherdess and a souvenir teaspoon. It's not worth the hassle."

Adams nodded. "Seems a bit unfair, that. You do all the work, and they turn up to grab an inheritance without so much as visiting."

"Maybe. Maybe not. Relationships go both ways, don't they? And we never know what they look like from the inside."

Adams nodded slowly. She was starting to see why Olly was welcome company. "Does Gladys have any family that you know of?"

"No. It's just her. Apparently she worked in the house for years, and was essentially a daughter to Verity."

"So it'd probably be reasonable to assume you'll get something in the will."

Olly frowned. "I don't quite understand where you're going with this. Gladys isn't dead, and the necklace has been stolen. If you're suggesting I thought I was going to get the necklace in her will, then surely I'd just bump her off rather than stealing it."

Adams raised her eyebrows at him, and he flushed, his nose going painfully pink.

"Look, I'm her carer. There's plenty of ways I could do her in if I wanted to."

A startled silence fell over the flat, broken only by Dandy's claws as he put his paws up on the window to stare down at the street. Olly covered his face with both hands. "I didn't mean it the way it sounds. It came out wrong. I read a lot of murder mysteries."

Brilliant, Adams thought to herself. Murder mysteries and little old ladies not wanting to go to the police. Temper was right, this one was on-brand for her. "Right," she said aloud. "I'd probably advise you not to say that sort of thing to a police officer."

"Yeah. I kind of realised even as I was saying it. I just … I write them, too. Murder mysteries. Not published yet, but Gladys really likes them. That's one of the reasons she thought we could sort this out ourselves. Because of my research, you know."

Adams sighed. "In other words, don't look at your search history?"

"Please don't."

She was starting to think the north was positively infested by people who couldn't keep their noses out of her cases. They were going to sort it out themselves because Olly wrote *murder mysteries?* She put that aside as well as she could and said, "I suppose I should just be grateful the bloody shop called us in."

"We would've done it eventually," Olly protested. "It's only been a couple of weeks."

"Long enough. Do you know of anyone else that comes

around the house? Visitors? Anyone who might have seen the necklace?"

He shook his head. "Gladys doesn't really know many people. Verity was her life, and she was pretty much a hermit before I started helping. Plus she never wears it at home."

"What about going out?"

He scratched his jaw. "I only ever saw her wear it out a handful of times. When she was buying the TV and so on. She gets dressed up for anything where she has to deal with people who might not take her seriously and treat her like some barefoot old hippie or something."

Adams smiled slightly at that. "She didn't seem too worried about it when we met her."

"I suppose she thought you'd already be invested in the case."

"I suppose I am, at that. Do you know where the necklace was kept?"

Olly shook his head. "It would've been in her safe, but I don't know where that is. I know she has one, but I'm always really careful not to get involved with things like that. It's not worth the risk if something does go missing, and I end up the perfect suspect."

"I can see how that might happen," Adams said, and looked around the little flat thoughtfully. It was a bed-sit, really, although just big enough that it probably billed itself as a studio. "How long did you say you've been doing this?"

He followed her gaze. "Since school. It doesn't exactly pay well. Better than a flat share, though. Having your own space, you know?"

Adams nodded. She did know, and she was going to have to start looking for her own place soon. The generosity of the police force in helping her relocate was going to run out along with the rental contract. "Is there anything else you can tell me?" she said aloud. "Any clubs or groups she went to, anything like that?"

Olly shrugged. "She's not really a group activity person. I think she goes to a poker game or something like that once a week, though, or did for a bit. She likes cards."

"Did you ever see her wear the necklace to that?"

"It's at night, so no," he said. "I've normally left by six latest, or if I stay it's because we're just hanging out."

Adams wondered what a man in his early thirties was doing hanging out with a woman who was well past sixty, but whether it was for work or friendship hardly mattered. It wasn't getting her any answers. "Alright," she said, and handed him a card. "Call me if you think of anything. And keep your investigations to your bloody books, okay?"

"Sure. Sorry," he said, and watched her head down the hall to the stairs before he closed the door. Adams heard the lock roll over the creak of the floorboards under her boots. He hardly gave off a guilty vibe even given the murder mystery shenanigans. If anything *she* was feeling guilty, and had a strong urge to call her gran.

That was a good way to a three-hour interrogation regarding her eating habits, dating status, and long-term life plans, though, as well as a lecture on the horrors of the north, so she just got back into the car and called James.

"Anything new?" she asked when he answered.

"I was reading the notes from the Apple Store – have you read them?"

"I started to," she admitted. "But it was really long."

"They're interesting."

"Interesting how?"

"Well, nobody remembers seeing anyone walking out with a laptop."

"They had a medical situation, didn't they?"

"Exactly. Patrice Claiborne, the associate who served the

presumed thief, had such a severe migraine he ended up in hospital and can't remember anything about the person he served."

Adams had her hand on the gear stick, the indicator already ticking, but she didn't pull out into the traffic. "Another migraine?"

"Yeah. Look, what if they really are using some sort of scrambling thing, and maybe it's got a certain frequency that affects the brainwaves? Or they've got some sort of chemical agent they spray on people to kick off these migraines?"

Adams didn't answer, resting her forehead against her hands on the wheel.

"Adams?" James said finally. "Have I lost you?"

"Do you write murder mysteries in your free time?"

"No," he said, a little huff in his voice. "It's *possible*."

"I'm sure it is. You know, in Hollywood. Don't you think it's more likely that these are inside jobs, and the whole migraine thing's a bit of handy acting?"

"Well, I suppose. Not as interesting, though, is it?"

"We're not after interesting, James. We're after what actually happened. What else did the shop assistant say?"

"Associate. And I haven't spoken to him yet. Technically he's on sick leave, but I think that means he's suspended. Giving away several thousand pounds worth of kit probably had some consequences."

"Yeah, that'll do it. Have you got his address?"

"I have."

"Meet you there?"

"Absolutely," he replied, a note of relief in his voice. Adams hung up with a small pang of guilt, thinking that maybe she was being a little unfair sticking him on phone calls and searching computer files, but someone had to do it. And if she had to deal with murder mystery writers and bloody difficult women of a certain age, she at least had earned enough seniority to not be stuck on the computer the whole day.

She pulled out of the parking spot, sliding back through the streets without really thinking about it, the roads of Leeds already becoming more familiar, the routes through them automatic. Two migraines. Two lots of scrambled cameras. Or two incidents of something that couldn't be picked up on camera, anyway, which pointed to something she already knew about. As did the migraines.

But she couldn't be jumping to magical bloody conclusions just because she didn't know what was happening. She was still a detective, and that meant she had to look at the facts, tricky as they were, not at folklore. Even if she knew by now that the two were far more closely linked than she really wanted to think about.

8

ALLIANCES FOR THE WIN

The Apple Store worker lived in Headingley, not far from the road that charged northwest out of the city, pouring through Otley and Ilkley and on toward Skipton, shaking off the towns and villages and industrial estates as it reached for high fells and hidden valleys and old, secret places. For a moment, Adams wondered whether she should be allowing herself to be swept along by the fleeing road rather than hurdling it, if she should be asking questions of dragons and cats rather than simply continuing this relentless circling of the city.

But she didn't wonder for long. It was just a missing necklace, for a start, but more importantly she did *not* want to get dragons involved, because then they'd be *involved.* And they never came unaccompanied, and the next thing she knew she'd have mystical beasts stomping through her evidence and ladies of a certain age being disapproving at her suspects, and probably taking tea in their houses, too. Plus she still didn't quite trust the cat.

So she reached a hand back to pet Dandy and said, "Just you and me, then."

He licked her hand, then dropped something small and slobbery onto her lap.

"Bloody hell—" She jerked her leg, knocking his gift to the floor, but not before it had left wet, slightly gritty streaks on her trousers. "Great. That's just great."

Dandy whined, and she ignored him, pulling up behind a neat little electric Nissan that was parked outside a row of red brick terraced houses adorned with big, white-framed bay windows, one of many that had been turned into student lets in the area. James was leaning on the Nissan with his face tipped up to the sunshine and his sleeves rolled to his elbows, looking too big to fit inside the car.

Adams climbed out and looked up at the building. "He here?"

"Assume so. Anything from Olly?"

"Not really," she said. "He went and saw Meredith, though. Apparently he and Gladys were having their own little investigation before they called us in."

James frowned. "Meredith didn't mention it."

"I know. I'm wondering if he's saying that so that if she *does* mention it, he's already covered himself."

"You think he and Meredith are in it together? The whole looking-like-Gladys thing's just some sort of really badly done misdirection?"

"Maybe," Adams said. "Possible, anyway. But I'm not really liking him for it. I think he'd come up with a better plan than that."

"You give criminals a lot of credit."

"Only some of them. Olly also said that Gladys wore the necklace when she was out shopping for big-ticket items, so maybe someone clocked it then."

"And then set up a whole jewellery shop heist? Who was it, a professional dotty old lady impersonator?"

"Had a good morning, have you?" Adams asked, and James cleared his throat, looking at his feet.

"Sorry. But you did dump me with all the bloody paperwork, *and* dealing with Isha."

"Isha's fine."

"She's fine with *you.* She calls me Posh Boy and made me go back and get her a different coffee because I got hazelnut syrup instead of caramel."

Adams tried for a sympathetic noise, and James glared at her.

"I am *not* posh."

"You are a bit. You went to public school."

"I'm not the one who only goes by their last name."

"That's not posh."

"Keep telling yourself that." He pushed himself off the car. "Also Lindsay wanted to look at what we had so far, and Isha basically strong-armed her out of the office, so you'll have that to deal with."

"Fun," Adams said. "Anyway, let's talk to Apple Boy."

She led the way up the steps to the front door, knocking sharply. The door was painted dark green, the paint slightly scuffed at the bottom, and there was a recycling box sitting just outside, overflowing with half-crushed beer cans and a couple of empty vodka bottles. There was no immediate answer, and she knocked again, a little more insistently.

Finally there were footsteps beyond the door, then fumbling with the lock. It was pulled open by a young man with messy hair, wearing nothing but a pair of baggy tartan boxer shorts, who squinted against the sunlight as he stared at them. "Hello?"

"Patrice Claiborne?" Adams said.

"Yeah," he said, rubbing one hand over his chest absently, and tried to focus on the ID Adams and James were holding up. "Oh, I already spoke to the police," he said. "I told them, I don't remember anything."

"Well, you haven't told us that yet," Adams said. "So we'd like to come in and ask you a few more questions."

He sighed, a great full body sigh that washed stale alcohol over the threshold. James stepped back and Adams wrinkled her nose, while beside her Dandy sneezed and gave Patrice a reproachful look.

"Come in," Patrice said, and stepped back from the door, wandering away. "I'm going to put some trousers on."

"That'd be appreciated," Adams said, stepping inside as he wandered up the carpeted stairs that took up most of the hall. A couple of empty carrier bags were living by the door, along with a pile of unopened mail, and the old red carpet had some predictably suspicious stains. There were a couple of cigarette burns in one corner, and a lingering scent of stale alcohol and congealed grease hung over everything, like the ghosts of old takeaways. It was like every student house Adams had ever been in and she ambled through to the living room, looking for lurking Apple computers or bags from jewellery shops without any expectation of actually seeing any.

The place was cursorily decorated with curling posters on the walls and some old floral curtains that would be hand-me-downs from someone's mum. It was stuffed with too many chairs and a table piled with abandoned textbooks and a bewildering array of chargers, empty beer bottles and discarded glasses, and a stack of half-empty takeaway containers. A girl in a summer dress with one strap hanging off the shoulder wandered past them with a cup of tea in her hand, nodding slightly.

"Alright," she said.

"Alright," Adams replied, and watched her pad barefoot

up the stairs. She shuddered slightly. She wouldn't like to be barefoot anywhere in this place.

A moment later, Patrice came stumbling back down the stairs, wearing a T-shirt and a pair of running shorts that weren't much longer than his boxers had been. "Ah … tea," he said. "Tea?"

"No thanks," Adams and James said together.

Patrice shambled across the living room and into the kitchen anyway, flicking the kettle on, and found a relatively clean mug in the sink. He set it on the worktop, added a teabag, and spooned an excessive amount of sugar into it straight from a split, stained bag. "I don't know what else I can say. I was completely wiped out by a migraine or something. I don't remember *anything.*"

"Feeling better now?" Adams asked.

"Yeah, back to normal," he said. "That was an absolute nightmare, though. Never felt anything like it. I thought I was having a stroke." The kettle boiled, and he slopped water mostly into the mug, then pawed through the fridge in search of some milk. He sniffed a couple of bottles that were in the door, put them back again with a grimace, then found one that was apparently acceptable.

"Do you get migraines often?" Adams asked.

"No, first time. It was like the worst hangover I've ever had, only even worse. Felt like my head was going to split in two."

"Horrible," Adams said with feeling, although she was mostly directing that at Dandy, who was standing in the middle of the floor with his floppy ears back as far as they were able to be and his nose twitching wildly.

Patrice led them back to the table and sat down, pushing aside a jumble of junk mail, fliers and coupons. "Yeah. Not super fun."

"Can you walk us through it?" James asked.

Patrice took a sip of tea and made a satisfied sound. "Sure. I just work part time, around uni. I was meant to be on from two, and I went in as normal. And I'd been there, I don't know, like an hour? Two hours? Something like that. And I kind of remember all of that fine – usual stuff of people coming in with questions or because they've locked themselves out of their phones or whatever." He frowned. "Then ... Then I think I remember someone coming in and asking about the latest MacBook. And I know there was something about having the whole ecosystem, you know, titanium watch, titanium phone, everything. All the top spec. And I was thinking, you know, I'm going to get *such* a good commission on this. And then ... nothing."

"Really?" Adams asked.

"Really. Even that's pretty foggy, to be honest. The next thing I remember is being in the ambulance with my head feeling like it was going to explode." He touched his fingertips to his forehead gingerly, as if the attack might have left traces. "They took me to hospital and did an MRI. Didn't find anything, though. I swear I thought it was a brain tumour."

James had been taking notes and now he looked up and said, "A brain tumour and a stroke?"

"I don't know, do I?" Patrice asked. "I'm studying computer science, not medicine."

"So you don't remember anything about the person you were serving when this happened?" Adams asked. "Male, female, anything?"

"Nothing," he said. "It's completely blank. The migraine just wiped everything out. Do you think it's like, brain damage or something? They said it wasn't at the hospital, but maybe they were just trying to stop me freaking out."

Adams sighed, leaning back against the chair, then immediately straightened up when something squished against her shoulder blades. "I'm sure they'd have told you if there was anything serious wrong."

"I hope so. I mean, it's bad enough that I'm probably going to lose my job. I got good discounts." He stretched out his arm to show them his Apple watch. "Not like I can buy this at full price."

"I imagine," Adams said. "The report from the store says that no invoices were signed or details taken from anyone for the kit that vanished. I suppose you don't remember anything about that either?"

"No. I don't even remember showing them any of it."

This was getting them nowhere. Adams took a card out and slid it across the. "We'll be in touch. Let us know if you do remember anything."

"Sure," Patrice said, then looked around, frowning slightly. "How many classes d'you think this can get me out of?"

OUTSIDE, the heat was baking off the pavement in a distinctly non-English manner, and James plucked at the collar of his shirt lightly. "Didn't get us far, did it?"

"The similarities are there," Adams said. "Do you really think there's something that could do that? Trigger a migraine?"

"I think maybe," James said. "All sorts of things out there now."

"There's the memory loss too, though, which is really weird. And his seems to be worse than Meredith's."

"Heavier dose?" James suggested.

"We don't even know if there is a dose."

"I can look into it. See if there's anything that might do it?"

Adams ran a hand over her face and sighed. "Yeah. The incidents are too alike to be unconnected. But you can do that later. For now let's head back to the station, drop your car, then we'll have another word with Meredith. See what she has to say about talking with Olly. Then we'll track the silversmith down, too. Make sure he's clear."

James nodded, already beeping his car open. "See you back there."

She went back to her own car, checking the to-go mug in the cupholder hopefully, but it was empty, which felt very much aligned with her day. They were running into dead ends everywhere. Olly with his earnest integrity, Patrice with his memory loss, Meredith with her migraine, and the increasingly anxious Gladys. It was all connected, but not in any way that made sense. It was like scratching at a roll of tape, trying to find the seam that would allow her to unravel it, and Adams couldn't find the seam. She was just going round and round in pointless circles, covering the same old ground repeatedly.

Coffee. She needed coffee. And if she was getting coffee, she may as well get Isha coffee, and see if she had anything new to say about James Bond scramblers and … brain scramblers? Adams shook her head, checked the road and pulled out. If she was clutching at straws that fragile, she was going to have to entertain some different straws. She looked at Dandy, who was staring fixedly down at her feet.

"You dropped it," she said. "I'm not hunting for your slimy little treasure."

He whined, and she ignored him. Moody dogs were the last thing she needed.

Isha looked up as Adams pushed through the door and placed a large iced coffee and equally enormous chocolate muffin next to it on her desk. She poked the coffee and said, "Bloody hell, I'm going to have to switch to decaf if you keep stalking me like this."

"And I thought I'd heard all the horrifying things I could already," Adams said, moving a potted fern off the chair so she could sit down.

"Be careful with him. He was getting crowded out by the others."

Adams looked at the plant, then set it gently on the corner of the desk. "Anything on the Apple Store CCTV? Or anything else?"

"And here I thought you were coming by because you liked me."

Adams opened her mouth, shut it again, and took a sip of her own coffee.

Isha waited a moment, grinning, then gave a surprisingly witchy cackle and said, "I've got nothing."

"Nothing?"

"Nothing. And that's what makes it interesting."

Adams sighed deeply, and gave a *carry-on* wave.

"I can't tell how they hacked in."

"And that's interesting, is it?"

"Love, if *I* can't tell, no one can. And there's no sign of anything in either the Apple Store or the jewellery shop."

"But there should be?" She tried to unobtrusively push Dandy away from the fern with one foot.

"There should. Everyone leaves some little traces of themselves behind, fingerprints as it were. But there's nothing. Not so much as a whisper."

Adams nodded. Fingerprints she could get behind. "So your theory is …?"

"So I'm starting to think your lad James's theory about the *Mission Impossible*–style scrambler could have some legs."

"Really?" Adams asked, and felt slightly disloyal for how surprised she sounded.

"Yeah. I've asked around, done a little bit of research. It's possible. You know, if they knew what the Wi-Fi signal for the cameras was, which wouldn't be that hard to find out."

"Right," Adams said, and picked up the fern as Dandy tried to take the pot in his teeth. "But then it could be anyone, right?"

"Yes and no. The people who have the knowledge and ability to set that sort of thing up are pretty limited. Who was your Apple Store lad?"

"Huh. Computer science student."

"Worth looking into," Isha said. "He'd definitely be able to sort the cameras there. Not sure about the necklace connection, though."

"Student debt's a good enough reason," Adams said. "If he knew a way to flog it, anyway." She liked the idea of it. Just a straight up heist.

"Suppose the jewellery shop woman would have a bit of knowledge of that," Isha said.

"Wouldn't surprise me." Adams waited for that tell-tale prickle of anticipation, the tightening in her belly that told her something had snapped into place, but it wasn't there. Too many loose ends still, she supposed. "Lindsay was going to check in with her contacts, see if anyone was trying to shift the necklace through art channels, so I'll see what she's got."

Isha had leaned back in her chair, inspecting the muffin bag, but now she looked up with a scowl. "I wouldn't give her too much info."

"Why?"

"She's a right vicious garden snake, that one."

"She seems alright."

Isha raised an eyebrow. "She giving you the whole sisterhood runaround?"

"A bit," Adams admitted.

"Wouldn't think you'd fall for that, Adams."

"Well, she's not wrong, though, is she? There is a bloody boy's club, and it doesn't hurt for someone to have your back."

"The only reason Lindsay has anyone's back is to stab it," Isha said.

Adams took a sip of coffee to hide her sigh, but the way Isha was watching her she doubted she'd got away with it.

"Fine, figure it out yourself," Isha said. "Thanks for the muffin."

Adams nodded and got up. "Anything else come up?"

"Not so far. But someone just gave me a call and said they were sending over some questionable CCTV files. I'll let you know if that links up to anything."

"Where were they from?" Adams asked.

"Porsche garage."

Adams blinked at her. "They've lost a car?"

Isha clicked a few keys on her keyboard. "Someone took a test drive without signing any papers. They're calling it clerical error."

"No mention of anyone with a migraine?"

Isha scanned the report. "No. Apparently the salesman in question was indisposed. The report was filed by the manager."

"Indisposed?"

"Yeah, whatever that means when it's at home."

"But surely they must have some sort of tracking system on the car?"

"Oh, yeah. The car's been picked up already, but there was

some damage, and they have to claim on the insurance. Hence the police report."

Adams was momentarily distracted by *hence.* More people should use words like *hence,* she thought. "Can you send me the report?" she asked finally.

"You'd have to request it from the officer who took it," Isha said, clicking a few things. Adams' phone dinged. "And he'd have to do his big man thing and insist you did paperwork requests and so on." She looked at Adams. "Just so you know."

"Thanks," Adams said, grinning.

"Bollocks to sisterhood, Adams. Alliances are where it's at. Sisters are nightmares."

"I only had brothers."

"Well, just trust me on this." Isha gave her a sudden wink. "On most things, really."

Adams wondered if she should wink back, realised she'd thought about it for too long, so just nodded and turned to the door.

"Adams?"

"Yes?"

"Can I have my fern back?"

Adams looked down at the pot, still clasped safely in her hands. "Sorry, yes," she said, and put it back on the chair before heading out of the room, chasing Dandy ahead of her as unobtrusively as she could.

9

ASH & YEW & DEAD ENDS

MEREDITH BUZZED THEM IN WITH A TIGHT, ANXIOUS SMILE ON her face. The shop was even hotter than the day before, and either the little fan from the office had been moved out here to sit on one corner of the counter, or they'd bought another one. It lifted Meredith's fine, straight hair as she fiddled with the necklaces she had set out on a cloth in front of her.

"Hello, detectives," she said. "Can I help you?"

"Possibly," Adams said. "How do you know Patrice Claiborne?"

Meredith gave her a blank look that seemed quite genuine. "Patrice who?"

"Patrice Claiborne. He works at the Apple Store up the road."

She shook her head. "I don't have anything Apple." She reached under the counter and produced a Samsung phone in a pearlescent case. "I just have this."

"Maybe you know him from uni? He does computer science?"

"I did a BA in English literature. Eighteenth-century poets." She was frowning, and as far as Adams could tell she really did seem to be genuinely bewildered. It was impossible to be certain, of course, and if she was a good enough actor to fake the migraine and throw her boss off then she'd definitely be good enough to pretend not to know Patrice, but Adams didn't like her for it any more than she liked Olly, which was disappointing. She managed not to sigh, and gave Dandy a hopeful look, but he was just staring at the fan, letting it lift his dreadlocks off his snout. She was starting to think he was quite a useless magical sidekick.

"I thought everyone was into Apple watches and so on now," Adams said. "Not your thing?"

Meredith extended her arm, showing them a small gold watch with no markings on the face, just barely visible hands creeping across it. "Really not my thing."

"How about your boss?" James asked. "He into Apple stuff?"

Meredith glanced toward the door at the back of the shop, an involuntary little twitch. "You were in his office. Did you see his computer?"

"Maybe as gifts? For his kids or something?"

She scrunched up her face. "I don't think he could. He's always complaining that the divorce cleaned him out, and I know things are kind of tight. We used to have a cleaner, but he can't afford it anymore, so I have to do it." She stopped, throwing another of those glances at the door. "I mean, I don't mind, though. And he's never missed my wages."

Adams looked around the shop until she spotted the camera, and turned her back to it, looking at Meredith levelly. "Are you sure there's nothing you'd like to share with us, Meredith?"

"No," she said, her voice quiet but firm.

"You seem a bit nervous. Has Scott told you not to talk to us?"

"No! No, not at all. But I just don't know anything. I don't know this Patrick—"

"Patrice."

"*Patrice,* and I don't know anything about Apple, and I don't know where the necklace is, and I don't know *anything!*" Her voice had gone up on the last few words, her hands clenched by her sides, and she stared at Adams, her cheeks pink and her breath audible in the quiet shop.

"How about Olly?" Adams asked, keeping her tone friendly.

"*Who?*"

"He works with Gladys. He came in and asked about the necklace too, apparently."

Meredith looked bewildered for a moment, then nodded. She took a breath, evidently getting herself under control. "Oh, him. Yes, he did, and I explained that she picked it up herself. Then Scott came out and talked with him."

"What did Scott say to him?"

"I don't know exactly. Just that he had the wrong idea if he thought we'd stolen it, I imagine." Her eyes were drifting to the door again.

"Is Scott here?" Adams asked.

"Um."

"We'd like to talk to him."

Meredith sighed and picked up the phone, but before she could even push the intercom the door at the back of the shop opened, and Scott emerged, giving them both a jovial smile.

"Detectives! Have you made some progress?"

"You could say that," Adams said. "Mind if we have a word?" She pointed at the door, and Scott dipped his head and waved at it, as if he were a waiter showing them to a table.

"Do come in."

Wedged back in the little office, weighted down with heat, Adams glanced at James. He was examining the office thoughtfully, looking from the slowly collapsing file boxes to the cluttered desk. He didn't seem to be coming up with anything more than she was, though.

"How can I help?" Scott asked, settling himself back in his chair. He had his suit jacket on, and Adams could see sweat sticking his shirt to his belly beneath it.

"You didn't mention that you talked with Olly, Ms Hudson's carer, the other day."

He frowned. "It didn't seem relevant."

"Can you tell us what happened?"

"There's very little to tell. He came here asking about the necklace, and we explained she'd taken it. I assume as her carer he must be aware she's … well. *Impaired*."

"He doesn't seem to think she is."

"She must be if she doesn't remember picking up her necklace." Scott looked from Adams to James.

Dandy was snuffling at the safe, and Adams looked at it. "Do you keep customer's items in there, Mr Samuels?"

He followed her gaze. "Yes."

"Can we have a look?"

He frowned. "Why?"

"Because I'd like to see what you have in there." She held his gaze, and he looked away first.

"Of course. I don't see why, though." He got up and crossed to the safe, blocking their view with his back while he entered the combination, then pulled the door open and stepped back. "There we are."

James got up to check the interior, while Adams tried to peer past him. He turned in a moment and shrugged, and she nodded. Now he'd moved, she could see even from here that there were a few small jewellery boxes inside, and nothing else. Nothing big enough to hold the necklace. Evidently Scott didn't keep much in stock.

"Have you ever handled a piece like Ms Hudson's before?" she asked.

"Antique pieces? Yes."

"Ones that are works of art. That might be in high demand in certain markets."

Scott looked at her for a long moment, colour rising in his cheeks, then he said quietly, "If that's all, I'd like you to go now, please."

"I hear you're having some financial difficulties. It must be tempting."

"I will not be insulted like this," he said in the same quiet tone. "Kindly leave. And I'll be talking to your supervisor."

James looked at the ceiling, then turned to the door. Adams got up and followed him, stopping to look at Scott. He stared back at her, his mouth a hard pinched line, and she couldn't quite tell if it was fury or fear. They sat uncomfortably close at times.

"THAT WENT WELL," James said, as they walked back to the station.

"Had to ask."

"Did you, though?"

She supposed not, actually. But Scott hardly struck her as a hardened criminal. If he'd had anything to do with it, he'd be flustered now. He'd make a mistake, try to move it too quickly, and that'd be their best chance for it to be turned up by Lindsay's contacts. She took her phone out and scrolled through her contacts, hitting dial. Lindsay answered after a few rings.

"Adams," Lindsay said.

"Hi. Just checking in – anything turning up on that necklace?"

"Not so far. Anything your end?"

Adams considered it, thinking of Isha saying, *I wouldn't give her too much info.* She didn't know what high school rubbish those two were involved in, and she couldn't be bothered to find out, but on the other hand, she didn't *really* know anything worth passing on, anyway. "Not so much," she said aloud. "Just poking a few things, seeing if it gets anyone jumpy."

"I heard you were looking into the Apple Store robbery, too. How's that going?"

"It's going. I don't think your art contacts'll have much interest in a flashy watch."

Lindsay laughed, a quick, light sound. "No. But if you need someone to bounce ideas off or anything, let me know."

"Thanks. James is working it with me, though."

"Well. If you need a bit more insight than a DC can give you." She laughed again, as if to take the bite out of the words. "Better go." The phone clicked off, and Adams shoved it back into her pocket.

"How's your new bestie?" James asked.

"Not much help."

"No surprise there."

Adams frowned at him. "Why's everyone got it in for Lindsay? She's fine."

"She's not. You should've seen when she made DI. She wasn't even in line for the promotion, but the DS who was ended up with an evidence bag in his locker. Destroyed a case and tanked his career."

Adams grimaced. "If Lindsay did that, it'd have tanked her career too."

"Only if anyone could prove it."

They walked the rest of the way back in silence while

Adams wondered how much weight to give to station rumours, particularly when it came to ambitious women. Not every lie was without its truth, but the ones where certain women were concerned seemed to have less than most.

ADAMS TOOK her notebook out and found the silversmith's card tucked inside it. She dialled the mobile number as they walked. It rang half a dozen times, and she was just deciding whether or not to leave a message when a deep voice answered.

"Charles Worthington," it said.

"DI Adams, West Yorkshire Police," Adams said. "I wondered if we could have a word."

"The missing necklace at Samuels's," he said, more statement than question.

"That's the one. Are you available?"

"I'm at my workshop," he said. "In York. I can be back down to Leeds tomorrow, perhaps."

"That's alright," Adams said. "We'll have a bit of a day trip. Whereabouts?"

He sighed slightly and reeled off an address, along with the name of a jewellers, that she scrawled in her notebook. "I'll be here all afternoon."

"We'll be about an hour," Adams replied. She hung up and looked at James, turning the notebook so he could see it. "Recognise the name?"

He examined it. "No. But that's in The Shambles."

"The what now?"

"The Shambles." He grinned. "It's the old, touristy bit. High rent, tiny shops, lots of footfall."

"Shops that might be making their money less than legitimately?"

"You ask that as if there's anywhere that *doesn't* have shops like that."

"Fair point." She put her notebook away and took her car keys out as they approached the station parking garage. "Need the loo before we leave? I'm not stopping along the way."

"You don't know how to make friends, do you, Adams?"

"I do. But you're my colleague, anyway."

"That does not make it better." She just looked at him, and after a moment he said, "Yeah, actually. Won't be a moment." He vanished toward the stairs at a jog, and she watched him go, grinning, then frowned suddenly. She should probably go herself and all. She hurried after him.

She'd just popped out of the toilets, drying her hands surreptitiously on her trousers, when Temper loomed in front of her. She barely stopped herself taking a step back as he glared down at her.

"Boss?"

"Care to explain to me why our best tech is spending all her time combing through CCTV footage of unrelated cases?"

"Not necessarily unrelated—"

"Oh? Because I tried to check your case notes to see what this spurious connection was, and there is nothing. *Nothing.* Not even an update to the original jewellery shop complaint, which is what you're meant to be working on."

"I am," she protested. "Something happened to the cameras at the shop when the necklace went missing, then the same thing happened during a robbery at the Apple Store. It seems unlikely to be unconnected."

He scowled at her. "And the necklace?"

"Still missing."

"Any leads?"

"Well, I'm hoping that the connection to the other robbery might turn something up."

He considered it. "And the necklace's owner? Sure it's not her?"

"Pretty sure," Adams said. "I'm going to talk to the silversmith, see if I can get some insight into the shop itself."

"You think they stole it then reported it themselves?" Temper spoke slowly, as if thinking she might not have grasped just how ridiculous that was, and wanting to give her a chance to do so.

"I know, it seems unlikely. I'm just following all leads."

They stared at each other for a moment, then Temper sighed. "Stop tying up all Isha's time and find that necklace, Adams. I thought this'd be your sort of case, but I'm starting to wonder." He turned away, raising his voice as he left. "And finish your bloody reports."

"Yes, boss," Adams said, and watched him stomp down the hall. A good thing she hadn't had to mention brain scramblers. She'd've been fired on the spot.

THE SHAMBLES WERE APTLY NAMED, Adams thought. Not that they were *shambolic,* exactly, but the heart of York, deep within its city walls, was a tangle of cobbled streets sprouting chaotically in all directions and giving off an unavoidable sense of everything being just a little off true. Things angled left where they should be right, whitewashed walls bulged around sunken windows, and buildings leaned toward each other to whisper secrets over streets that wore the scuffs and shadows of footsteps long gone.

Although there were plenty of modern, trainer-clad footsteps too. The place was rife with tourists, stopping every two paces to peer into the old, distorted glass of the shop windows or to snap selfies of themselves with ice creams and oversized lollipops and Viking helmets. Adams and James worked their way through the crowd single file, James muttering apologies as he bumped into Germans in sensible shoes and Americans in baseball caps and visors. Adams didn't bother too much with such niceties. For a start, she was a lot smaller than James, so she was getting jostled more than she was inflicting any jostling. And second, she'd lived in London far too long to get precious about bumping into tourists.

So she was well ahead of him by the time they reached the jewellery shop, and she examined it while she waited. The sign hanging from a frame above the door was delicately painted, silver on lavender – or lilac, she wasn't sure. Pale purple, anyway – and read *Ash & Yew*. There were falling leaves in the same silver paint drifting softly across the sign, and small gold lights shone like glow worms on the wrought iron support. A white-framed door with small glass panes gave her a glimpse of the interior, which was all cream shades and warm lighting, and chubby bay windows with heavy, bulls-eyed glass panes pushed out over the streets. It certainly didn't look like it was doing brisk trade in stolen goods out the back door, but then again, it didn't look like it was doing brisk trade at all. Not enough souvenir Viking steins, she imagined.

James joined her, his face pink and his collar askew. "How did you get through so quick?"

"Elbows and ruthlessness," she said, and rang the bell.

The door wasn't buzzed open. Instead, a form approached from the other side, indistinct in the old, warped glass, and the lock rolled. A woman wearing a long, soft dress in multiple shades of green smiled at them both, stepping back as she did. "Welcome," she said.

"Cheers," Adams replied, feeling as dishevelled as James looked.

The head jamb was so low she almost felt she should duck as she stepped in, and James certainly had to, not coming up until he was well inside. The woman shut the door behind them, locking it again, and the steady surge and swell of the crowds outside faded to near silence, no more than the hum of the sea captured in a shell. Low, warm light washed from delicately wrought fittings that seemed almost organic, smooth and driftwood-like, gleaming on freestanding cases and their contents, and the scent of vanilla and sea salt rose around them.

Adams took a slow breath, looking for Dandy instinctively. He sat next to her, his snout pointed at the woman and his stance suggesting attention, making her feel vaguely better. Something about the place prickled at her senses, raising the hair on her arms, but not entirely in a bad way. She didn't think, anyway. She had to admit she wasn't exactly an expert at these things, but she suddenly wished James wasn't with her. Having a clingy partner was proving annoying.

The woman smiled at James, then as she turned her gaze to Adams she paused, examining her carefully.

"Welcome," she repeated, with quite a different emphasis.

Adams frowned at her. "Do I know you?"

"Oh, not yet," the woman replied.

Adams had that uneasy sense of perspectives shifting again, just as she had at Gladys's house. That soft clicking into place as the world of Folk and humans overlapped. She closed her eyes, searching for that connection, that clarity that made the world come into focus, and opened them again. Nothing had changed. The woman just looked like a woman, the loose curls of her long brown hair streaked with grey, tumbling over her shoulders as she smiled at Adams.

Maybe she was a little bit more clear-cut than average, but Adams thought she could've walked past her on the street and not thought anything of it.

"How may I help you?" the woman asked.

"DI Adams, DC Hamilton. We're looking for Charles Worthington," Adams said. "He's expecting us."

"Of course. He's out the back." She indicated a simple, white-painted door behind her. It wasn't a security door, no keypad or lock or anything that might've been expected in what was evidently a very high-end jewellery shop (Adams was convinced it had to be high-end, as she hadn't seen a single price tag yet). The door was just a door, with a simple, black metal handle. It looked like any bedroom door in an old country cottage, and despite the display cases the whole place gave off the sense of being someone's front room. There weren't even any cameras that she could see. Which didn't mean there weren't any, of course. They could simply be very well hidden. But she didn't think so. Adams had the feeling this place was more secure and had better protection than any security shutters and alarm systems could offer. It was a different sort of protection, was all. And she really didn't want James to come in with her. It was the same feeling she'd had at Gladys's house. This wasn't for him. She looked at the woman, not speaking, and the woman smiled.

"It's rather tight back there. These old buildings, you know." She looked at James. "I think maybe you should stay here."

James looked at Adams, his eyebrows raised, and Adams nodded at him. "It's fine," she said. "I'll be back in a minute."

"Alright," James said, looking around at the cases. "I need a present for my mum anyway."

"I'm sure you'll find something quite wonderful," the woman said. "And we do offer a discount for the police, of course. Don't be afraid to ask." She smiled at him, a warm, expansive smile, and James visibly relaxed, smiling back at her. The woman turned back to the door and opened it, revealing a low-ceilinged, softly lit hall with pastel paintings on the walls and bare wood floors.

"Enter," the woman said to Adams, and offered her the same smile she had James.

Adams had slipped her hands into her pockets, and now she found herself squeezing her keyring, the one with the little brass duck on it. The duck from London, the one the woman from the river had given her. The one that could bring down monsters. She returned the woman's smile with her own, a little toothier and harder. "After you," she said.

The woman's smile blossomed into something far wider and less goddess-of-the-old-town, her eyes bright, and she walked ahead of Adams into the dim lighting, her back very straight. Her feet were bare under the long skirt of her dress, warm and brown and hardened.

Adams, Dandy, and the duck followed.

10

A DUCK ISN'T JUST A DUCK

The scent of eucalyptus and tea tree oil continued into the hallway, but over it Adams could smell hot metal and solder drifting from an unseen workshop. A couple of white, wood-panelled doors led off the hall, both closed, but at the far end one lay open, spilling an altogether brighter and more industrial light over the wooden flooring. When they reached it the woman stepped to the side, allowing Adams to join her on the threshold. They were looking into a large workshop which appeared to take up the whole width of the shop, and was as much given over to finely made but hulking sculptures as it was to jewellery. A tall, skinny man curved over a workbench, hunched as a vulture. A part of Adams' brain tried to tell her that the pale light flaring from under his hands was nothing more than a soldering iron, but she wasn't entirely sure she believed it. She'd never seen a soldering iron that lit up like that, or required the sort of eye protection the man was sporting. The whole place stank of metal and ozone, and it made the hair on her arms stand even further to attention.

She shot a wary glance at the woman, keeping her hand on the duck.

"It's alright," the woman said, sounding less to be offering reassurance than simply stating facts. "You're welcome enough here. We prefer to keep on the right side of … law enforcement." The pause was strange, as if she were thinking of a different term than *law enforcement.* Adams was almost certain she'd *said* something different – that she herself had *heard* something different – but it was another one of those sliding feelings, the world not quite in focus. She looked at Dandy, who was standing at her side, paws spread solidly. The woman didn't seem to have noticed him, or she certainly hadn't acknowledged him.

"What's your name?" Adams asked her.

"Heather," the woman said.

"Heather …?"

"Just Heather." She was still smiling steadily, and it was starting to grate on Adams. No one had that much to be happy about.

But aloud she just said, "What is this place?"

"The oldest jewellery shop in York," Heather replied. "We've been here since the first person carved a ring out of stone and gave it to her lover."

"Right," Adams said, with the sneaking feeling that *we* wasn't really generic, but obviously that was impossible because the woman looked like she was in her fifties, max. Definitely not old enough to be chasing around stone rings. But then again, in a world of dragons and useless invisible dogs, who knew?

"Charles?" the woman said, raising her voice slightly. "You have a visitor."

The man set his tool (Adams didn't look at it too closely, because she thought it might be a *pencil,* with absolutely no wires attached to it, and *pencils* do not solder things) on the workbench and turned to look at Adams. He was wearing chunky, dark glass goggles with leather frames, and he pushed them up onto his forehead, exposing a pair of small wire-rimmed spectacles. His face was as long and lean as the rest of him, other than a set of astonishingly bushy eyebrows, one of which was looking slightly singed.

"I did say you needed to trim those," Heather said. "You'll set your face on fire if you're not careful."

He touched his eyebrow lightly. "It's a very effective grooming technique."

She shook her head and said, "Detective Inspector Adams is here to talk to you."

"Of course. The missing necklace." He examined Adams, his gaze evaluating, and she stiffened slightly under its weight, folding her arms over her chest and returning his stare, waiting for him to speak first. It was always better if they spoke first.

"What can I say?" he said, apparently satisfied by whatever he'd seen. "I brought it here. I replaced the clasp – quick, simple job. I handed it back, and filed my invoice."

Adams nodded, and said, "Did anyone seem particularly over-interested in it? Scott Samuels, for instance?"

"*Over-interested,*" Charles said, and looked at Heather. She shrugged, a smooth, easy movement. "It's the sort of piece anyone could get over-interested in, if they weren't careful, I suppose."

"Because it was so valuable?" Adams asked, and even as she said it she could feel the way the words fell into the room, like the blatantly wrong answer in some high-stakes quiz final. *Who Wants to Be a Folk-y Friend,* maybe.

"In a way," Charles said. "It's certainly a rare piece."

"What can you tell me about it?" Adams asked.

"I repaired it, I returned it," Charles said, inspecting a thermos mug whose plastic sides were scorched and stained.

Apparently the contents were still okay, though, as he took a sip.

It seemed she was getting the questions wrong as well as the answers now. "What about the stone? We don't seem to have a straight answer about what it is."

"It's a very *specific* stone. You're not going to find it in your average gem book."

Adams wondered if threatening to arrest someone would drag some answers into the air. It was quite appealing, either way. "Why not?"

Charles tipped his head to the side slightly, then looked at Heather.

She smiled at Adams and shook her head. "I don't think there's much to discuss if you don't know that."

Adams scowled at her. "I know enough. I know Ms Hudson claims it vanished from the shop before she picked it up. I know that Meredith swears it was Ms Hudson who picked it up. And I also know that both of those things can't be true." She looked at Charles. "What have your dealings with Meredith been?"

"Meredith's very sweet. She's nothing more than what she appears."

"You haven't heard that she's had money troubles or anything like that?"

Heather shook her head. "Even if she did, what would she do with a necklace like that?" There was a note of disappointment in her voice, as if Adams were being deliberately obtuse.

"Well, she works in the jewellery business," Adams said, "Perhaps she knows somewhere to sell it."

"Yes, because we're all doing backstreet deals with stolen goods on the side," Charles said. "Positively pirates, us jewellers."

Heather chuckled softly, and arched her eyebrows at

Adams. Adams immediately felt even hotter and more unkempt than she had when she'd walked in, and she took a steadying breath.

"Do you have CCTV in the shop?"

"No," Heather said. "We find it doesn't work very well here."

"Handy. I'd have liked to see the necklace come in and out."

"No helping it. Call it atmospherics." Heather smiled.

Adams didn't smile back. "Would you happen to have heard anything about how someone might get rid of a necklace like that?"

Heather's smile faded. "I hope you're not accusing us of anything, Detective Inspector. This is a very old jewellery shop, and we've been doing this for a very long time. We certainly wouldn't risk our reputation."

Adams nodded, looking around pointedly. "Not very busy, are you? No customers since we've come in, and you're slap on the main street."

"We don't cater to the average main street shopper. This is where people come when they want something special."

"Such as a necklace?"

Heather started to say something, her face tight, and Charles spoke up first. "We're not really getting anywhere here, are we? You've asked some questions, we've given some answers. And I need to get back to work."

Adams shook her head. "Not great answers, are they?"

"Not great questions."

"If I dragged you down to the station, would your answers improve?"

"No," Charles said. "Probably deteriorate, in fact."

"I imagine it'd be at least a bit inconvenient, though. Noted silversmith hauled in by the coppers in relation to a missing necklace."

"*Hauled in*," Heather said. "How gauche."

Adams thought the whole situation was a bit gauche. But she kept her gaze on Charles and said, "I don't really believe you've been working in the industry this long and have never so much as caught a whiff of someone operating a little loosely when it comes to legality."

"Can neither confirm nor deny," Charles said, giving her a half smile, and Heather crossed her arms, looking away with a huff.

"Alright. So, theoretically, *if* someone were to steal that necklace, where might they go to resell it?"

"It's not as easy as that," he said. "Something so particular would require a specific buyer. And that's assuming you even wanted to sell it."

"Well, no one would just keep it," Adams said. "It's a bit bloody distinctive."

"It is," Heather agreed. "But sometimes a necklace isn't just a necklace."

Adams frowned at her. "What?"

"Similar to how sometimes a duck's not just a duck."

Adams almost gagged at the sudden swell of nausea at the back of her throat. Copper and salt and stale mud, and the horrible, bitter surge of adrenaline. She steadied herself, her hand clamping down on the duck keyring in her pocket convulsively. And she didn't know why she was surprised, not with the bloody pair of them, each as sharp-edged as the other, wearing their years so lightly. Deceptively so, she was oddly sure.

"Well, this hasn't exactly been helpful," she said. "A two-hour round trip to be told a duck isn't just a duck?"

"I did tell you I'd be down in Leeds tomorrow," Charles said comfortably.

"By which point some other place will've been robbed and its CCTV gone squiffy."

"Not squiffy," Heather said. "Some things just don't show up that well on camera."

"That's really helpful. Super," Adams said, then held a hand up. "Sorry. Unprofessional."

"Much more interesting, though," the other woman said.

Adams wondered if she should've gone south when she left London. Southampton had bridges, but it might not've had people encouraging her to be unprofessional, or trying to feed her excessive amounts of tea and baked goods. "There must be some shop, somewhere, that doesn't ask too many questions about where things come from."

"There are plenty," Charles said. "But not when it comes to this sort of thing. Anyone who's got their hands on it won't be selling it, anyway."

"Why not?" Adams asked, and neither of them answered. "*Why not?*"

"It's no use asking when you won't accept the answer," Heather said. "It won't get you anywhere."

Adams opened her mouth to ask what the hell she was talking about, a nauseous roll going on in her belly, and Charles said, "There's a shop in Leeds market called The Occult Onion. Chloe might be able to help."

"You do need the help," Heather said in a conversational tone.

"The Occult Onion?" Adams asked, ignoring her.

"It's the sort of place people go when they can't find something through the usual methods," Charles said.

"That's it?"

He spread his hands out in front of him, the knuckles gnarled and scarred, and a fresh burn marring one wrist.

Adams sighed, and handed them each a card. "Please get in touch with me if you think of anything else."

"There's no point," Heather said. "Not if you're still thinking this is just any old necklace." Then she turned and led the way back down the hall, her back as straight as ever and her long hair swinging.

Adams followed, rubbing the back of her neck to settle the prickles running across her skin. She wasn't thinking it was just any old necklace, not really. There was too much weirdness about this, too much that smacked of the Thames and toasties and Yorkie bars. Of ducks that could hold back monsters. But she didn't want it to be that. She'd left London to get away from it, after all, not to find herself chasing around up here after ghosts and fairy tales. And dragons were one thing, even goblins were just criminals with big teeth (or the ones she'd met had been), but this was something else. This was her, in the middle of an investigation *again,* and the slow yet insistent escalation of necklace to laptops to cars that wasn't going to stop anywhere soon. Not unless she did something about it, because there wasn't anyone else. She couldn't exactly report it to Temper, after all. He'd probably send her back down to London in a padded wagon.

The front room seemed rather less strange and beguiling than it had before, after the dim mystery of the workshop. James was leaning over one of the displays, and he looked up as they came in. He pointed at a thin gold bracelet, wrought into interlinked butterflies.

"Do you think my mum would like that, Adams?"

She stared at him. "How would I know? I've never met your mum."

"Okay, but is it a mum thing? Would your mum like it?"

Adams leaned over for a closer look, and shook her head. "Too fussy for her. But I'm sure yours will like it."

He considered it for a moment, then looked at Heather. "Can I take it out to look at it?"

"Of course," Heather said, and took an old-fashioned key from a pocket in the depths of her dress to unlock the case.

Adams sighed. "I'll wait for you outside."

She pulled the door open and stepped out onto the cobbled street, hissing in annoyance as someone's oversized backpack smacked her in the shoulder. She stepped back, under the overhang of the building, and stood there in the shelter of the wall, rocking on her heels slightly. The shop had felt hot and claustrophobic, the ceiling too low and the walls too close. And she still had that cloying taste in her mouth, a hangover without any of the slightly dubious fun.

A duck's not always just a duck.

A Yorkie bar's not always just a Yorkie bar.

And a necklace isn't always just a necklace.

The idea that this was somehow Folk-related, *magic*-related, was as sticky and unwelcome as the taste. Not just because, well, *magic*, but also because of the fact that if this necklace had some funky properties, it wasn't just a simple robbery, someone nabbing a bit of jewellery so they could flog it to some fancy art dealer or melt it down for gold. And if that wasn't the case, how did she even start? Where was the end of the tape then, the bit that would unroll the whole case?

She had to know what the necklace did, she supposed, other than muddle up cameras and give people migraines and memory loss. Which was nasty enough to start with, but hardly seemed worth pulling a full-on robbery over. There had to be more to it. She pulled her phone out and swiped to contacts, hitting dial.

"Adams," Isha said. "This is getting to be a habit. Are you going to invite me to your book club next?"

"I don't do clubs."

"That's something. What d'you need?"

"Any progress on the Porsche garage?"

"Not really. Recordings are as mashed up as the others, and the cameras aren't wireless this time."

"Meaning?"

"Meaning no one could just tap into the signal. They'd have to access the hard drives and the recordings manually. Which there's no sign of having happened."

"Anything in the notes about any of the staff getting a sudden migraine?"

Isha sighed, deep and heartfelt, and Adams heard her clicking keys. "Yeah, they did," she said, sounding at least mildly curious. "How did you know?"

"Hunch. I'll be back soon. See if anything else has come in with the same MO, alright? On any case over the past week."

"Yes, ma'am," Isha said, and disconnected before Adams could try and soften her phrasing. She frowned at the phone and shoved it back in her pocket. Migraines and people just handing over flash cars and fancy computers. And the necklace itself, of course. What did Olly say? That Gladys wore it when she went out to buy big-ticket stuff so that people took her seriously and didn't think she was just some aging, penniless hippie? Adams had an idea that wasn't at all the reason why she wore it. And it was time that they talked to Gladys again.

Or rather that just *she* talked to her. Because all of this was treading far too close to London and Toot Hansell. Partly, she didn't want to have to try and somehow explain it to James without making it sound like her mental health break was very much not over. More than that, though, she didn't want him to start *seeing*. Because there was no going back once one did, not really. A certain cat she knew of could do some fancy hypnosis stuff to ensure casual encounters were forgotten, but it was apparently just as likely to turn someone's brain to mush if they'd really seen things properly.

So if James got wind of what was really going on, the odds were he wouldn't be able to unsee it. She thought that some people could handle it, and some couldn't, but, more to the point, no one should *have* to. And she didn't want to be the person that dragged James into a situation where he *had* to.

The shop door creaked open, and James emerged with his neatly brushed, schoolboy hair, clutching a little white gift bag adorned with a pink ribbon.

Adams looked from it to him. "Is it her birthday?"

"No," he said, "I just like getting her a little something sometimes."

"You're sickening," Adams said.

He grinned. "I know. What now?"

"Back to Leeds. There's a shop in the market that might have a few ideas about missing goods, apparently."

"A jewellery one?" He frowned. "I can't think of anywhere in there that'd deal with something like this. It's a bit of a specialty item, isn't it?"

"I think so too," Adams agreed. "But it's not like we have anything else."

He gave an agreeable shrug, and Adams turned to lead the way back to the car, threading a winding path through the tourists, with James struggling along in her wake, attempting to protect his bloody fancy gift bag. She hated to admit it, but while she still didn't know how she was going to find the gap that would wedge her into the case, things suddenly had shape. As if she'd been staring into fog and now the sun was coming up, rendering the world still murky but discernible, shadows beneath water.

It wasn't an entirely welcome feeling.

11

AN INCOMPREHENSIBLE SORT OF SENSE

Back in Leeds with the plodding trip from York behind them, tourists evaded, and a variety of caravans and camper vans overtaken along the way, Adams parked her car in the station garage and said to James, "Do you want to head in and check how Isha's doing?"

James gave her an unimpressed look. "No," he said. "Backup, partners, all that, remember?"

Adams wrinkled her nose. She was evidently going to have to work harder to shake him. But checking out one shop, even if it was called The Occult Onion, hardly seemed risky, so rather than argue she just headed across the road toward the market with him ambling next to her. It was quiet in the lull of the afternoon, the lunch rush gone and the afternoon shoppers mainly made up of a few older women haggling over papayas and pineapples in the specialty greengrocers, and a man in a snazzy pinstripe suit buying metres of gaudy cloth from one of the haberdasheries.

Adams wasn't entirely sure where in the market The Occult Onion was going to be, but she bypassed the butchers' row and the fishmongers' area, already empty and cleaned down for the day, because it was hardly going to be in there. Instead, she skirted the edges of the market, examining the smaller, more furtive shops tucked into alcoves along the walls. Everything looked vaguely forgotten, faded and a bit dingy around the edges, as if the years had rushed on beyond its borders, leaving them undisturbed within. There was a tea shop that looked as if there'd be more cobwebs in their offerings than there already were in its windows, a sweet shop with humbugs congealing in jars on the display shelves, and a DIY shop that was still selling rabbit ear TV antennae. Adams wondered what else these shops were dealing in, because surely no one was buying their actual stocks, but they were surviving somehow.

She'd almost finished a full circuit of the market edges when she found, tucked up in a corner equidistant from the doors that led up onto the main street and the ones that led down to the outdoor market square, a small shop spilling warm light and incense onto the dull floors outside. The windows that looked onto the empty, dim alleys of the market were clean enough, and beyond the display the interior was shielded by purple curtains. The glass door rested slightly ajar, and someone had hand-painted *The Occult Onion* on it in gold. The window display held a chipped Ouija board, a collection of crystals which looked like they needed a polish, and some slightly tatty books proclaiming five easy steps to alchemy, and top ten herbal tinctures.

It didn't exactly look promising, and it certainly didn't look like the sort of place anyone would go to flog a highly precious necklace, even if that necklace wasn't exactly a human one. Adams pulled the glass door open, letting them onto a floor of peel and stick tiles, a little scratched and stained. The shop wasn't big inside, and was cramped by shelves running along the walls and dreamcatchers descending from the low ceiling above them. James had to duck and dive around them as he followed Adams in.

The cramped room pushed back into one of the alcoves that pocked the market's external walls, and was joined to the next one along by a low arch. Through it, Adams discovered an eclectic-looking library full of books about interpreting dreams, understanding astrology, and certain practices of botany that she thought were probably borderline illegal. At the back of this section, a counter had been set up, and more purple curtains were drawn behind it, shielding the very back of the alcove from sight. No outside light reached in here, just reluctant lamps in a mix of shades and brightness, and piled on the counter were bunches of sage, carefully stacked voodoo doll kits, and little velvet pouches holding runes and stones.

A couple of jewellery cases stood in the corner, and Adams went over to inspect them without any sort of hope that they might yield anything interesting. They held standard-issue heavy silver rings and necklaces, wrought into skulls and cats and bats, some of them with cheap gems embedded in them, or more likely pieces of glass. In among them, though, were a few pieces that looked older, some of them bearing small cards that told stories about where they'd been discovered, who had made them, or how they'd come to be in the shop. She skimmed a couple of them, eyebrows raised. Of course, they could have just been done up to look old, but she didn't think so. There was an *otherness* to the shop, and as James looked around, he said, "Do you know, I've never seen this place? I've been in this market so many times, I don't know how I missed it."

Adams didn't reply. She was pretty sure she knew how he'd missed it. It was the same way that people missed dragons, or beasts under bridges. The same way people missed anyone that slipped through the edges of society, or fell through the cracks of reality. "Doesn't exactly jump out at you," she said aloud, and James nodded.

He looked back at the jewellery display. "I'm glad I got Mum something from the last shop. I don't think she'd fancy any of this."

Adams pointed to a bracelet in one corner, formed of a constellation of differently coloured, polished stones. It was chunky and set in silver, and she said, "That's more my mum's style."

James examined it, tipping his head to one side, making her think of Dandy. "That's pretty, I suppose," he said in an encouraging sort of tone.

"Can I help you?" someone asked, and they turned to find a slim young woman with long dark hair watching them. She was wearing sandals with skinny black jeans and a black T-shirt that made her look even more slight, and her arms were bare, tattooed, and pale. She examined them with open curiosity, her gaze drifting over James and then fixing on Adams with something that almost felt like recognition.

Adams returned the gaze and said, "I hear this is a good place to find things."

The woman smiled. "It depends what you're looking for. We've got a good collection of crystals, some decent arcane books. What exactly can I interest you in?"

Adams decided there was no point being subtle about it. "Necklaces," she said, and pulled the photo up on her phone. She turned it so the woman could see, watching her face as she did so. She didn't react, but she certainly took more than a cursory glance at the image.

"Interesting piece," she said. "Looks a little bit rich for the tastes of my clients though."

Adams smiled slightly. "You are Chloe, aren't you?"

"Yes."

"I was told you might be able to help people find things.

Say, a buyer, if someone was looking to sell one of these." She shook the phone lightly.

The woman snorted. "How many of *those* do you think are rocking around out there?"

"I wouldn't know," Adams replied. "I'm just interested in this one."

"Selling, are you?"

"Not me personally," Adams replied, and Chloe grinned, revealing slightly pointed canines.

"No, I wouldn't have thought so. There's a whole thing about not being able to sell evidence, isn't there?"

James grinned. "She rumbled you there, Adams."

Chloe looked at him. "Oh, you as well. You two positively stink of bureaucracy."

The corner of Adams' mouth twitched up. It was better than the usual *I can smell bacon,* at least. "DI Adams, DC Hamilton. Does that mean that you won't help us?"

The young woman pointed at Adams' phone. She had short-cropped fingernails, painted a luminous shade of purple and decorated with little speckles of silver glitter. "I haven't seen it," she said. "Any other questions?"

"Your last name was?"

"McGill," she said. "Just call me Chloe, can't be doing with the Ms stuff."

"All right, Chloe, this necklace has been stolen. So if no one's brought it to you even though you're known as a place to go, where might they take it?"

Chloe folded her arms, tapping her fingers on her biceps. There were smudges of purple ink on the sides of them and what looked like a blood blister on one thumb. "It's a bit stuffy in here," she said. "Crowded for three, like."

Adams looked at James, and he gave her an unamused look.

"Really?" he said.

"She's right, it's tight in here," Adams replied.

"I don't even know why you bother having a partner," he said, but turned and walked out. Adams waited until she heard the bell over the door go, and a moment later Dandy came trotting around the corner, looking from Adams to Chloe with evident interest. He was chewing on something, and Adams just hoped it wasn't anything that might open holes in reality. Expensive seemed unlikely in here, at least.

She looked at Chloe. "Better?"

"Yes, actually. He's very unaware, isn't he?"

"He's a very good detective."

"I didn't say he wasn't," Chloe replied. "But there are different ways of being aware."

Adams sighed. "Just like ducks aren't always ducks."

"What?"

"Never mind. What can you tell me about the necklace now he's gone?"

"Well, it's not just an ordinary necklace," Chloe said.

"I've kind of gathered that," Adams replied. "Can you be more specific?"

"Show me the picture again," Chloe said, coming around the counter to join Adams and peering down at the phone. "Yeah." She tapped the photo, zooming in a little. "That's a very particular pattern. Come on."

She turned to the shelves, running her fingers along the spines of the books. There were some newer ones on meditation and breathing and being a modern Wiccan, but there was a much larger section of not only second-hand books, but books that looked like they'd been second-hand before the city was born, with stained spines and tattered edges, leather fraying softly and fading in the dusty light. Chloe dug through them, standing on tiptoes to reach the highest shelves, with her shirt riding up to show heavy tattoos coiling down her back, soft with muted colours and movement.

Finally she said, "*Ha,*" and grabbed a book by its spine. It was a heavy thing, and she clutched it to her chest with both hands as she turned around to face Adams. "I'm no sorcerer," she said.

"Good to know," Adams said. "Are you also not a wizard?"

Chloe examined her for a moment, then shook her head. "You're very odd."

"It's been said. In what way specifically this time?"

"You're aware, and yet you're not," Chloe replied.

"You're talking about *sorcerers,*" Adams said. "I mean, how am I expected to react to that?"

Chloe hugged the book, tapping her fingers on it, not replying.

Finally, Adams said, "What? I don't know anything about sorcerers. I mean, other than the fact that obviously they don't exist." She could hear the question mark in her own voice.

"Well," Chloe said, "I can tell you're aware-ish, that you can see some things at least. Plus you've got something in here with you." She looked around the shop, her head tipping to one side, then the other, as if she were trying to find the right angle. Adams looked at Dandy, who had picked up a voodoo doll. He offered it to Adams, and she took it, pinching it between two fingers.

"I'm sorry," she said to Chloe. "I'll buy it. It's got slobber on it now."

"What is it?" Chloe asked.

"A voodoo doll?" Adams replied.

"*No*. What took the voodoo doll?"

"You can't see him?"

"No," Chloe replied. "I can feel something, and I think I can maybe smell wet dog?"

"He's not wet," Adams said, patting Dandy's head. "He might stink a bit, though. I think I've got used to it. I was sort of hoping that the invisible looks would also go with an invisible smell."

"Well, I wouldn't worry," Chloe replied. "Most people probably don't smell it. But coming back to the point, you have an invisible dog even I can't see, an awareness of this world, you're hunting for a magical artefact, and you're taking the mick out of *me* for talking about sorcerers."

Adams scratched her forehead. "I really did hope this was just a jewellery robbery," she said.

"Oh, it is," Chloe replied. "But if it's that necklace, it's a very targeted robbery, and you're going to have to expand your definition of criminal activity."

"Oh, that's just bloody wonderful," Adams said, and when Chloe just shrugged she added, "What can you tell me?"

"Well, like I said, I'm not a sorcerer. I'm not completely versed in this."

"So what … are you?" That felt very strange to say, and Adams wondered if there was some sort of etiquette to this.

"I'm a magic worker."

"So you're a magician. Or a witch?"

Chloe thought about it. "Yeah, let's go with the witch label. It's a term that's been misused a lot over the years, and I quite like reclaiming it. I'm good with witch. Hedge witch, technically, though."

Adams nodded. She was all for reclaiming labels, even if it was a hedge witch, although she wasn't quite sure what that meant.

Chloe said, "Here's the thing. Sorcerers are like super, mega-powerful magic workers. Most of them are so ancient they're not even human anymore, although they were once. And as they grow older, they keep accumulating power, and they sink that power into items and places. Normally it's a book. They have a book of power, a spell book, a *grimoire* if you want, and they put a lot of the excess power into that so they can still pass as pretty much human and also not spontaneously combust."

"That sounds unpleasant," Adams said.

"Trust me, you do not want to clean up an exploded sorcerer."

Adams stared blankly at Chloe. "I'll take your word for it. What's the necklace got to do with this, then?"

"Right, so. Plenty of sorcerers, especially the really old ones, distribute their power in different places. That way, if they lose one thing, they've still got power waiting for them elsewhere. Often they'll have a house or a property that soaks up a lot of the excess, which also acts as a haven for them, because that power's really sunk into the earth, and the house then protects itself. Then they'll have their book, and sometimes they have artefacts like this." She set the book on the counter, flipping through it, and a moment later lifted it to show Adams. It was a drawing, and not an exact copy of the necklace, but more than close enough.

Intricate, heavy gold strands looping and twining around each other, in a pattern that deceived the eye, that stole away with it, and right at the base was a stone. In the drawing, it was rendered in the multicoloured, multi-layered colours of an opal. Blues and reds and greens and something even darker shining deep within. The artist had captured it beautifully, and it was certainly nothing like the black hole that had appeared on the camera. Adams looked at the picture on her phone again. "It doesn't photograph well, does it?"

Chloe snorted. "These things never do. I almost guarantee that stone is going to be very similar. It's a stone of power, and *that* is a sorcerer's necklace."

"Right," Adams said. "So we're looking for a sorcerer

then?" She almost looked over her shoulder, in case Temper had appeared from somewhere with the padded wagon.

"Not necessarily," Chloe said. "But it belonged to one, yes?"

"I'm not entirely clear on that," Adams said. "I don't think the current rightful owner is one, but she inherited it."

"Interesting." Chloe thought about it. "But it also makes sense. A sorcerer would have serious safeguards on something like this. Once it's out of their possession, the power in it is accessible for anyone who can claim it. So if someone's got this necklace, and they've got the slightest idea of how to use it ... well, they could get up to all sorts."

Adams took a breath. "Could they, say, convince someone to give them a laptop?"

"Sure," Chloe said. "I mean, that's pretty small, but they could definitely use it to influence people. The problem with things like this is that if you use it once, you tend to keep going. It's addictive. You might start with one small thing, but then it snowballs, because the artefact takes over. That's why you don't touch a sorcerer's stuff, because a sorcerer is the only one who can dictate to the power. For everyone else, that power is dictating to them."

"So this is going to escalate," Adams said.

Chloe nodded. "Absolutely. And the other thing is, I'd put money on the fact that whoever's got this doesn't know how to use it properly. Not if they're using it on *laptops.*" She almost sneered the word. "This thing could topple governments. Using it for a bit of petty theft's like using a tank to break into a letterbox."

"Which means they don't know how to control it."

"And they'll be leaving traces. There'll be magic workers out there who *do* know how to use it, how to harness the thing. And if they get the slightest whiff of what's happening, they'll be chasing down whoever has it."

Adams scratched Dandy's head as he leaned against her leg. "So they're going to be in danger from these other magic workers?"

"Exactly," Chloe replied. "Now you're getting it. That necklace isn't going to come through my shop. I doubt it'll come through any shop. Not unless someone really has taken it with no idea what they've got their hands on. But again, the necklace has its own will. So even if they don't know how to use it, *it's* going to use *them*."

Adams sighed. "Tell me it's not a sentient necklace."

"No," Chloe said. "Semi-sentient, maybe."

"Fantastic," Adams said. "That's something to look forward to."

Chloe grinned at her. "You got an answer, didn't you?"

Adams wanted to say that she didn't *like* the answer. At the same time, the palms of her hands were prickling, and it wasn't from the heat in the shop, or from the sticky bloody voodoo doll that Dandy had given her. It was because this was something. This made sense. In some weird and incomprehensible way, this made *sense,* and things were connecting, the way they hadn't earlier when she'd still been looking for scams and human deceptions. "Can you let me know on the off chance that it does come in here?"

"Sure," Chloe replied. "I'll keep an eye out."

"Thanks," Adams said, and turned to head for the door.

"Be careful," Chloe said, and Adams stopped, looking back at her.

"Of what?"

"You're still thinking too much like police. You keep that up, there's no way you'll find this thing. Or if you do, it'll swallow you whole."

"The necklace?"

"Everything," Chloe said.

Adams tried to find something to say to that, but in the

end she just nodded and let herself back out of the shop again. James was slouching around outside, his hands in his pockets, frowning at a woman with two chihuahuas, one of which was weeing on a watermelon display.

"Alright with your girls' club there?" he asked.

"Eh," Adams replied.

"That useful?"

"Not really," she said. "Back to footwork. We speak to Meredith again. We speak to Scott and Gladys again. And we start putting a bit of pressure on. Someone's going to give."

"Bloody hope so. This thing's going nowhere fast." He looked around. "Fancy an ice cream?"

"Oh yes," Adams said. "Mint chocolate chip."

"So boring," he muttered.

12

SAME QUESTIONS, NO ANSWERS

ADAMS TRACKED LINDSAY DOWN TO AN INTERVIEW ROOM AT the station, where she had various files and reports spread out on the table in front of her and was typing on her laptop. She looked up as Adams came in, giving her a quick, businesslike nod.

"How's that jewellery case coming on?" she asked.

"Yeah, making progress," Adams said. "Don't suppose you've heard anything back from your art contacts?"

Lindsay gave her a regretful look, taking a sip from a cup of tea. "I'm afraid not. Nothing's surfaced yet. I've asked them to be on the lookout for it, though."

"Fair enough," Adams said. She hadn't really expected anything else. It seemed almost inevitable now that the necklace wasn't going to be found in any art gallery or pawn shop, not even of the most illegitimate or poshest varieties.

"What progress have you made on your side?" Lindsay asked. "Are you still liking the jewellery shop assistant for it?"

Adams frowned slightly. "I never really liked her in the first place. She doesn't seem like the type."

"They never seem like the type," Lindsay pointed out, and

Adams shrugged in acknowledgment. "Who else have you got?"

"Following a few leads still," Adams said vaguely, since *trying occult shops and hoping the invisible dog comes up with something* seemed inadvisable.

"I heard you'd gone up to York."

"Just following up on the silversmith. Bit of a dead end there too, really."

"Oh, well." Lindsay went back to what she was doing. "Let me know if I can help with anything. You know, if you want some fresh eyes on your notes or something. A bit of perspective."

Adams grimaced slightly. "Thanks. I'll let you know." She'd have to actually type them up first, of course.

"Sure."

Adams left Lindsay to her paperwork and trotted downstairs to see Isha. The door to her office was closed and locked, though, and Adams checked her watch. The long summer days meant she hadn't realised that it was past six already. They'd spent the whole day coming up with nothing more than more dead ends. She sighed, and looked at Dandy, who was sniffing the door looking plaintive.

"You leave her ferns alone," she said in a low voice, and headed back upstairs.

James was sitting on the visitor side of her desk, tapping at a tablet with a frown on his face.

"You may as well get off, then," she said to him.

He looked up. "Really?"

"Yeah, fresh start tomorrow and we'll start re-interviewing. Nothing's happening at any great pace for now."

He nodded, and turned the tablet toward her. "That necklace is some sort of occult artefact, isn't it?"

She looked at the picture he had up on the screen. It was a black-and-white photo of an imperious-looking woman walking up a set of carpeted stairs in a clinging black dress, with a necklace that looked distinctly similar to the one they were searching for glittering on her neck. She looked directly at the camera, less in challenge and more with a sort of amused superiority, and the stone at the heart of the necklace was as dark and empty as it looked on Adams' own phone.

"Who's this?" she asked.

"Verity Sullivan in 1922," James replied, and Adams blinked at the screen. It was hard to tell with the quality of the photo, but she doubted the woman could be under forty.

"Why do you say occult?" She was really hoping he wasn't going to point out that Verity must've been a vampire if she only died a couple of years ago, then remembered he hadn't been with her at Gladys's to hear that particular timeline.

"Well, she's at the Occult Society Ball," he said, swiping down to the caption.

"Oh. Right."

"Which is why you were sniffing around that shop. Do they deal in artefacts like this?"

"Possibly," she said.

"Why not tell me, though? I could've been looking into underground occult markets and things like that, rather than us waiting on bloody Lindsay and her art contacts."

"It just seemed a bit … I didn't fancy putting it in a report, say."

James nodded, looking back at the tablet. "Right. London."

"London."

"Want me to look into it? See if there's a market out there for that sort of thing? I mean, there will be, but as to if anyone's up to nicking things …"

"Cheers, James," Adams said. "That'd be helpful, actually. I mean, never know, do you?"

"Exactly." He gave her a sideways look. "Do I still get to knock off now, though?"

"Yes, go," she said, grinning, and watched him jump up, hurrying for the hall as if he were afraid she'd collar him and haul him back at any moment. He couldn't get in much trouble poking about a few magician's sites, could he? Or she had to hope not.

Adams opened her computer and stared at her unfinished reports for a while, then closed it again and got up. It was no good. She could never think through things on the computer. She was going to go home, lay out her favourite sticky notes and see if anything came of it.

THE NEXT MORNING dawned with that same heavy heat haze, everything feeling sticky and uncomfortable, heavy with humidity and tension as Adams stepped out into the early morning. That sense of barely contained violence had grown since the day before. As she ran, she spotted blood on the pavement outside one of the pubs, and broken glass smashed from a corner shop window, the inside hurriedly repaired with plywood. The car horns were sharper, sirens shriller, and two men were screaming at each other outside a greasy spoon, veins standing out on their necks. A woman with too many teeth watched them, her eyes glittering with indifference. This heat was going to need to break soon, because the whole world was slowly cracking at the corners with the weight of it.

But no one interrupted her as she ran, neither the humans nor the ones that only seemed human when she didn't look too closely. She couldn't stop thinking of Chloe, telling her she was both aware and not, and Heather with her evaluating gaze and dismissive *I don't think there's much to discuss if you don't know that,* which felt like it could apply to her understanding of the whole world at the moment. Or both worlds, although she was less and less convinced that there was any sort of division between them at all, other than that of seeing or not seeing. She'd left London to get away from this, yet it had been here waiting for her when she arrived. It was what had dragged her out to Toot Hansell, three times over now, helpless to ignore it, or to let others tumble into a world she wasn't sure she wanted any part of at all.

But there was something deeply instinctive about protecting that hidden world, she found. Not just in standing between the dragons and the humans who would no doubt exploit them, but in shoring up a barrier that held back chaos and panic and, more than likely, all-out bloody war. Because it wasn't as if everyone was going to take nicely to fauns and faeries, was it? She knew full well humans were bad enough with differing skin tones, or belief systems, or pretty much anything that marked a person as *not one of us.* Throw some tails and wings in there and all hell would break loose.

And, of course, even in that hidden world, laws were broken, and whether they were human laws or Folk laws didn't really matter. They were still laws, written or not, about not hurting kids, and not kidnapping people, and about lives mattering no matter who they belonged to. And about not taking what wasn't yours.

Although in this particular case she had a feeling it was less about ownership and more about protection. Because if that necklace really could *persuade* people, then that meant it couldn't be out there in the wrong hands. Whoever had it now likely didn't even realise they were using a chainsaw to pluck some daisies. They'd think it was a game, nothing more than a magic trick, pocketing watches and joyrides in equal measure. Adams could feel, somewhere deep and certain, that it was a whole lot more than that, felt it with the same certainty that she'd felt the connection to Dandy and that fierce protective urge when she had to face the things under the bridge. She had to take this on, and she had to protect those who didn't know what they were walking into, and that meant making sure that James was otherwise occupied while she went and dealt with everyone else.

DESPITE THE HEAT, she sprinted the last stretch home, and when she got inside she was sweating so much she had to wait quarter of an hour before she could even get in the shower, grumbling to herself about it not being nearly grim enough up north. Eventually, though, she was done, dressed, and hurrying back down the stairs to her car with Dandy loping behind her. It was still early, but rush hour had started. She wasn't going into town, though. She was going out of it, swinging through the streets against the flow of traffic, only occasionally hitting snarls at junctions and traffic lights, until she pulled into the quiet leafy lanes where Gladys's house crouched.

She fancied she could feel it, even before she pulled into the kerb outside the gate, and what Chloe had said about magic sinking into the soil made an awful lot of sense. So did Dandy hanging back as she approached the gate, and this time she didn't try to persuade him up the steps. She just let herself into the garden and stood on the path for a while, watching the house. *Seeing* it. She wasn't certain, and maybe she hadn't been paying enough attention before, but she thought the koi pond had an extra little island in the middle, as well as a new waterfall tumbling from a raised pool into the main one. It was also possible that the willow in the corner was hanging a bit lower, the shadows underneath it deeper and richer. Perhaps that was just down to whatever the gardeners were doing, but she also remembered Olly saying he'd never seen anyone working on the grounds. It could just be scheduling, as he'd said, but she had a feeling the garden was self-governing, rather like the house. Other than its additions of rather newer and more modern amenities.

She glanced back at Dandy, who was peering in the gate. "Coming?" she asked him softly, and he whined. She wondered what a sorcerer's house smelled like, even if the sorcerer was gone. She supposed it was old, deep magic, the same things that raised the hair on her arms and sent chills shivering up her neck despite the heat. Dandy must be feeling it a hundredfold, and who knew what he was smelling. So she just said, "Good boy," and headed for the door.

She didn't have to wait long after she knocked. Olly opened the door, and she blinked at him.

"You're here early," she said.

"I work around the best hours for Gladys, and she's an early riser. I assume you're looking for her?"

"Yes, I'd like to have a word."

"She's doing yoga on the patio." He stepped back, and Adams followed him into the lingering coolness of the house, wrinkling her nose slightly. The last time she'd been confronted by yoga on the patio, there'd been dragons involved, and she didn't fancy that again.

But there were no dragons to be found on the stone flags that met the living room and overlooked the garden. The lawn on this side of the house was smooth and luminously green, meandering between elegant trees and trellises of climbing roses and islands formed from riotous beds of flowers. Gladys was doing sun salutations in a pair of cropped leggings and a loose singlet, her sinewy arms stretched above her head. She bent at the waist and folded forward, placing her hands firmly on the ground, making Adams think that she probably should have done a few stretches after her run. It always seemed like such a waste of time, though.

"Gladys, it's Detective Inspector Adams," Olly said, raising his voice slightly, and Gladys straightened up, shading her eyes against the already warm sun.

"Inspector, wonderful to see you," she said. "Do you have my necklace?"

"I'm afraid not," Adams said. "I just wanted a word."

"Of course," she replied, and smiled at Olly. "Can you get us coffee, dear?"

"Coming right up," he said. "Iced?"

"Ooh, yes. With extra chocolate syrup. Inspector?"

"Just black," she said. Olly ambled off, his hands in his pockets, and Adams watched him go. He certainly wasn't acting like someone who had been off joyriding in a Porsche or knocking off Apple Stores, but who knew?

She turned to Gladys. "What can you tell me about the necklace?"

Gladys frowned. "Nothing more than I have already. It's a family heirloom, and it's vitally important that I get it back."

"Nothing else?" Adams asked. "No particular properties I should know about?"

Gladys's frown deepened. "Properties? I mean, it's gold, if that's what you mean. We've already been over this."

"What about the stone?" Adams asked. "Can you tell me more about that? Why it doesn't show up on the video properly?"

"I'm sure I don't know," Gladys replied. "It's an opal of some sort, I believe. Perhaps the light was bad." She sat down cross-legged on her mat and waved to Adams to join her. Adams sat down rather less gracefully, tugging her legs close to her as she did so, and Gladys tipped her head. "You should do yoga, dear. It's fabulous, the flexibility. And you want to start now before you get any older."

"Thanks," Adams said. "I'll bear that in mind."

Olly reappeared with the coffees, handing Gladys a large glass complete with ice cream, cream, and chocolate syrup, then offered Adams a cup. "Can I get you anything else?" he asked.

"No, that's alright, Olly," Gladys said, and busied herself with her drink until he'd vanished back inside again. Only then did she look back at Adams, her gaze direct. "I'm not really sure how I can help you further, Inspector," she said. "I've given you all the details. This is rather in your court now."

"The thing is, investigations go in all directions," Adams replied. "I understand you weren't too keen to go to the police initially."

Gladys sighed. "Olly told you that, I imagine. He may be very discreet in many things, but he's entirely incapable of keeping a secret from anyone in authority. He confessed to a museum guard that I took a selfie on a taxidermy tiger when we were in the British Museum last year. I was embarrassed, is all. A little old lady losing her finery."

"I see," Adams said, momentarily distracted by the vision of Gladys riding a tiger. "I've also heard from other sources that the necklace may be a little *persuasive*."

Gladys gave her a puzzled look, and dipped her little finger in the chocolate syrup, then licked it off. "I did tell you that I wear it when I'm shopping. One has to take every advantage one can with these salespeople. They can be very *dismissive*."

"I'm sure they can," Adams said. "But how does the necklace affect that?"

"I'm sure I don't know. But many people are influenced by outward signs of status."

Adams really hated it when difficult women of a certain age voiced her own thoughts on things. It didn't bode well for the future. "You're sure there's nothing more to it?"

"DI Adams, I think you'll have to be a bit clearer if you have something to ask me. I'm not a mind reader."

Adams took a deep breath, considered simply coming out and saying *just tell me if the bloody necklace is magic and how to nab it, will you,* and once again decided against it, feeling vaguely cowardly. Not that Gladys was likely to go to Temper about her, but what if she did? In London her DCI had known that there were things that required tackling *differently.* Here, Temper was still getting to grips with the concept of a debrief being more than a few rounds down the pub. She didn't fancy springing anything else on him.

"Did Verity leave you anything else? A book maybe?"

"She left me the entire house, and there are plenty of books in it. She was quite a bibliophile."

"Any particularly special ones?"

"Well, there's some first editions and so on."

They looked at each other for a moment, Gladys still sipping steadily away on her drink, her gaze level and guileless, and Adams found that the moment to say *I think your necklace is magic* was gone, if it had ever been there at all. Part of her was glad she couldn't say it, because maybe that meant she wasn't as far gone as she could be, but on the other hand, this was seriously putting a kink in the investigation.

Aloud, she said, "I don't suppose Olly's mentioned any interest in Apple computers, or Porsches?"

Gladys frowned. "He helped me to choose a nice new computer last year, but it wasn't Apple. And he's not very into cars that I've seen. Why?"

"There's been a couple more incidents that could potentially be related."

"Incidents," Gladys said, and put her glass down. "What sort of incidents?"

"Things taken and malfunctioning cameras," Adams said. "We're following up, of course, but anything at all you can remember about anyone who was particularly interested in the necklace, or was around when it was taken would help. Anything at all."

Gladys gave her a thoughtful look and folded her hands together in her lap, as if about to start meditating. "I've told you all I can, Inspector."

Not all she knew, Adams noticed. She supposed, if one were already concerned about being branded a dotty old lady, talking about magical necklaces to anyone in a position of authority wasn't exactly one of the better ideas. So here they both were, each of them carefully saying nothing.

She sighed, finished her coffee, and got up, not without a little difficulty. "Alright," she said. "If you think of anything else, please let me know."

"I will do," Gladys said. "I'm sure you'll find them." There was a certain thoughtfulness in her voice, and Adams stopped, examining her.

"Are you sure you can't tell me anything else?"

"Not at all," Gladys replied. "You go on, we'll get to the bottom of this."

Adams left feeling thoroughly dismissed, and it wasn't until she was climbing into the car, pushing Dandy out of the driver's seat, that she thought, ***we'll*** *get to the bottom of this,* and rested her forehead on the wheel. She had an unsettling suspicion that the *we* didn't include her in any way. She was going to need to keep a closer eye on Gladys.

But for now, she needed to go and talk to the Porsche garage about the missing car. Not that she really thought it was going to get her anywhere, but one never knew. Good old-fashioned police work sometimes turned up the most unusual of things.

She called James on the hands-free as she pulled onto the street., and he answered almost immediately, sounding irritatingly perky. He evidently hadn't spent half the night shuffling Post-its around the kitchen bar and making zero progress.

"Adams," he said.

"I need you to go to the Porsche garage, re-interview everyone, make sure nothing was missed earlier."

"Good morning to you too," he said. "But shall do. What're you up to?"

"I'm going to catch Meredith at home before she heads into work. She might speak a bit more freely without Scott hiding out in the back room like a gremlin." Or she might have more to say about how the necklace *felt* without earnest, normal, James smiling and nodding encouragingly in front of her, looking like he couldn't wait to give her a gold star for effort.

"You don't want company for that?"

"I think I can handle Meredith."

He sighed audibly, but she was already hanging up. Let him think she was rude and overly individualistic. It was partly true anyway, and it might just keep him safe.

13

ABDUCTION THE FIRST

Adams parked in front of a bungalow crouched in the centre of a flat, neatly trimmed lawn, and headed up the concrete path to the door. The flowerbeds were painfully neat, not a weed daring to make its presence felt, and there was an alarming number of garden gnomes, which she eyed with well-earned suspicion. They seemed to be stone, or concrete, or whatever regular garden gnomes were made of, though, and in addition there was a bird bath, a couple of feeders, and a fake wishing well wedged into the rockery. Even if she hadn't known Meredith lived with her parents, she'd have been able to guess.

The door was opened by an older man in broken-down slippers, his glasses sliding down his nose and his polo shirt tucked into his jogging bottoms.

"Good morning," he said, far too cheerfully. "How can I help?"

"Detective Inspector Adams," she said. "Is Meredith still in? I just want a word. Following up on the jewellery shop incident."

The man barely glanced at her ID before opening the door wide. "Henry Williams. Come on in. She seems to have overslept this morning, actually. My wife just went to get her up." He bustled down the hall, raising his voice as he went. "Meredith! Meredith, move yourself, love. There's someone to see you."

A pretty, thin-faced woman came rushing down the hall from the opposite direction, her cardigan clutched close to her, as if she were pinning herself together with it. "She's not there," she said, transferring her grip to her husband's arm. "*She's not there.*"

"What do you mean she's not there?" Henry asked, cupping the woman's arms in a gentle, almost delicate gesture. "Has she gone in early?"

She shook her head. "Her bed's not made, and her work clothes are still on the chair. I don't ... she's just gone."

Adams already had her phone in her hand, the soft-lit hall suddenly bright and the heat forgotten. "Did she come home last night?"

"Oh, yes, we had dinner together," the woman said.

"Did she go out again?"

"Not that we know of," the man said. "It was a work night. She didn't say anything about going out, did she, love?"

"No," the woman said. Henry was still steadying her, and Adams could see a fragility to her, not just in her uneven voice, but in the dark shadows under her eyes and the deep lines at the corners of her mouth, deeper than her age demanded. "No, she didn't, and she'd have said if she was going out."

"Is she dating?" Adams asked. "Anyone she might have gone to meet last minute?"

The woman shook her head. "I don't think so. She was seeing that nice girl from the Co-op, but they broke up."

"Alright," Adams said. "This still doesn't mean anything's happened, though, okay?" She was feeling distinctly out of her depth. This wasn't the sort of conversation she'd been prepared to have, and she'd never been particularly good at them even when she was prepared. "Have you tried her phone? She might be more likely to answer you than me."

"Of course." The woman rushed into the kitchen, leaving a faint trail of panic behind her. Meanwhile, Dandy drifted down the hallway, heading for the room the woman had just come out of. Adams and Henry followed the woman into the kitchen, Adams taking her notebook out as they went.

She scribbled the details down quickly and checked the time, then looked at Henry, who had one hand on his wife's back as she clutched her phone to her ear. "What was your name?" she asked the woman.

"Patricia," she whispered. "She's not answering."

"Could she have gone out for a run or something?" Adams asked

"She doesn't run." Patricia hung up. "Is this something to do with what happened at the shop? I knew she shouldn't be working at a jewellery shop. I mean, anything can happen in a jewellery shop, can't it? People come and steal diamonds. Hold people hostage!"

"I'm sure that's not the case," Adams said, although she wasn't sure of anything of the sort. "And the theft at the shop seems to be more of a misunderstanding than anything else. No violence involved at all." She tried to smile encouragingly, but at the word *violence* Patricia dropped the phone and covered her mouth with both hands.

Henry put an arm around his wife's shoulders. "I'm sure she's okay, dear," he said. "Meredith's smart. Whatever's happened, she'll work it out."

"What do you mean, she'll work it out?" Patricia asked.

"There's nothing to work out. She should be in her bed or getting ready for work, and she's just *gone*. We didn't even hear anything!" Her voice was rough and rising, like a storm front coming in.

"Well, you do wear earplugs," Henry said, and she scowled at him.

"That's because you snore."

"I do," he admitted, but Patricia took a deep breath and leaned against him.

Adams tapped her notebook against her leg. "Let's not jump to conclusions," she said. "There's lots of possibilities as to what happened. She may have gone in early to work, or be meeting a friend for breakfast."

"Meredith doesn't meet friends for breakfast," Patricia said. "She likes her sleep."

"Try her again, and leave a message this time," Adams said. "I'll call the jewellery shop and make sure she wasn't called in early for something." She was already flicking through her phone. It rang half a dozen times before it was answered.

"Scott Samuels, Samuels's Jewellers. How can I help you?"

"Mr Samuels, DI Adams," she said. "Have you seen Meredith this morning?"

"No," he replied, his tone bemused. "She's not due in until ten."

Adams looked at her watch. It was only nine o'clock. "Call me back if she comes in, alright? You've still got my phone number there?"

"Yes, I do," he said. "What's this all about? Is she alright?"

"We're hoping so. Just call me, got it?" She hung up before he could reply, and looked at Patricia and Henry.

"She's not there?" Patricia whispered. Henry leaned his head against hers. They were clutching each other now, and Adams couldn't tell who was comforting whom, or whether they were merely trying to find a way to anchor themselves to the world.

"There's still no reason to panic," she said. "If she calls, you let me know immediately. I'm going to have a look at her room, then I may send someone to go over it properly."

"To go over it properly?" Patricia said. "You think something's happened, don't you? That she's been abducted? Oh, *no*, she's been abducted. What if they hurt her? What if they ..." She stopped herself, pressing one hand to her mouth, and Henry hugged her a little more tightly.

"She'll be fine," he said. "She'll be absolutely fine. Maybe ... maybe she's decided to join a gym."

They looked at each other doubtfully, and Adams made some small noise of encouragement then headed down the hallway. Dandy was already there, standing in the middle of the bedroom and looking up at the window. Adams followed his gaze. There was nothing to be seen there that she could tell. A couple of smudges on the glass, not even fingerprints. The lock wasn't forced. The glass wasn't broken. She peered out, but the flowerbed below the window was packed with bark to stop any weeds sneaking through. Even if anyone had stood there, there'd be no sign of it.

She leaned back into the room and examined it. The bedside lamp was off, and still standing. More worryingly, a phone lay next to it, half-hidden under a copy of *On Earth We're Briefly Gorgeous*. Adams used a corner of the sheet to pick the phone up and turn it over. It was on silent, and the missed calls from Patricia lit up the screen. She put it back with a sigh and resumed her inspection of the room. A few other books were stacked beside the bed, and more filled a bookshelf on the opposite wall. Some clothes were hanging over the back of a chair, looking very much like the outfit Meredith had been wearing the day before. Photos and art prints in frames peppered the walls, but they were all hanging straight and neat. Adams crouched down to peer under the bed without finding anything more than some shoeboxes, then prowled the room, looking for anything that seemed out of place, but it was impossible to tell.

When she was sure there was nothing obvious, she called down the hallway. "Patricia, Henry, can you help me out here for a moment?"

They came to join her, walking side by side despite the hall's narrow confines.

Adams tried her encouraging smile again, but it didn't seem to have improved. She thought Patricia might've actually flinched this time. "Don't touch anything, but can you see anything that looks out of place?"

They both examined the room, then looked at each other.

"No," Patricia said. "It all looks just as it normally would." She pointed at a chest of carefully painted drawers in the corner, on top of which were arranged some necklaces on a hanging tree, and a clutter of moisturisers and make-up. "She hasn't even put her contacts in. That's the pot there."

Adams squinted at it. "She wears glasses?"

"Yes, but they're there," Patricia pointed at the side of the bed, and sure enough, a pair of light, wire-framed glasses were hooked onto one of those fake nose glasses holders. "She's not going to be able to see *anything*."

Adams nodded. Well, that certainly put paid to the idea that Meredith might have gone out on her own. She didn't say it aloud, but she could see the realisation dawning on the couple's faces. "This still doesn't mean that anything untoward has happened," she said.

"No," Henry replied. "I'm sure she just walked outside in the middle of the night, in her pyjamas, barefoot, and without being able to see more than a couple of metres."

Adams grimaced. "I understand. But we really can't panic just yet. I'm going to get someone to come and go over the room and the house properly, though. Please try not to touch anything. In fact, if you have somewhere you could go and wait, that would be the best option."

They looked at each other, then back at her. "What do you think they did to her?" Patricia whispered.

"There's no sign of a struggle," Adams said. "So maybe nothing at all." She smiled at them as well as she could, aware of how empty that sounded.

"Please," Henry said. "What do we do? How do we help?"

"By keeping out of here in case there's any evidence," Adams said, ushering them back into the hall. "Is there a neighbour you could wait with?"

"I suppose we could go next door," Henry said.

"There we go," Adams replied. "Good start."

ADAMS STOOD on the doorstep and watched a short, rotund woman open the door of the house next door. She was wearing a broad smile, but it faded rapidly as she put both arms around Patricia, staring past her at Adams.

Adams sighed, pulled her phone out, and hit call before she could think about it too much.

Temper answered just as she was thinking she might get away with a message and calling in the crime scene officers herself, even if that meant a bollocking later. He sounded even more put out than usual, scratchy with the heat. "Adams, what is it? Have you finally got hold of that bloody necklace?"

"No—"

"It's just some sodding missing jewellery," he interrupted. "We've got other cases, you know? It shouldn't be taking this long. I heard you were off on a jolly up to *York?*"

"Not a jolly, that's where the silversmith was, and—"

"You do know you can just make phone calls? And where are your notes? Lindsay said something about helping you out and I can't find a single bloody case note on the system to decide whether that's even justified or not, you dragging other detectives in."

"*Boss*. I think we've got an abduction. This case is bigger than I expected."

He was silent for a moment. "You're sure it's connected to the theft?"

"Pretty certain," she said, hoping she was right. But it couldn't not be, could it?

"What's your evidence of this abduction?"

"Meredith Williams, the assistant from the jewellery shop, wasn't home when her parents got up this morning. She hasn't taken her bag or her phone, plus her contacts and glasses are still in her room, and apparently she's pretty much blind without them."

There was a pause, then Temper said, "How do you know she hasn't just gone out to shag her boyfriend or something?"

"Girlfriend," Adams said. "And again, no glasses. No phone."

"Oh, girlfriend, boyfriend, same thing," Temper said, then fell silent. Finally he sighed and said, "So what do you want?"

"Well, I've asked the parents to leave the house, and I'd like the CSOs to go over it and see what they can come up with."

There was another long pause, and she pulled the phone away from her ear in time for the explosion of swearing at the other end. When she put the phone back, Temper said, "Do you know how much budget that is? For a missing *necklace?*"

"Missing person."

"How long has she been missing?"

"Since last night sometime. She went to bed around ten, according to her dad."

"That still sounds like she's just gone out for a shag. Maybe she's got a spare pair of glasses. Maybe she put new contacts lenses in and hasn't thrown the old ones away. Have you considered all of these possibilities, Adams?"

"I have, sir," she said. "But her phone's still here. What twentysomething leaves their phone behind, even for a shag? Plus, she's meant to be at work in the next hour, and it looks like her work clothes are still here. By all accounts it's *way* out of character."

"Well, maybe she finally decided to just be a twentysomething," Temper said.

Adams didn't reply, waiting. Dandy sat in front of her and looked from her to the side of the house, his ears expectant.

Temper drew a deep sigh. "You better be right about this, Adams."

"I'm sure I am, sir," she replied.

"Oh, the confidence of youth," Temper said, and hung up.

Wondering whether she should be complimented or insulted by the youth comment, Adams put the phone back in her pocket and nodded to Dandy. He jumped up and padded around the house. She followed, watching the ground carefully, but between the hard pathways and well-kept garden there was nowhere for a footprint to be left, and she didn't spot any dropped receipts or cigarette butts or anything at all that might help them out. Whatever Dandy had found, it wasn't anything she could see.

He stopped under Meredith's window, gazing up at it, and she crouched down next to him, pretending to examine the flowerbed. "What can you smell?" she asked him in a low voice. "Recognise anything?"

He tipped his head slightly, the dreadlocks over his eyes shifting and giving a glimpse of that red LED glow.

Adams shivered. "That will never not be creepy," she told him, and he huffed at her. "Well, you're not very helpful," she said, straightening up. "Lassie has given me very unrealistic expectations. Even Timmy was better than you."

He growled, a deep and reverberating sound, pointed his nose back at the corner of the house, and loped off. Adams followed him, but all he did was head back to the car and stand there on the sidewalk, looking expectantly down the road with his nose pointed toward the centre of Leeds.

"Brilliant," she muttered to herself. She probably could have figured out that they'd had a car herself. Most kidnappers didn't escape on foot. She took some crime tape out of the back of the car and strung it across the gate, then headed next door and knocked.

Henry appeared almost immediately. "Yes? Have you found something?"

"No," she replied. "But there's going to be a team coming to have a better look. They'll probably want to take your fingerprints and DNA for elimination purposes. But if you can just hang here until they're done, that would be best."

"But where are you going?" he asked. "You need to find our daughter."

"I will," Adams said. "But I'm not getting anywhere by staying here."

Henry grimaced at that, deflating. "Of course." He gave her an awkward little wave as she headed back down the path, leaning against the car as she took her phone out again. Dandy panted at her from the front seat.

James answered almost immediately. "Ay-up Adams, anything?"

"Meredith's gone," she said. "Probably abducted. I've got a team coming to check the house out."

"Abducted? Seriously?"

"It looks like it, and I'm kind of hoping I'm right because

otherwise Temper's going to string me up for wasting police resources. I've requested a crime scene team."

"Oof. Yeah, I hope you're right, too. What's the next move?"

Adams thought about it for a moment, tapping her fingers on the steering wheel. "Why attack her?" she said. "Can't be the person who's got the necklace. They've already got it. So someone else is chasing it." She was thinking of Gladys saying, *we'll get to the bottom of this*. But surely Gladys wasn't going to be sneaking around the place, abducting young women. And if she was, she'd already taken things into her own hands before Adams' visit that morning.

"Maybe there's more than one person after it," James suggested. "Maybe someone else saw it was taken into the shop and decided to get after it."

Like magic workers. Not that she could say that. "What, like rival art gangs or something? Are we moving on from James Bond to Sherlock Holmes?"

"Do you have a better theory?" he asked, and she sighed.

"Unfortunately not." Or not one she could share, anyway. Sorcerers? Magicians? Magic bloody faeries? "Meet me back at the jewellery shop," she said aloud. "We'll talk to Scott, maybe review a bit more of the CCTV footage and see if there were people hanging around when the necklace was brought in."

"See you there." He hung up, and Adams climbed into the car but just sat there for a while, staring through the windscreen and down the mild, nondescript little cul-de-sac. She didn't know where to start. It wasn't rival art gangs, she knew that much, but what magic workers did she know? None. And if the use of the necklace at the Apple Store and the Porsche garage – and maybe some other places they hadn't turned up yet – had attracted attention, how had it been traced back to Meredith? Who knew everything had started at the jewellery shop? The only person who ticked all the boxes was Gladys, and Adams still couldn't quite believe she'd actually be chasing around abducting people.

But one thing she had learned since moving north was never to underestimate ladies of a certain age. Anything was possible when it came to them.

14

EVERYONE'S AN INTRUDER

THE PHONE RANG AS ADAMS DROVE BACK TOWARD LEEDS CITY centre, and Lindsay's name came up on the display. Adams hit answer, but not without some reservations. It wasn't because James and Isha had both been less than enthusiastic about Lindsay. Workplace politics were ever-present, no matter what industry you were in, and she was fairly certain the police were about the worst of them. Everyone was always whinging about something, and Lindsay had been nothing but helpful to Adams since she had arrived.

No, what annoyed her was the fact that Lindsay had been asking Temper about her case notes. Bad enough she was trying to get hold of the notes themselves without asking Adams, but it had also drawn Temper's attention to the fact that Adams hadn't actually written any notes, which had done nothing to improve their earlier conversation.

But she answered anyway and said, "Morning?"

"Morning to you too. Anything new to report?"

Adams considered it. It would be common knowledge pretty soon anyway. "Yes," she said. "The assistant from the jewellery shop seems to have been abducted."

"Abducted?" Lindsay said, making it sound as if Adams had mentioned an intriguing new dish at the local cafe rather than someone being snatched out of their home. "That *is* an interesting development. What're you thinking?"

Adams didn't answer for a moment, weighing the different possibilities of how she could answer. And why was she even worried about Lindsay anyway? There was no reason to be. Her job was the same as Adams' in the end. "I think there's more than one person after this necklace," she said. "There's got to be, because whoever's actually got it wouldn't be chasing Meredith. And the woman who it belongs to, Gladys, she's in her late sixties. She's hardly going to be stealing away twenty-year-olds in the middle of the night. Not to try and get information out of them anyway," she added, mostly joking.

"I suppose not," Lindsay said, sounding slightly confused, and Adams thought maybe the other woman hadn't been as exposed to ladies of a certain age as Adams had. "So you have no idea where the necklace is still?"

"No," Adams said. "More concerned about the abduction, to be honest."

"Of course. But if it's all linked—"

"Has to be, but not going to be the same party, is it?"

"Sure," Lindsay said, in a patient tone that made Adams scowl at her phone. "But if you get your hands on the necklace, they've got no reason to be abducting anyone, do they? The necklace is out of reach. So surely the best way to get Meredith *un*–abducted is to find the damn thing."

"Oh. Right." Adams' ears were unaccountably hot.

"So where are you with that? If it's not Meredith, who might have it?"

Adams didn't answer straight away. She still had no solid suspect, not now that Meredith was out of the picture, not that she'd been that suspicious in the first place. "I need to think this through a bit."

"Do you want to hand something over to me? You can send me your notes and I'll take on the abduction angle, start seeing what I can do to track Meredith down. You can keep after the necklace."

"No," Adams said thoughtfully. "No, I think it's all very much intertwined. James and I'll stick with it."

"Suit yourself. I mean, I've worked abduction cases before, though, so I might be a bit more useful on that side of things than James."

"Cheers," Adams said. "We'll be fine. But can you check in with your art dealer contacts and just see if there are any rumours about that piece popping up?" Because who knew how much overlap there was between Folk and human artefacts?

"I already have, but sure."

"Doesn't hurt to ask again. I'm going to see if Isha can find any video footage of the abduction."

"Good luck," Lindsay said. "I can never get anything out of that woman."

"You have to bribe her with coffee," Adams said. "It's the only currency that works."

Lindsay laughed. "All right, well, keep me updated and let me know if I can help."

"Thanks," Adams said. "I appreciate it. It's good having someone around here that doesn't just treat me like the intruder from the south."

"We're all intruders in one way or another. Got to stick together."

She hung up, and Adams' smile faded. She did feel like an intruder, not made to fit the shape of the north and this city. And of course it'd take her time to settle here. Maybe she never would, too moulded by the London that had birthed her, that had breathed soot and metal and strange magics into her bones, to be able to reshape herself to this place with its roads that fled to moors and fells and wild places, as if the city could never quite untangle itself from their influence, feral and deep and unknowable.

So Lindsay could say they were all intruders, probably meaning the boy's club she was so fixated on (and right to be), but Adams had a feeling that she was more so than others. And it wasn't about being a city cop from down south, and it wasn't about the colour of her skin. She wasn't even sure it was about the mental health break, marking her like a scarlet letter.

She had a sneaking feeling it was to do with the way some people were more real than others, more in the world. Because she thought that even if people didn't necessarily *see* it, they felt it. And it was why they turned away from those who were different. It was why some people passed under the notice of society, or were deliberately ostracised by it. Because humans above all else are still animals, and different is dangerous and not to be trusted. And she had a feeling she wore her difference a little too close to the skin.

JAMES WAS WAITING at the jewellery shop when she got there, and she parked in a loading bay, sticking her permit in the windscreen.

"Have you been in?" she asked him as she climbed out.

"No, waiting for you," he replied. "Haven't seen any sign of Meredith though."

Adams checked her watch. "Still early. She's not meant to be here until ten. She's got another half hour."

James looked at her. "You think a half hour is going to help?"

"Probably not," Adams said. "But you never know."

He nodded. "Temper will do you if you've pulled out the tech team and she does just walk in here a bit hungover."

"I realise this," Adams said, and rang the bell.

There was a glimpse of movement behind the door, then it buzzed open. She pushed her way through. Scott was standing at the counter wearing a light blue jacket over his shirt, and he looked from Adams to James with his face pale, lines drawn at the corners of his mouth.

"What's this about Meredith?" he asked. "I mean, she's not even meant to be here yet. Are you sure she's missing?"

"Pretty sure," Adams replied, trying to gauge him. His hands were rubbing on his trousers as if to wipe off sweat, and his forehead had a soft sheen on it. He was definitely uneasy about something. But why would he abduct Meredith? Unless it really had been a set-up, and she was getting cold feet, so he'd had to silence her.

Aloud, she said, "Anyone unusual been hanging around? Perhaps coming back a bit too often, especially since the necklace was brought in?"

He spread his fingers. "I didn't notice anyone," he said. "But you can have any of the recordings you need to check."

"That'll be good," Adams said. "Let's have a quick look now, then we can send them on to the lab and see if anyone can pick up any familiar faces from it."

Scott led them back into the office, where the old computer was groaning away through a backup. It sounded like it was winding up to explode, and Scott hit pause, giving it a moment to recover before he pulled up the right program. He turned the screen toward them, and Adams leaned over the desk as he scrolled through the files, trying to find the right date. She let him get on with it, not really looking at the images. She wasn't actually expecting that they'd see anything, but rather wanted to let Scott feel he was being helpful, and to think that he was in the clear.

She glanced at James, who was trying to look at the screen as much as he could in the close confines of the office without actually putting his chin on her shoulder. "Do you recognise anyone?"

"No," he said. "But Isha can probably do a bit of facial identification on it."

Adams nodded. "I wonder how many iced coffees that's going to cost me?"

"I'd invest in a home set-up," James said. "Or stocks in the cafe."

Adams stayed where she was, her palms on the desk, all of them crowded into the corner. Scott sat back in his desk chair, leaning away from her as much as the wall would allow him. She wasn't sure if she could actually smell the anxious sweat on him, or just sense it.

"When did you last see Meredith?" she asked him.

"Yesterday," he said. "She was working all day."

"And she wasn't worried about anyone?" Adams asked. "Didn't mention anyone hanging around, feeling like she was being followed, anything like that?"

"No, nothing. I mean, she's been a bit nervous after the whole necklace incident. It's really affected her. But she seemed fine otherwise."

Adams nodded, still not moving, Scott trapped between her and the wall. "Things been a bit tight for you recently, haven't they?"

He frowned at her. "We've been through this. I didn't take the necklace. I wouldn't destroy my own business over something that I probably wouldn't even be able to sell on."

She smiled at him, a baring of the teeth. "Checked into it, have you?"

He folded his arms over his chest and tried to glare at her, but quickly dropped his gaze to the screen. "I'm a jeweller. I've been doing this all my life. I wouldn't even know what to do if I had to find something else, so I wouldn't risk my business. And I certainly wouldn't risk going to jail over it." He grimaced. "Also Meredith has been the most fantastic employee, and if anything's happened … Well. I'm really worried about her, is all."

Adams kept her gaze on him until he looked up reluctantly and met it. He still had that nervous sweat going on, but there was an indignant edge to his tone which seemed perfectly genuine. She wasn't sure if she believed him about the necklace, but she did believe him about Meredith. She straightened up.

"Alright. If she comes in, let us know straight away."

"I will," he said.

He followed them back through the shop, closing the door behind them a little more firmly than was necessary. Outside, James and Adams stood in the shadow of the shopfront, out of the worst of the morning heat. It was building enough that Adams could feel it baking off the pavement and soaking into the bare skin of her arms and face.

"Now what?" James asked. "How do we find Meredith?"

Adams didn't answer straight away, considering it. There was Scott, there was Gladys, and there was the question of where the hell this necklace was, and how taking Meredith was helping anyone.

"I think we get someone watching Scott," she said finally. "See if he leads us anywhere. I don't think he was lying about Meredith, and it still seems way too obvious for him to have taken the necklace, but at the same time …"

"Yeah," James said. "Sometimes obvious is just the way of things."

"Criminal masterminds are thinner on the ground than Sherlock would have us suspect."

"Have you met any?" he asked, as he followed her to the car.

"Not a one," she said, beeping the car open. James climbed into the passenger seat and she added, "Did you follow up with the Porsche garage this morning?"

"I did, but there wasn't anything we didn't already know. Someone came in, the salesman signed them out for a test drive, then was stricken down by a migraine that was so severe the manager didn't know anything about it until she came in from lunch and found him lying on the floor behind his desk. A car was gone and the only signature on the paperwork was his."

"Sounds like a bit of a fireable offence," Adams said.

"Yeah, haven't talked to him, but he's home watching Netflix on sick leave apparently. I don't imagine he'll be going back."

"Okay, check in with him and get his story, and tell him to stay in with his Netflix, or make sure he's around people. I don't imagine our kidnappers are going to be chasing down everyone involved, but best to be sure. Call Patrice too, and make sure he's safe."

"You don't want to put someone on them?"

"Temper's going to have conniptions over me putting someone on Scott. He'll have an actual meltdown if I ask for someone to babysit those two. We don't have any reason to think that they're going to be targeted, really. Even our connections between these cases are tenuous at best."

"Fair point," James said, taking his phone out, and she looked at him.

"On you go, then."

"What're you doing?"

"I'm going to talk to the silversmith again. See if he can shed some more light on Scott."

"Alright," James said, still not moving, and she sighed.

"Do you want me to drop you back at the station?"

"No," he said, "I can make phone calls while we're driving."

"I don't need you to come with me to York. You didn't even come in last time."

"I didn't not come in, I wasn't *allowed* to come in," he pointed out. "And at the very least, this way I can be in the same general area when the silversmith stabs you with a soldering iron and runs out the back. It'll help with the paperwork, and possibly mean you don't get dumped in the River Ouse."

Adams thought about it. "Can you actually stab someone with a soldering iron?"

"Probably if you got them in the eye or something," James replied.

"Not really your point, I suppose," she said, and he spread his fingers, still not budging. Annoying little jobsworth. If he wasn't such a generally decent bloke she'd have definitely hated him. Technically, she could order him out of the car, she supposed, but all she needed was for him to go complaining to Temper, and then she'd be off the case before she could even fully get to grips with it. Besides, she needed to save her ordering him away for when she *really* needed it.

"Fine," she said. "But it's not a shopping trip this time."

They headed back out through the disgruntled traffic clogging the main roads, picking up the dual carriageway as they turned toward York. Adams settled back into her seat as the traffic thinned, her fingers light on the wheel as she overtook lumbering lorries and pottering estates, and scowled at white vans ducking and weaving through the traffic like they thought they were Formula One drivers. She flicked her lights at one who pulled in too close in front of her, and an arm emerged out of the driver's window, gesticulating rudely. Figured.

James hung up and looked at Adams. "Patrice is in an engineering lecture. He's with friends, doesn't seem worried, hasn't seen anyone hanging around. And Kelvin, the guy from the Porsche garage, says he's not planning on going anywhere."

"Alright," Adams said. "Someone on Scott?"

"Requested. You're liking him for all of it?" James asked.

"I think so," Adams replied. "I can't figure out the Apple Store and the Porsche thing, though. If he's got the necklace, surely he'd just shift it and get the cash, not run around using whatever this tech is and creating more of a trail for us."

"Maybe he's sitting on it until things calm down. And he's got kids, doesn't he?"

"Alright, so that explains the gadgets," Adams replied. "What about the Porsche?"

"Well, his sports car did get repossessed. And it was a Porsche from that garage."

"Oh," Adams said. "Interesting."

The phone rang, Isha's name coming up on the display. Adams answered it on the hands-free.

"Alright, Isha."

"Alright, Adams. How much extra work are you going to keep giving me? I've just got a load more videos in from that bloody jewellery shop."

"Yeah, I know," Adams said. "We're actually liking the owner for the theft, but the shop assistant's gone missing on top, and that doesn't seem to fit. Can you see if you can pick up anything suspicious? Someone hanging around, or following her when she left last night?"

"Yeah, can do, but never mind that right now," Isha said. "Take me off speakerphone so I can talk to you properly."

"I'm driving."

"Oh no, you'd better not break the law. I mean, you might

get arrested or something. Pity you don't know a police officer who could get you off."

James snorted, disconnected the Bluetooth, and held the phone to Adams' ear.

"What?" Adams asked.

"Right. Don't want Public School there listening in on this."

Adams managed not to laugh, and looked at James. He hadn't reacted, so either he couldn't hear or he wasn't about to take offence. "Go on, then."

"I was actually poking around the footage already."

"Okay, why?"

"Because I noticed something. I thought the camera just wasn't very good quality when your Gladys went in there with the necklace. But when she leaves, perfectly clear once she's out of the shop."

"Well, that's a different camera outside the shop, isn't it?" Adams said.

"You misunderstand me. When she arrived, it was just a bit *off*. Not bad, not like when the necklace was taken, but not great. When she left, could have read the watch on her hand."

"Huh," Adams said. "So you think the necklace is what's causing the interference?"

"Exactly. And it seems to have a certain constant level of interference, whether it's being used or not."

Adams could hear the quotation marks around *used*. "You think the necklace itself is the problem? An electronic device of some sort?"

"Maybe," Isha said. "But there's still nothing I know that can do this. And the fact that the Porsche garage had *wired* CCTV cameras is annoying me so much that I swear I can't sleep. I was thinking about this all night."

"It's definitely weird."

"It's *impossible.*"

"Do me another favour?" Adams asked.

"Why not?"

"See what you can find from Meredith's address last night. I don't know the timing of it, or even if there's any cameras around her house. I think someone went to her window, though. Can you just see if anything comes up?"

"Sure," Isha said. "But you owe me a beer, some wings and an explanation about what the hell is going on."

"Deal," Adams said. "Call me when you get something."

"Oh, I will. This is the most interesting thing that's happened in bloody ages."

Adams hung up and James gave her a curious look. "Isha thinks the necklace is the device?"

"Maybe," Adams said.

"Is she a bit freaked out by how weird it all is?"

"Maybe," Adams repeated.

"I kind of understand that," James replied. "Although calling me Public School's a bit off. It was only day school. I wasn't *boarding.*"

Adams didn't have the heart to tell him either how posh that still made him, or just how strange the whole situation really was. She was struggling with it enough herself as it was.

15

A LITTLE PERSUASION

HEATHER OPENED THE DOOR OF ASH & YEW AND REGARDED them, eyebrows raised. "You're becoming quite the regulars."

"Is Charles here?" Adams asked.

"He is." She stepped back to allow Adams in, then held a hand up. "You can stay out here," she said to James. "Unless you're looking for something else for your mum."

"No," he replied, and looked at Adams.

"It's fine," she said, and Heather swung the door shut on him, turning the lock as she gave Adams an appraising look.

"You're not going to find what you need here," she said. "Running around asking questions isn't getting you anywhere. You have to *do* something."

"That's what I'm trying to do," Adams answered, her tone sharper than she intended.

"If you're here, that means you still haven't found the necklace."

"I think that's fairly obvious."

"You're running out of time."

"What for?"

Heather shook her head, and Adams had that feeling she'd

disappointed her again. "Charles is in the workshop. Go on through." She picked up a bracelet and started carefully threading silver and coloured glass beads onto it, her hands steady and sure.

Adams watched her for a moment, then let herself through the door at the back of the shop and walked down the hall to the workshop, where Charles hovered over his bench, his T-shirt torn on one arm and his arms thin and long. "Hello?" she said, hoping he wasn't in the middle of doing something vital.

He looked up, the goggles making his face distorted and unnatural, the dark glass reflecting the lights. "Again," he said. "I'm starting to think you're making excuses to see me, Inspector." He pushed the goggles up onto his head, and Adams saw that he'd managed to singe the other eyebrow almost fully off. "What can I help you with this time?"

She leaned against the door, folding her arms. "Tell me about the necklace," she said.

"Gold, and one unidentified stone," he said, looking back at her levelly.

"Only a necklace isn't just a necklace."

"You're learning," he replied.

"Meredith's missing."

The smile vanished from Charles's face. "What do you mean?"

"She vanished last night. She doesn't have her glasses or her contacts with her, so I don't think she's just wandered off."

"No," Charles said. "That wouldn't be Meredith's style."

"You know her quite well then?"

Charles shook his head. "Not that well. I only go in there once a week. But she's a nice girl. I normally stop for a cup of tea with her. Her mum's sick, you know."

Adams winced. It explained Patricia's haggard, delicate

face, and Henry's protectiveness. "So Meredith wouldn't worry her."

"Definitely not," Charles replied, peeling his heavy gloves off. He patted his pockets and said, "Come on."

Adams followed him out a door at the back of the workshop that led onto a small, cobbled alley, equipped with a couple of bins and some hopeful weeds.

Charles looked around, lit a cigarette, and leaned against the wall. "You really want to know about the necklace?"

"I know a bit already. It's *persuasive,* apparently. Who would want it?"

"Pretty much anyone who knows anything about magic," Charles replied. "It has power, that necklace. She shouldn't have brought it into the shop. It was just too tempting for anyone to pick up."

"What does it do, besides being persuasive?" Adams asked. "Is it what's scrambling the video?"

"Probably," Charles replied. "It can convince people to see what the holder wants them to see. It's not going to work like that on a TV camera, but Folk things tend to have their own protection against human devices." He looked at her, drawing heavily on the cigarette. "You know about Folk?"

"A little."

"You should learn more."

"Not sure if I want to."

He grinned at that, his teeth crooked and as stained as his burnt hands. "You may not have a choice. But anyway. The necklace would've probably just looked like a bit of boring jewellery on the camera, unless someone was using it to disguise themselves. The disguising bit is what would've busted up the camera image, and is why Meredith would've been sure she saw Gladys." He tipped his head. "Bet your eyes went a bit funny when you checked the signatures, too."

That explained a lot. "So basically someone's running

around with a necklace that lets them get exactly what they want, all the time."

"To start," Charles said. "That's pretty harmless in itself. But *persuasive* means, among other things, that it can convince people to do whatever the holder wants them to."

Something cold and coiling shifted in the pit of Adams' belly. That wasn't the sort of thing you wanted out there. Not for just anyone to be holding onto. "Why the hell would Gladys bring that into the shop?"

"Basic high street shop, really. She probably thought no one would recognise it for what it was."

"You did, though," she said, looking at him levelly. "Weren't you tempted?"

"No. There's always a price for these things." He looked at his cigarette, then flicked ash onto the cobbles. "Most magical things aren't worth the cost you pay for them. Folk know that, generally. But there are always those who are looking to build power."

Adams sighed. "But this isn't Folk, is it? Apple computers and cars and things."

"I doubt it."

"Could it be Scott?"

He considered it, eyes squinted up at the sky, then shrugged. "The necklace, maybe, although I don't know how he'd have recognised it for what it was, or known how to use it. Things like that have their own ways of working on people though, so it's possible. But Scott wouldn't hurt Meredith. That I'm sure of." He hesitated, then added, "And if he does have the necklace, he's going to be drawing some really unwanted attention pretty soon. And not just from you."

"Can you help me find out whose attention it might have drawn?"

"Absolutely not," Charles replied. "Heather and I have a quiet life. We intend to keep it that way."

"Not even for Meredith?" she asked.

Charles didn't answer for a moment, still puffing quietly on his cigarette. Eventually, he stubbed it out in an empty baked bean can and looked at her. "I'll ask some questions. That's as much as I'm doing."

"Thank you," Adams said.

"Not for you. For her."

Adams nodded her understanding, and headed back out through the shop. Heather looked up to watch her pass, but didn't say anything, and a moment later she was outside, where James pushed himself off the wall of the shop opposite and came to join her, hands in his pockets.

"Well?" he asked. "Did he give you anything?"

Since *it's magic* wasn't any sort of answer she just said, "Nothing. He didn't notice anyone around the shop. And he's certain Scott wouldn't hurt Meredith, although he says he wouldn't put it past him to take the necklace."

"Right," James said. "So do we pull Scott in?"

"I think so. If he's feeling trapped he might not be as well-intentioned as Charles seems to think."

"Call it in?"

"No, we'll do it ourselves." She set off before he could argue, pushing through the tourists as she struggled her way out of The Shambles, feeling trapped and dragged back by the crowds and the heat and the uncertainty, the sun burning the back of her neck but doing nothing to warm that chill, twisting feeling in the base of her stomach.

It can make people do anything you want them to. Make people see what you want them to. That was the sort of thing you didn't want out there in the world.

THEY WERE HALFWAY BACK to Leeds when James's phone rang.

He answered it and said, "DC James Hamilton."

Adams could hear someone talking rapidly on the other end of the line, and James said, "Slow down. Take a breath. I'm just going to put you on speaker so my colleague can hear you." He looked at Adams, frowning, and hit the speaker button. A man's voice blared out, panicked and unfamiliar.

"Hello? Are you still there?"

"Yes," James said. "Detective Inspector Adams is with me, too. What's your name?"

"It's … um, it's … my name's Dan. I'm a friend of Patrice." He was stumbling over his words, gasping them out in a rush then stopping again.

"Alright," James said. "Deep breath, Dan. Are you okay?"

"No," he said. "No, I'm not okay. Or I am, but Patrice is gone."

"What do you mean, *gone?*" Adams asked.

"We finished a lecture and were heading to the cafe. Our usual cafe, you know?"

"Sure," Adams said, since he seemed to require some acknowledgment.

"Just as we got to the door these two guys stopped him, and he … he just walked off with them. Like, they didn't even say anything. He just *left*, and when I tried to stop him one of them shoved me right into some bins, knocked me down."

"They didn't force him to go with them?" Adams asked.

"No, he just turned around and left. I was shouting at him, but he didn't even answer, just climbed into a car with them."

"Had you seen them before?"

"No. I … I'm not even sure what they looked like. But it was two … I think it was two men? Maybe?"

"You're not sure?"

"I was panicking, okay?"

"Okay," Adams said. "I understand. It's fine." It wasn't, of course, but they weren't getting anything out of him by stressing him more. "Then what happened?"

"By the time I got up they were already driving away, but he dropped his bag when I tried to stop him, and it was still on the ground. This number was on his phone, and he'd told me you called earlier to check on him, so I thought I better call you rather than just the police. Is this something to do with why you wanted him to stay around people?"

"Maybe," Adams said, thinking of the necklace again, and how it could *persuade* people. But why were they taking Patrice if they already had the necklace?

"Did you notice the car?" James asked. "See the number plate?"

"Yes," Dan said. "I took a photo."

"Well done," Adams said. "Send James the photo, and try to remember anything you can about the people who took him."

"I'll do that now. You're going to find him, aren't you?"

"We're going to do our absolute best," Adams replied.

James hung up. "That's two," he said. "We need to check on Kelvin."

"Who?"

"Porsche man."

"Right. Get him on the phone, then call that number plate in as soon as Dan sends it to you." Adams was already accelerating.

"What about Scott?"

"This doesn't sound like him, does it?"

"No, but—"

"I'll deal with Scott," she said, her tone terse. And she knew she couldn't excuse it or explain it if they lost Scott because she hadn't called it in, but there was also no point sending anyone else after him. Not if he had the necklace.

Because all he had to do was wave it about and go *oh, no, don't arrest me,* or however it worked, and that would be it. It had to be her, although she supposed she wouldn't be any better able to resist it. At least she'd be prepared, though.

Kelvin answered on the sixth ring, sounding half-asleep, and James told him to stay put. Not that it was going to help if someone turned up with a bit of *persuasion* and suggested he join them, though, so Adams kept her foot down all the way there, jumping red lights and swerving past cars and buses and lorries, leaning on her horn as she went. James clung to the door handle but, to his credit, only swore once, when she slammed the brakes on to avoid hitting an elderly man being towed across a pedestrian crossing by six dogs, each of which looked like they outweighed him by about twenty kilos.

Kelvin's flat was on the canal, not that far from Adams', although in a much fancier and better outfitted building. She pulled into the loading bay at the front, slapping her permit in the windscreen. James was already out of the car, running for the door to the building, and he slammed every button on the intercom, shouting, "Police!" as soon as someone answered. By the time Adams reached him he was pulling the door open, and they ran up the stairs, James taking them two at a time and Adams racing after him, cursing her parents for not having taller genes. They burst into the hallway one after the other, checking numbers on the doors.

James found it first, pounding on the panels with the side of his fist. "Open up! Police!" He was still knocking when the door was pulled open, and Kelvin stared out at them, looking bleary. "What?" he asked.

James sagged against the doorframe. "You need to come with us."

"Why?" Kelvin asked. "What's going on?" He scratched his

chest. He was shirtless, his stomach ribbed with unnaturally tanned abs.

"Just put your shirt on and move yourself."

"Ugh. Really?"

"*Police,*" Adams said, waving her ID at him.

"Am I in trouble?"

"You will be if you don't get a hustle on," she said. "You think we're here for the fun of it? *Move!*"

He moved, fleeing inside, and James looked at Adams. "How much coffee have you had today?" he asked.

"Not enough."

"That was my diagnosis, too."

She scowled at him, and Kelvin reappeared in a pair of skinny khaki trousers and a white shirt, still buttoning it.

"Do I need—" he started, and Adams cut him off.

"Keys?"

"Um, yes?"

"Good." She slammed the door behind him and headed for the stairs.

Kelvin followed her, phone clutched in one hand. "I don't understand what's happening," he complained.

"We can explain it all later," Adams replied, not entirely truthfully. They clattered down the stairs, and she scanned the foyer before heading for the door onto the street, beeping the car open as she went. There was no one outside that she could see, so she pushed the entrance door ajar, checked the street again, then hurried to the car. She skirted around it to open the driver's door and swung inside, jamming the key in the ignition. The engine rumbled into life, and she called, "James, can you call ahead and see if there's been any movement from Scott?"

James didn't reply, and neither passenger side door opened. She looked up, frowning, and something *shifted.* It was as if she blinked, closing her eyes on an empty pavement, other than Kelvin with James behind him, one hand on the shorter man's shoulder, then opened them again to a woman standing in front of the two men, her form oddly indistinct.

Oh, she thought, rather disinterestedly, and watched the woman slip her arm companionably through Kelvin's, pulling him away from James while the detective constable stared at her somewhat stolidly, one hand hanging loose at his side and the other still outstretched, even though Kelvin's shoulder was gone. On some level Adams felt there was something wrong with this picture, and that she should probably be doing something, but at the same time the only thought that occurred to her was that same *oh,* as if someone had hit pause on her thinking process, setting it stuttering with static.

The woman started to walk away, Kelvin ambling along with her, and Dandy shoved his face into Adams', slapping a warm, wet tongue across her cheek.

"*No!* Bad dog!" she yelped, and the world surged into motion again, a crisp packet fluttering across the road and the woman snapping her head around to stare at Adams. James was still frozen, Kelvin moving but blank-faced, and Dandy surged over Adams and out of the car.

Adams' body caught up before her brain did, and she threw herself after the dog, shouting, "Police! Stop!"

The woman threw something at her, and Adams ducked behind the car, but didn't hear anything hit. She just had a sudden moment of vertigo, a swinging, seesawing motion that made her stumble to one knee. But then she was up again, even as Dandy grabbed the leg of Kelvin's trousers and hauled on them. Kelvin staggered, half-falling, and the woman lost her grip on his arm, swearing. She grabbed for him again, and Adams couldn't have said what the colour of her hair was, or her eyes, couldn't have even really said if she was looking at a woman at all. But what she did know was that another oddly indistinct form was swinging out of a white van to help her, and neither of them seemed to be aware of the hulking dog trying to drag Kelvin off by one leg. Adams decided there wasn't time to worry about what any of them should've been seeing. She just threw herself around the car and charged at the woman.

The man altered course from running to help his companion, who had hold of Kelvin's arm and seemed to be confused by why he wasn't moving, to heading for Adams, and she barely managed to swerve around him. He made a grab for her and she landed a good sharp kick on one of his legs, setting him staggering.

"Leave it!" the woman shouted, and Adams tried to make sense of her voice, to place an accent or a dialect, but there was nothing there. The man spun and broke into a limping sprint for the van, the woman already ahead of him, and Adams bolted to intercept them. The woman heard her coming and dropped into a sudden crouch, turning as she did so and coming up fast, before Adams had a chance to react. The woman's shoulder slammed into Adams' side even as she tried to turn away, Dandy arriving an instant too late to intercept the blow. Adams yelped and staggered, trying to keep her balance, then collided with the dog, sending herself tumbling over his back and to the pavement.

By the time she'd rolled back to her feet, both attackers were in the van and it was screeching away. Adams swore, running a few steps after it as she squinted at the number plate. Dandy ran with her, then stopped in the street and looked back at her, his head tipped apologetically. She sighed. He'd saved Kelvin, and shaken her out of whatever trance she'd been in. She couldn't be *that* angry.

The van vanished around the corner, and Kelvin sat up, looking down at himself. "What happened?" he asked. "Did I pass out?"

"Something like that," Adams said, and looked at James, who had one hand on his head. "Are you alright?" she asked him.

"What the hell happened? It feels like I blacked out there for a second."

She nodded slightly. "Chemical agents."

"Seriously?"

"I think so," she said. "It's alright, we've still got Kelvin. And I got the plates."

James rubbed both hands over his face. "I didn't even *see* anyone."

"I didn't see them either," Adams said. "They must've been in the back of the van."

"But I mean I didn't see them grab Kelvin. I remember stepping through the doors, then *nothing.*"

"Chemical agent, I told you. Got to be."

"It didn't affect you."

"I was in the car," she replied. "Whatever they were using wouldn't have reached me."

James looked at her doubtfully. "I'm really sorry."

"It's fine," she said. "You couldn't have done anything."

She could have though. She should've been straight in the car, giving chase. She shouldn't've let the van race off without her on its tail. She should've left the two men on the pavement and just *gone.* Because sure, she had the number plate, but it wouldn't do them any good. She was certain of that.

"What happened to my trousers?" Kelvin asked. "There's holes in them! And … did something *bite* me?"

"That seems unlikely," Adams said, and headed for the car, one hand reaching out for Dandy. "Good boy," she whispered, as quietly as she could.

The number plate was the same as the one Dan had sent them, and by the time they got Kelvin into the station they had a match. But sure enough, the plates didn't belong to the van. They belonged to a Mini, so that wasn't getting them anywhere.

But what Adams did know was it was time for her to fully discount there being any art gangs or electronic scramblers or jewellery thieves behind any of it. Whoever the would-be kidnappers had been, they'd been hiding themselves in a manner that owed nothing to human technology or knowledge, and whether they had the necklace or not, they were most certainly involved. And she might not know what was going on, but she was going to work it out. That was her job, after all.

And the kidnappers had been human-shaped enough to arrest, so that was good enough for her.

16

SPRINGING A LEAK

At the station, Adams left James to deposit Kelvin in an interview room. He was still complaining about his torn trousers, and Adams didn't feel she could be responsible for her actions if he kept whinging.

"But how long will I be here?" he asked, as she and James hurried him into the station.

"As long as it takes," she said.

"As long as *what* takes?"

"Finding whoever hit you with a chemical agent?" she suggested, and he stopped so sharply that James ran into him and swore.

"What, like that Russian bloke who got stabbed with an umbrella?"

"No umbrellas involved."

"Was it a dog? Did they attack me with some sort of chemical-carrying dog?" He looked down at his ankle, pulling his trousers leg up to show them. "Is it rabies?"

"It's not even bloody bruised," James said, who seemed to be taking the whole situation somewhat personally. "Now will you just *move?*"

"It is too bruised! Look, you can see the teeth marks—"

"Do we need to arrest you for your own good?" Adams asked.

"You can't do that!" Kelvin looked from one of them to the other, then added, "Can you?"

Neither James or Adams answered, and Kelvin started walking again, throwing in a limp that hadn't been there a moment before. Adams and James exchanged glances, and Adams waved them on, then veered off toward Isha's office. She wasn't *certain* James wouldn't give the silly sod a slap if he kept up his moaning, but he was less likely to do it than she was.

Isha's office door was closed, and Adams knocked lightly.

"Enter," Isha called, and Adams slipped around the door, holding both hands up.

"I come empty-handed," she said.

"That's alright, I'm holding you to the beer and wings," Isha replied and nodded at the seat across the desk. "Plus I've still got a caffeine headache from yesterday." She examined Adams as she sat down. "What've you been doing to yourself?"

Adams looked at the scuffed knees of her trousers and gave them an ineffectual brush, then tried to unobtrusively nudge Dandy away as he investigated the fern, which was on the corner of the desk. "Almost had a third abductee."

"Third? Who was the second?"

"Oh – Apple Store worker. Nabbed in Headingley. We kept hold of Porsche Man, but there was a kerfuffle."

"A what?" Isha asked, grinning broadly, and Adams grimaced.

"An altercation."

"I think you should put *kerfuffle* in your report. Himself will love it."

"I'm sure. What've you got?" Adams asked.

"No kerfuffle at Meredith's."

"Good to know."

"Barely even call it an abduction," Isha added. "But first – definitely some issues with the cameras outside her house. But not like you'd think. Or not like we've come to expect, which is still doing my head in."

"What do you mean, not like you'd think?" Adams asked.

"It's not the glitching like before. Not even the out of focus that I was telling you about. You can see detail on everything except the abductors." She turned the screen so that Adams could see it. It was frozen on a white van with three people at the back of it. Isha zoomed in, and at first Adams assumed things just got pixelated. But then she frowned and looked a little closer. One of the stranger's faces was in profile, the other mostly turned toward the camera, and they were less pixelated than *blurry*. The van, however, was in perfect detail, and Adams could even see the cartoon cats printed on Meredith's pyjama bottoms. They were cavorting about with flowers, which seemed unlike Adams' experience of cats.

That wasn't the only strange thing, though. Meredith was standing there with her head hanging slightly, but she wasn't being restrained, and as Isha hit the play button Adams watched her climb docilely into the van. No one pushed her or dragged her, and her body language didn't seem to indicate she was at all concerned. She might've been climbing into a cab.

"Would you say it looks like she knows them?" Adams asked.

"More like she's sleepwalking," Isha replied, scrolling back through the recording. "Look."

There wasn't a camera on the house, but Isha had found

one close enough that Meredith was visible coming down the path. From the wide angle, Adams had a feeling it was one of those doorbell cameras, probably from a house across the road, and she decided not to ask where Isha had dug that up. She focused on Meredith instead. Two figures flanked her, but they weren't dragging her along, or even touching her. She just pottered along between them quite happily. The only thing that seemed off was her hanging head and slightly uneven gait.

"Drugged, I reckon," Isha said. "Unless you've got some dab hands in hypnosis out there."

Adams managed a dutiful snort of laughter and said, "You can't clean it up to see the faces better?" There was the same smudginess to the abductors on this camera, too.

"Nope. And there are some things out there that mess with facial recognition, but normally we can pick up what they're using at least. This is like it's happening within the tape, as if something's causing it to degenerate."

"That seems like pretty hefty tech."

"It's *impossible* tech. And it's really annoying me."

"What about the van, then?"

"Nothing," Isha said. "Generic white van, and they must've changed plates. I tracked it to the ring road, then lost it in traffic."

Adams sighed. "Yeah, that doesn't surprise me."

Isha leaned back in her chair and said, "You going to clear any of this up for me?"

"Not sure I can."

"Try."

Adams rubbed the back of her neck, digging her fingers into the tender spots where the tension collected. "Can I say I'll tell you what I can once I'm finished?"

Isha watched her for a long moment, then said, "*What I can* doesn't fill me with confidence."

Adams spread her hands apologetically, but didn't answer.

"*Fine*. But don't forget the beer and wings. Proper ones."

Adams grinned and got up. "Those I can promise."

"You bloody better."

UPSTAIRS SHE WENT to the interview room to check on Kelvin. He jumped to his feet as soon as she opened the door. "There you are," he said. "That other detective is a right mardy bum."

Adams tried to remember if she should know what that particular piece of northern slang meant, but couldn't. Judging by James's expression when she left, though, he probably meant grumpy. "Are you alright in here? Need anything?"

"I need to leave."

"Oh, sorry. Did you want to be abducted?"

"Look, it was just a mugging, right? Why would anyone want to abduct me?"

It was a reasonable question, really. She was almost wishing they'd succeeded, though. "It wasn't a mugging, and we're working on the why. Could be your Porsche thieves think you can ID them. But until we're sure, sit tight."

"Aw, *come on*. This is ridiculous. I haven't done anything wrong and you're keeping me locked up in here like *I'm* the bloody kidnapper."

"It's for your own safety."

"Can't I just have a police guard or something?"

"You're not a bloody celebrity."

He scowled. "I'm meant to be going out tonight."

"Well, you *can* go out," Adams said. "Then you can get

abducted, murdered, and dumped in the river. Or you can just sit here until we sort this out. What's your preference?"

Kelvin heaved out an enormous sigh and dropped back into the chair. "This sucks so much," he muttered, mostly to himself.

Adams shrugged slightly and left, making sure the door was locked behind her.

James was in the staffroom, making a cup of tea, and he looked up as Adams came in. "Want one?" he asked.

"No." She poked the coffee machine, but the jug was empty again, and a faint burning smell was drifting from it. She narrowed her eyes at Dandy, but he just wagged his tail. "You feeling alright?" she asked James.

"Sure. Just not sure what happened."

"You need to get yourself to the doctor. Get checked over."

"I'm fine. What's the next move?" He leaned against the worktop, sipping his tea, and she examined him. He did *look* alright, but who knew what the inside of his head was like after that little incident.

"It wasn't a suggestion."

"Oh, come on—"

"No, James. You blacked out. I can't in good conscience let you go back out there until you've been checked out. It's not just about you."

He scowled. "I *barely* blacked out. *If* I did."

"We're not discussing this. You're going to get checked out now, or I get you put on leave until you do."

He stared down at his mug, his jaw working. "And what're you going to do?"

"I'll take Lindsay and bring Scott in."

He took a sip of tea. "You're actually going to take her? Not do your Lone Ranger thing?"

"What are you, my keeper? Get yourself to the bloody doctor."

"I don't like it," he said.

"You don't have to. You just have to bloody well do it." She left him there and headed for the stairs. At least that got him safely out of the way and gave her time to deal with Scott. Not with Lindsay, of course. Not with anyone.

She headed out onto the street, hurrying across to the cafe with her takeaway mug and ignoring Dandy sticking his head into the grounds bin while the barista made her coffee. She got a hummus wrap as well, and took a bite while she scrolled through her phone and hit dial.

Charles answered quickly enough, his voice smooth and formal. "Charles Worthington."

"It's DI Adams," she said. "Have you found anything?"

He sighed. "Not really. I told you I'm not prepared to dig too much, not even for Meredith. No one's interested in doing business with those who can't be trusted to mind their own."

"But you found something?"

"Rumours. The incidents at the Apple Store and so on are being noticed."

"How? That wasn't even in the news."

"You think the police are so leak-tight?" He sounded amused. "Someone's always passing information. It's how the world works."

Adams blew air over her bottom lip and accepted her coffee from the barista with a nod, heading outside. "I suppose. Any hint on who might be after the necklace?"

"Now that *is* being kept very quiet. But given the fact it's undeniably a sorcerer's property, a lot of magic workers are very interested indeed. You need to get a wiggle on, Detective Inspector, or it'll be gone forever, and who knows what use it'll be put to."

"I'm going as fast as I can. Can you give me any details on the magic workers? Names, descriptions, what the hell they are?"

"The sort of people you're not ready to go up against, even before they get hold of that necklace. You need to get it back to its rightful owner, fast."

Adams took a bite of her wrap as she walked, and said indistinctly, "Could these magic workers hypnotise people? Make them freeze, say, or obey them?"

"There are charms that can do that. You don't even have to be a magic worker to cast them. You can buy them ready-made if you know where to go."

"Where would that be? If I can find who sold them—"

"Pocket towns, for the most part, which are Folk towns left over from old times. But you won't find them without a guide, and I don't advise you try. Forget that approach."

Adams grimaced. "Meredith walked out of her house with two unknown people, quite willingly. I need to find her."

"Trying to get into a pocket won't do anything but get you vanished, DI Adams. Concentrate on Meredith. She'd have had to open a window or door to them. They couldn't just heft a charm at the house and hope it worked."

"So she must've known them."

"Either someone she trusted, or thought she had a reason to trust. Someone in authority, maybe."

"That's still not hugely helpful."

"It's all I've got. Good luck."

"Great." Adams hung up and took another bite of her wrap, not really tasting it. It was time to talk to Scott. With any luck, she'd even get to arrest him.

It would have been as quick to walk to the jewellery shop as to fight her way through the traffic, but Adams wanted the car handy, so she looped her way through the one-way system, growling at delivery trucks and waiting impatiently at lights for dawdling pedestrians. Eventually she pulled into the delivery bay in front of the shop and popped her permit in the windscreen, looking around for the officers who had been set to watch Scott. She couldn't spot them, either on foot or in a car, and she wondered if Scott had left. If so, no one had told her.

She got out and stood on the pavement for a moment, looking up and down the street. There was no back door to the shop, she knew that much. It backed onto another building, so the officers wouldn't be watching a different entrance. And there should be one out the front anyway, even if there had been a back door. She frowned, hit the buzzer, and stepped back to wait.

The lights were on beyond the glass, and the security shutters were up, revealing the glittering displays of gold and stones and pricey tat, but she couldn't see any movement in the shop itself. She waited a moment, then hit the buzzer again, holding it for longer this time. There was still no response, and she cupped her hands over the glass of the door, peering inside. The place seemed caught in a freeze-frame, the cases glowing softly with the lights within, the floor neatly swept, the door at the back of the shop firmly shut, but the place was absolutely empty.

She tried the buzzer one more time, knocking as well for good measure, and watching the door at the back of the shop as she did so, trying to see if there was any movement. Still nothing, so she took her phone from her pocket and tried the shop number. It went straight to voicemail, prattling on about opening times and leaving a message, with nothing to indicate that the shop should be shut now. She checked her notebook, looking for Scott's mobile number, and tried that. It went straight to voicemail as well, and she stood there for a moment, looking at the empty shop and frowning, tapping her fingers on her leg.

She could call James and find out who he'd talked to earlier, who was meant to be watching the shop. But hopefully he was on his way to the doctor's, or even already there, and the last thing she wanted was for him to use this as an excuse to come back and join her. She considered her other options, then pulled Lindsay's number up on her phone.

Lindsay answered after a few rings. "Adams," she said. "How're you doing?"

"Yeah, good," Adams said. "I just wondered if you could look into something for me?"

"Whatever I can do to help."

"Are you at the station?"

"Yes."

"Okay, good. I asked James to get someone watching Scott Samuels. He was at his shop when we made the request, but there's no one here now. I haven't heard anything back from whoever was assigned to it, which is odd. Can you check and tell me who was meant to be on him, and if they're on the move or what's happening?"

"Give me a minute," Lindsay said. "It should be in the logs." Adams couldn't hear the clatter of a keyboard or anything, so maybe Lindsay was on her tablet. A moment later Lindsay said, "I don't see anything. Are you sure James requested it?"

"Definitely," Adams said. "He did it while I was in the car with him."

"Oh. Did he get a confirmation, though?"

"Not sure," Adams admitted. "We were a bit busy."

"Right. Well, something seems to have fallen through the gaps. Nothing here that I can see."

"Nothing? So no one was watching Scott?"

"Doesn't look like it."

Adams swore, and a young woman passing on the street gave her a startled look. She made an apologetic gesture and said to Lindsay, "Well, thanks anyway. I'll follow it up."

"Alright, then," Lindsay said. "Do you need a hand? Want me to come and join you?"

"No, I've got it." Adams hung up and stood there frowning at the phone. It didn't feel right. James wouldn't have lied to her about it, and neither would he have neglected to confirm it. Anyone else she might've thought they simply forgot, but this was James. He'd no more forget that than the best rugby plays of 2007, or whatever it was they taught in posh schools. Maybe someone had cancelled the request without telling them? Temper could've put a stop to it, especially as Adams hadn't cleared it with him, but surely he'd have called to bollock her about it. He wouldn't have just said no without the opportunity to do a bit of shouting.

She considered calling James again, but he was better off out of it. She'd follow Scott herself, if she could. She swung back into the car, calling Isha as she tapped the jeweller's home address into her maps.

The call connected, and Isha said, "Can't stay away for a second, can you?"

"Evidently not. Look, something's gone weird. James requested a couple of bodies to watch Scott Samuels, but there's no one at the shop. Lindsay's had a look for me, and she said the request was never put through. Can you follow up and see if it was cancelled, and if so who cancelled it?"

"Wish, command, etc.," Isha said. "You need backup?"

"No," Adams said. "I'm just going to see if Scott's home, then I'll call you back."

"Pretty sure—"

"Hi, is your name James?"

Isha snorted. "Fine. But don't come running to me when you get smacked over the head with your precious necklace." She hung up, and Adams hit start on the navigation, that crawling, uneasy feeling back in her belly.

Someone's always passing information.

17

SOME MILD BREAKING & ENTERING

Scott's flat wasn't in a bad area, but it wasn't great either. It inhabited the no man's land between Leeds and Bradford, where the tumbling expansion of both cities ran into each other, sending up crops of council estates and subdivisions and industrial parks. Scott's building stood with a few others, mired in tarmacked parking with a few patches of greenery chucked in almost as an afterthought. It looked like it was probably a council estate that had been made available for tenants to buy when the council ran out of money to maintain it, and the new owners didn't exactly have the cash spare for its upkeep, either. At least it was easy to park.

Adams found a spot in front of the building and tucked her collapsible baton into the curve of her arm to partially hide it as she climbed out of the car, thinking that the uncharacteristically hot weather really made things difficult unless you were into cargo trousers, and that seemed somewhat un-detective-like, if practical. At the door, she checked the flat number on her notes, then hit the buzzer a few times. There was no answer, not that she'd really expected there to be. Instead she poked a few more buzzers until an intercom clicked on. It was a woman's voice, wary and a little creaky at the edges.

"Who is it?" she demanded.

"DI Adams, West Yorkshire Police," Adams said. "I need access to the building."

There was a pause, then the woman said, "Who're you looking for?"

"Scott Samuels," Adams said. "Have you seen him today?"

"Oh, him," the woman replied. "Flash Man."

"Flash Man?"

"When he first turned up here he was driving a bloody Porsche," the woman said. "We all said to him, that one's not going to last long around here. And sure enough, he's got himself an old Vauxhall estate now."

"Right," Adams said, looking around the parked cars for it, but she couldn't see one that matched that description. Plenty of other old estates, though. "Do you know if he's in?"

"Doubt it. It's a workday, innit? He's got some flash jewellers in town, he'll be off down there."

"Can you let me in so I can check his place?"

She could hear the woman considering it, and finally she said, "Alright then. No trouble though, you hear?"

"I'll try to avoid it," Adams replied. "That's generally my job."

"No it isn't," the woman said. "You're police. It's your job to get in the middle of bloody trouble."

"Only to stop it becoming worse trouble," Adams protested, then shook her head. She wasn't here to argue with people who sounded like her auntie. "Look, just buzz me in, alright?"

"Keep your knickers on," the woman said, and the door buzzed open.

"Thanks," Adams said, but the intercom had already gone

dead. She pushed though into the lobby. It was clean enough inside, the walls scuffed but the floors clear of anything but a little scattering of gravel walked in from outside. A bike leaned against the wall at the bottom of the stairwell, but the rest was uncluttered.

On the second floor she found the right door, and knocked sharply. There was no response, and after a moment she knocked a little bit harder. "Scott," she called. "If you're in there, you need to answer."

Still nothing, and she put her ear to the door, listening for movement inside. If something had happened, if someone had tried to abduct Scott, she'd have a reason to enter. But right now, there was no reason why Scott would be the abductee, rather than the abductor. And she couldn't hear anything.

She was just straightening up when there was a crash from beyond the door, and she stepped back. "Scott," she called. "Mr. Samuels, are you alright in there?"

Something else fell over with a clatter, and she banged on the door with the side of her fist. "Open up!"

No response. The door to the next flat over cracked open, but no one came out, and Adams could feel eyes on her.

"Disturbances heard, reason to suspect Mr Samuels is at risk," she said for the benefit of her unseen audience, snapping the baton out. "I'm coming in."

She jiggled the handle with her baton hand, her other flat on the door, testing the lock. The door itself felt pretty solid, so it all depended what sort of lock it was. She could get her kit from the car and take a crowbar to it if need be, but with any luck a good kick in the right place might move it. It was amazing how many things responded to such treatment.

She took a step back, eyeing the spot on the door where she wanted to land her boot, and the door down the hall opened a little bit further. A man with a head of thick grey hair peered out at her and said, "Hey, now. Don't be trashing the place."

"There's a disturbance inside," she said. "Mr. Samuels is not answering his phone, and he's missing from his workplace. I have reason to believe that something may be wrong."

"Whatever you say," the man said. "You police can always justify anything. But just use the key, alright? Brings the tone right down, having busted doors about the place."

"What key?" Adams asked.

The man pointed up, and Adams looked at the top of the door, which had a thick frame running around it. She slid her fingers along the top and encountered a key stuck in place with a bit of Blu-Tak.

"Thanks," she said, her cheeks warm.

"He locked himself out the first week," the man replied. "Made such a fuss over the locksmith that I suggested a spare key would be a good idea." He shut his door again and Adams heard his own locks rolling.

She took the key down, slipped it into the lock and said, "Scott, I'm coming in."

There was still no answer from inside, and she opened the door, stepping into a short hallway. Everything was still and quiet, and a door opened off to one side of the hall, two to the other. She checked the first one, finding a double bedroom with an unmade bed, the walls plain and unadorned. The next had twin beds in it, superhero posters on the walls, and a clutter of kids' toys in the corner. The toys looked mostly shiny and unused, and expensive with it. Adams moved on to the next door, which gave her a bathroom with a toilet in one corner, and a short tub with a shower over it.

Then she was into the main room, which was as empty as the bedrooms. A pot was lying on the floor of the open plan living and dining area, next to a utensil holder with a spoon, a spatula, and a potato masher scattered next to it. Adams frowned at them, and Dandy padded out from behind the breakfast bar, wagging his tail at her.

"You're going to get me in trouble," she said, her voice low. Dandy just cocked his head at her.

She shoved the baton precariously into her pocket, took a pair of blue latex gloves from her pocket and pulled them on, then swept through the flat quickly. There wasn't much here. The main room itself had just the minimum of furniture that was needed, and the kitchen was more of the same, even the fridge empty of anything but a bottle of milk and half a block of cheap cheddar. Adams went back to check the main bedroom, being a bit more thorough this time. Clothes, shoes, and very little else, until she dug under the mattress and discovered the hard edges of something tucked well back from the edge. She pulled it out, revealing a MacBook. She wasn't exactly up with all the latest models, but it was large, heavy, and painfully shiny. She could almost smell the shop on it still.

"There you go," she said, smiling slightly, and took it into the main room to set it on the breakfast bar. Her phone dinged as she walked through, and she ignored it for a moment, opening the computer. While it booted up, she pulled her phone from her pocket. There was a message from James, with a picture attached, which she assumed would be him sending her a doctor's note, proving that he was fine. Or else some sort of rude meme about the Lone Ranger. Either way, she was going to have to think of a way to put him off joining her.

She almost didn't open the message, not wanting him to see that she had read it. But she couldn't avoid him forever, and the last thing she needed was him tracking her down. That'd be even worse. So she clicked on the image, and a moment later she'd completely forgotten the computer, blinking away next to her.

The image was of James, but it wasn't a smug, *doctor says I'm fine* selfie. It showed him sitting in the back of a van, his hands hanging loosely between his knees and his head drooping, so that he looked half-asleep.

The message that accompanied it simply said, *stand down*, and Adams found that sick, twisting sensation in her belly had wormed its way right into her chest, choking her breath.

Stand down.

But who was going to step into her place if she did?

SHE CALLED TEMPER. She didn't want to, because she couldn't explain any of this, but she also didn't have a choice. Not if James was in trouble.

"Yes, Adams," he said when he answered. "Calling to tell me you've stopped mucking around and found this necklace?"

"No," she said. "I know who took it, though."

"Progress! So why're you calling me instead of arresting them?"

"I've lost them."

Temper sighed, a great breezy sound. "And here I thought this was your sort of case. How?"

"I asked James to get someone watching them this morning while we followed another lead, but the request was cancelled somehow."

"That was a bit careless, then. And?"

She took a breath. "And James is missing."

There was silence for a moment, then Temper said, "Missing? What the hell do you mean, *missing?*"

"I mean missing," she replied. "I'm sending you a file." She hit forward on the message and heard it ding on Temper's end.

A moment later, Temper said, "Bloody hell, Adams. Was he drugged?"

"Maybe," Adams replied. "It's looks like the same as whatever happened when they grabbed the shop assistant."

"Right. Where are your notes?"

"Um."

Temper swore, roundly and creatively, and Adams winced. When he'd finished, he said, "Really? You've not done *any?*"

"I've got them in my notebook. I was going to do them later."

"Some bloody help that is. Take some photos of them and send them to me so I can get things moving. We're not losing James."

"We don't want to lose anyone," Adams said. "The shop assistant's still missing too, and the guy from the Apple Store. We've got to assume it's all the same people."

"Well, obviously. But a cop's always going to be a bit of a bargaining chip, isn't he?"

"Yes, boss. I'm sorry."

"Where are you now?" he asked.

"Scott Samuels's place."

"And where was James last seen?"

"I sent him to the doctor to see if he was alright after an altercation with two people who tried to grab the guy from the Porsche garage."

There was a pause, then Temper said, dangerously quietly, "You've had two missing persons and another attempted abduction, and you've been carrying on with just you and James? *And* you sent him off to the doctor and continued alone? Didn't even alert me to *any* of it?"

"It all just happened this morning. And I did request someone get on Samuels."

Temper took a deep breath. "Without following up to make sure it was happening. Well, you can most certainly stand down now, Adams. You're off this case and suspended. Go home."

"Boss, I can—"

"You can send your notes then bloody well do as you're told. We can discuss this further once we've got James back."

"Boss," she tried, but the phone went dead, and she stared at it for a moment, then at the MacBook, which looked back at her blandly. She considered it, then shut the lid and tucked it under one arm. She let herself out of the flat and ran down the steps, fleeing back into the sunshine and scrambling into her car, as if Temper's new team might materialise and come charging after her before she could make her getaway. She got the car started, but didn't back out of the space. She didn't know where she was going next – only that she might be off the case, but she wasn't standing down. Not when she was the only one who had the slightest idea what was actually going on. Very slight. She looked at the MacBook. With any luck there might be something on there that would lead her to Scott, but she needed a bit of time and privacy to look through it, somewhere other than here.

She'd just about decided home was her best option when her phone went. She almost ignored it, assuming it was Temper, but Isha's name flashed up, so she answered it.

"Adams, where are you?"

"Scott Samuels's—"

"Get yourself to Gladys Hudson's house."

"Why?"

"There was a report of a disturbance there earlier, and someone deleted it off the system. I only know because I was sniffing around trying to see who cancelled your call."

Adams shoved the car into reverse. "Who's doing it?"

"Still looking. But I hardly think this is unrelated."

"No," Adams said, and disconnected the call as she revved out of the parking space, slewing the rear end around and shoving the car into gear. No, she rather doubted it was.

Adams tried calling Olly and Gladys as she drove, but both phones went straight to messages, tightening the panic in her chest into something breathless and physical. She sped up, laying on the horn and screeching around corners, overtaking ruthlessly into oncoming traffic, and still it seemed to take far too long to circle around the north of the city and spiral into the leafy streets near Roundhay. But finally she was pulling up in front of the old house, serene behind its fences, and coming to such a sudden stop that Dandy pitched out of the back and into the gap between the front seats. She swung out of the car and jogged for the gate, letting herself in and running up the path, baton already in hand. The garden murmured around her, and she spotted a treehouse that had sprouted in the willow, a swing hanging beneath it, still moving softly as if just vacated by a ghostly inhabitant. She ignored it and headed straight for the front door, banging briskly on it.

There was no reply, and she tried the handle, but it was locked. She circled around the house instead, skirting the koi pond, which had developed a small bridge and seemed to be working on its water lotus game rather effectively. All the way, she was checking for broken windows or signs of struggle, but there was nothing. Just the slumbering, fragrant heat of the garden, baking her skin and raising sweat on her shoulders.

At the back of the house, the patio was empty, no yoga

mats or iced coffee glasses left out. She tried the folding doors, but, unsurprisingly, they were locked. She resumed her circuit of the house, and arrived back at the front door without spotting so much as a window left ajar, let alone smashed. She wasn't sure just how disappointed to be, as she had a sneaking suspicion that the house probably wouldn't take well to intruders. Maybe the report had been deleted because there had been no merit to it? But she couldn't just walk away. What if Gladys was inside, hurt? Or worse?

The phone rang, Temper's number coming up, but Adams didn't answer. She picked up a rock from by the koi pond instead, eyeing up the windows as she bounced it in one hand. Would it even work, or would the house drop a gable on her, or suck her into the flowerbeds or something?

A whine distracted her just as she was getting her courage up to take the shot, and she looked around at Dandy. He was standing on the path with his tail and head hanging, and she said, "What?"

He whined again, and she went to meet him, still clutching her stone. He pushed his snout against her fingers, pressing something hard and slobbery into her hand, and Adams caught it before he could drop it on the path. It was a key, hooked to a metal fob that said *Olly*. She stared at it, then at Dandy, remembering him dropping something in the car after their visit to Olly the previous day.

"You thief," she said admiringly, and he whined again, looking at the house. "It's really inappropriate, my having a criminal dog," she added, but without much feeling. She headed for the front door and Dandy followed her, so close he stepped on her heels a couple of times. She was okay with that. She didn't much like the idea of going in alone.

The lock turned easily and she pushed the door open, then stood on the threshold for a moment, feeling the regard of the house, heavy and quizzical. Finally she walked into the lobby, still trailed by Dandy, her footsteps muffled by the old carpet. No guard dogs appeared, no booby traps yawned underneath her, no ghosts of the ancestors came rushing out to drag her into the earth. It was just a house. Of sorts, anyway.

She checked the living room first, but it was empty, overstuffed and still, nothing overturned or broken (although she thought it'd take a whole team of movers to overturn those sofas anyway). In the kitchen the only noise was ice chattering into the storage in the big fridge-freezer, and the coffee machine hissing away to itself, and nothing looked out of place. In the snug she discovered a massive widescreen TV, almost ridiculously large, with a couple of virtual reality headsets sitting next to it, along with about three other game consoles, all untouched. She shook her head slightly and checked the next door along, which turned out to be the study. The desk was bigger than her bed at home, and probably twice as expensive as her entire flat, all heavy, antique carved wood. Perched on top of it was an incongruously modern computer.

Adams jogged the mouse, and the computer came straight on. It was open to a search for news articles for the area. The search terms were *unusual robberies Leeds* and *medical incidents migraines blackouts Leeds*. Adams sighed. *We'll sort it* was right. She should've been more on it.

She turned to go, then noticed one of the pictures hanging just slightly away from the wall, as if pushed out by something behind it. It was the first thing that had seemed out of place, and she frowned, crossing to it and using her phone to hook the edge. The picture swung out as if on a hinge, and behind it, the door sitting slightly ajar, was a safe.

"Huh," Adams said softly. She found her gloves again and pulled them on, then opened the door the rest of the way. Inside was an empty box made of old, worn wood, with indentations in it which suggested the necklace had once laid in it. Next to it was another box, this one bigger and heavier. Adams gingerly lifted the lid. There was nothing inside, but she thought of Chloe talking about books and how sorcerers could sink their power into them. A book could fit in here, and there was something about the feel of the wood, even through her gloves, that made the hair on her neck stand up. She doubted Gladys was a sorcerer, though. If she was, she wouldn't have been dropping her necklace off at the local jewellery shop. Which meant Verity was the one who'd left a very human woman with artefacts she didn't even know how to handle. It seemed foolish at best, deadly at worst. But maybe even ancient, all-powerful sorcerers weren't always sensible when it came to those they loved. No one else was, after all. The more pressing question right now was who had taken the book out. Gladys, or the causers of the disturbance that Adams still couldn't find any sign of?

She poked into the safe a bit further. There was a shopping bag at the back and when she opened it, there were an astonishing amount of twenty-pound notes in it, some bound into bundles but most just lying loose. She stared at them, then folded the bag back up again and left it where it was, straightening up and looking at Dandy, who was peering around the room anxiously.

The safe shouldn't have been left open like this. What had happened for Gladys to rush out so suddenly? Had she been dragged out? Maybe she'd opened the safe to try and get something to protect herself? Or she'd been forced to open it? It was impossible to tell, but what was sure was that Adams had at least one more missing person to deal with, and she was no closer to finding who had taken them, or where.

She was bloody well going to find out, though.

18

MIND THE KOI

Adams swung the door of the safe closed and looked around the study dubiously. The open safe was the only sign that things weren't right. Nothing was overturned. The screen of the computer was still standing. There wasn't so much as a broken glass on the floor, not here or anywhere else downstairs.

She headed out of the study and trotted upstairs, where she discovered far too many bedrooms for one person. Gladys evidently thought so too, as each had been allocated their own purpose. One was a library, the walls lined with books and sunlight flushing a big, comfortable-looking sofa that stood grandly in the centre of the floor, a coffee table in front of it stacked with art books and magazines and a jumble of hardbacks. Another had been given over to a workout room, complete with tall mirrors on the wall and rings suspended from the ceiling, the floor covered with heavy matting. Another sported a sewing machine, a cutting table, and a dressmaker's mannequin, and yet another was packed with racks of clothing and shoes and bags. Everything was tidy and clean, the windows shining and the surfaces clear of dust, and absolutely nothing looked disturbed. Even the big bedroom at the front of the house, replete with a four-poster bed, was made up as crisply as a posh hotel's. If there had been any disturbance, Gladys and Olly had evidently tidied it up before they left. Which should have made her feel better, but it didn't. What were they up to?

Adams walked slowly back down the stairs, frowning, then stood in the hallway listening to the deep stillness of the house. It was the quiet of a living thing, restful but watching, and judging by the way Dandy's tail was still at half-mast, he could feel it too. She wondered what would happen if she did something *wrong,* something the house didn't like, and even as she thought it, it felt as though the walls leaned closer to her. She took a quick, uneven breath, and when her phone went off in her pocket she let out a yelp that was matched only by Dandy's, as he bolted to her and collapsed at her feet.

"Oh, bloody hell," she whispered, fishing the phone out, her heart going too fast. She swiped to answer with a shaking finger, and found her words caught in her throat.

"Adams?" Isha asked. "You alright there?"

"Yeah," she managed, then cleared her throat and tried again. "Yes. All good."

"What did you find?"

"Nothing at all."

"Seriously?"

"Yeah. Were you able to pull the details of the report? What did it say exactly?"

"Oh sure, I recovered that," Isha said. "Some old boy walking his dog heard screaming coming from inside the property. He peeked through the gates, but couldn't see anything, so he called it in."

"Didn't enter the property at all?" Adams asked.

"No, he said he wanted to stay well away from anyone screaming."

"Sensible," Adams said. "My job would be much easier if everyone was that sensible."

Isha snorted, and there was a moment of silence before she said, "I hear you're out on your ear."

"Something like that."

"Don't suppose you should really be getting any updates then."

"Probably not," Adams agreed. "And I definitely shouldn't be here, investigating non-existent disturbances. I do believe I've been told to go home and sit quietly in the corner."

"No one puts Baby in the corner," Isha said, and chuckled.

Adams gave Dandy a slightly quizzical look, and he returned it. "Something like that?"

"Well," Isha said. "Can't hurt to tell you that Temper's beside himself, obviously. He's stomping up and down the stairs yelling about James."

"Yeah," Adams said. "That one's on me, but I only sent him to the doctor. I thought he'd be safe enough with that."

"It's not on you," Isha said. "He's a big boy, *and* a police officer. He should be able to look after himself. Whatever happened, it's on whoever took him."

"Any progress on it?"

"Not so far. I tracked his phone, but obviously it was dumped straight after they sent the photo. Found some kid with it, trying to claim it was his."

"That figures," Adams said.

"Yeah, and we can't get anything off the picture other than that it's a van. We can probably assume it's the same white van that was seen at Meredith's house and that you saw when Kelvin was almost snatched, but it doesn't help us. Thousands of the bloody things about the place, and obviously the plates we've got, from Meredith's and your kerfuffle, are both stolen."

"Obviously," Adams said.

"We'd be dealing with substandard crooks if they weren't," Isha replied, far too cheerfully for Adams' liking. Then she added, "Lindsay's getting pretty squirrelly."

Adams sighed slightly. She didn't know what it was between Lindsay and Isha, but she hated this stuff. Bloody high school girls' drama, and she had even less time for it right now than she usually did. "I'm sure she's just worried about James."

"Maybe. I think it's more likely she's setting you up, though."

"What?" Adams asked.

"Yeah, she's been dropping a lot of stuff about how you haven't been on it, you've missed a lot of things, you should have picked Scott up earlier, etc., etc. She's out for you."

"Well, I'm off the case. It hardly matters."

"It does. She's making noises that maybe you're behind James vanishing. That you're working with whoever took him."

Adams didn't answer. She didn't know *how* to answer. Because there was a warped sort of logic to it, the way she'd never written up her notes, and had been chasing around without checking in with Temper. She *had* been hiding things, just not the things she was being accused of.

"Then there's the whole thing of bringing Kelvin in and releasing him once James was out of the picture," Isha added. "She's really selling that one."

Adams found her voice somewhere. "I didn't release him. He was still in the interview room when I left to find Scott."

"He's not now. And we can't get him on the phone, and nobody knows where he is."

Adams pressed a hand to her forehead. "You've got to be kidding me. We've lost him as well?"

"Every single potential witness to any of the robberies," Isha said. "Only someone on the inside would have known about them. And definitely only someone on the inside would have been able to get Kelvin out. And then there's James, of course. It's not like he'd have had his guard down around anyone he didn't know. He's so posh it makes my teeth hurt, but he's not stupid."

"I didn't do any of this," Adams said.

"Oh, I know that," Isha replied. "But Lindsay's sneaky as all hell, and trust me – she'll find a way to make it look enough like you did that you won't be coming off suspension."

Adams looked around the still hall with its dreaming scent of furniture polish and dried roses, took a deep breath, and said, "I can't deal with this just now. I need to get on."

"Get on where? What're you doing?"

"I'm going to follow something up," Adams replied.

"What? And where?"

Adams hesitated. She wanted an ally – *needed* one, even – but she couldn't tell her. Not only would it potentially put Isha in a compromising position, it could even be a dangerous one, given the fact that James had been snatched in an attempt to stop her. She couldn't risk anyone else. Plus, there was the other possibility, that Isha would call in backup for her, unasked. The last thing she needed was a bunch of cops descending into what was quite likely going to be some mad bloody showdown between magicians and sorcerers and who knew what the hell else. Aliens and Loch Ness Monsters, given her luck. Bloody Yorkshire. Bloody women of a certain age and their secrets. Bloody *magic.*

"I'll let you know if anything comes of it," she said, and hung up before Isha could say anything else.

Dandy huffed, looking up at her with his red eyes half-exposed.

"I know," she said, and bent to scratch his ears. He seemed to have shrunk a little. She tried to think about that, rather than about Lindsay. Because there were two possibilities there.

One was that Lindsay was simply cashing in on the situation, trying to get an edge on Adams. Maybe she'd just taken a dislike to her, or felt Adams was standing in her way. Competitiveness was far more the rule than cooperation, after all.

But there had been all those questions. The requests for updates, the offer to look at her notes, all couched as *help*, but maybe it hadn't been about that at all. Maybe it had been information-gathering, but there was no telling for what reason, and no point making guesses. She could be the leak, the saboteur, but so too could Temper. He'd been around enough to still believe in the old ways being best, off-the-books deals and looking the other way when it suited him. And of the two, Adams couldn't help feeling he was more likely to know about the hidden parts of the world than Lindsay. Her DCI in London had certainly known.

Not that it mattered right now. Either Adams solved this and got herself in the clear, or she ended up permanently suspended over it, and, worse, the necklace would still be out there, being put to all sorts of uses that didn't bear thinking about. So all she could do was get on.

Adams let herself out of the house, locking it behind her, and trotted down the path to the car, Dandy all but sprinting ahead of her. She swung inside and pulled the MacBook out from under the seat where she'd stashed it, opening the lid to spark it into life. It woke up almost immediately, giving her a pleasing background of some lake somewhere, and requested a four-digit passcode. Adams considered it, then tried all zeros. Wasn't that meant to be the most common password?

Maybe it was, but it wasn't the right one. Fine. *One, two, three, four.* The laptop immediately opened to the desktop, and Adams allowed herself a moment of pride at her hacking skills, then realised she'd never used a Mac before and had no idea how to find anything. Plus the trackpad was weird. For one moment she considered calling Isha again, but this had to be within her tech abilities. She'd cracked the password, hadn't she?

There followed some swearing and googling on her phone, after which she had a hotspot set up, the MacBook connected to the internet, and she was poking through the settings looking for Find My Phone. Which was there, and a phone was connected. Adams hit *Find* then held her breath, willing it to work. If it didn't, she wasn't quite sure what her next move was going to be.

The result binged up almost immediately, displaying a map with the little tag of the phone sitting docilely in the middle of a load of greenery, apparently unmoving. She frowned and zoomed out, wondering if it had been dumped in a park or something. Still more greenery, so she zoomed out again, then again, until she could finally grasp where it was. There was a sketch of buildings around it, and a small road running past them, and the whole bloody lot was on the edge of the Yorkshire Dales. Because of course it was on the edge of the Dales. Every strange bloody thing in the north seemed to draw toward the Dales, like they were some magical magnetic north, all the weirdness trailing toward them like iron filings on a piece of paper.

But she had it. At the very least she could find Scott, and if she found Scott, she found the necklace. If she found the necklace, she had a bargaining chip, and that bargaining chip was what was going to save James's life. She closed the computer again, slid it underneath the seat, went to start the car, then hesitated. She didn't know what she was going to be dealing with out there. And somehow walking into it with nothing but her collapsible baton and her duck keychain seemed a bit less than well-prepared. She rested her hands on the wheel for a moment, then groaned and swung out of the car, heading back to the house. Dandy trailed reluctantly behind her, whining a protest, but she ignored him. She wasn't going to be long, anyway. Not that she was entirely sure what she was looking for, but even if it was just a bloody great cricket bat that she could whack someone on the head with, it'd be something. She quite fancied the idea of that, actually.

Adams let herself back into the house using Dandy's stolen key and headed straight into the snug, dismissing the kitchen. She wasn't about to start running about with butcher's knives or rolling pins, and this was the sort of house which posh people would've decorated with their forebears' old (or pilfered) weapons.

Sure enough, a couple of old-fashioned swords were crossed above the fireplace, faded tassels hanging from the handles, but the old steel was pocked with rust and they looked like they'd probably crumble to nothing the second she picked one up. Besides, she didn't really fancy the idea of stabbing someone with an antique sword. That seemed likely to involve an awful lot of paperwork and even more explanations.

There was nothing else of use in the snug unless she wanted to ride into battle wearing a wooden war mask, so she tried the living room. The fireplace in here was adorned with a collection of what she took to be war clubs of some variety, half a dozen fluted and embellished weapons carved into solid wood. She stood on her tiptoes to take one down, bouncing it in her hand. No chance of this one falling to pieces the moment she used it, but she wasn't too keen on just how much damage she could likely do with it. There was a definite heft to the thing, and after a moment she put it back, somewhat reluctantly.

She turned to head out of the room, and something in the corner by the door caught her eye. Not on display like the others, it was a long and intricately carved stick, for want of a better word. *Staff* popped into her mind, but she wasn't bloody Gandalf, so stick would do just fine. She crossed the room to examine it more closely, the wood smooth and untreated, but darkened with age and reflecting the light from an inlaid, intricate pattern of fragments of glossy shell and mother of pearl. A few bits were missing, but when she hesitantly placed a hand on it, half-expecting it to bite, she couldn't even feel the gaps in the warm wood. She picked it up, swapping it from one hand to the other, and looked at Dandy.

"Thoughts?" she asked.

He tipped his head to one side, which she decided to take as approval. A big stick seemed reasonable for mysterious countryside encounters.

Outside, she was halfway down the path when Dandy barked, a short, warning sound, and she spun around, the stick coming up instinctively as part of her mind shouted, *I knew it wouldn't let you leave! You've stolen from it!*

But no arms of stone and timber were scuttling after her, and the trees hadn't uprooted themselves to stalk in pursuit. Dandy was staring at the koi pond, his front paws forward and his chest low, his ears back as far as he could put them. He barked again, an exclamation of fright, and Adams jogged back to him.

There was a shoe floating in the pond. It was a trainer, undamaged and perfectly unremarkable, and it could've come from anywhere. It could've been Olly's.

Adams didn't think so, though. She grabbed a handful of Dandy's hair and pulled him away. If the koi pond had eaten someone, it was one less person to worry about, after all.

ADAMS CONSIDERED CALLING it in as she pulled away from the kerb, Dandy panting over her shoulder. There was no point, though. Whoever had cancelled the previous call-out would just cancel this one too. And the more she thought about it, the more sure she was that it had to be Temper. Other than Isha and James, he was the one who knew most about the case, and the only one who had the authority to countermand her requests. All that aside, though, even if the call-out wasn't cancelled, the end result would be just as bad as anyone else joining her in her chase after Scott. They'd be walking straight into a trap that they weren't prepared for, humans marching into a world full of ghosts and goblins and things that go bump in the night. At least in London, her DCI had been aware of such things and willing to let her tackle them. Not that she'd actually prepared Adams other than to give her a packet of bloody Yorkie bars, so how much difference that made was somewhat questionable.

Thinking that, Adams pulled over outside the next corner shop she saw and went in, examining the chocolate display next to the counter. There were raisin Yorkies as well as the plain ones, and she wondered briefly if one was more effective against hostile beasties than the other, or if any of them would help at all where she was going. But it couldn't hurt, and she knew the plain ones worked, so she picked up the entire box and put it on the counter.

The shopkeeper looked from the box to her and said, "Rough day?"

"You could say that," Adams replied.

Back in the car, she tried Olly and Gladys again, but there was no reply, not that she'd expected one. Either they'd made it out while the koi pond dealt with the intruders, and were up to their own mischief, or they were prisoners. She opened the Mac to check the phone, but it was still in the same place, so she settled herself back into the seat and drove as fast as she dared out of Leeds and onto the long stretch of road that led toward Harrogate, the routes around the city slowly becoming ingrained in her mind.

Nowhere near the way London was, of course. She had a moment of temporary homesickness. London had been her place, her patch. She'd known it so intimately she could have sketched her way through it in her sleep, the way the cabbies did. The proper cabbies, the ones that still did The Knowledge. And that was one of those things that always quietly charmed her. The fact that it still existed in the days of GPS and Ubers and ride shares. The fact that there were still men and women who could navigate the streets more quickly and efficiently than any machine, all of it based on the map in their heads. She missed it, but she was the one who had left. No one had chased her out, not really. And now *this* was her patch, and she was just bloody well going to make the best of it. Starting by getting to Scott before anyone else did and sorting this whole damn thing out.

She accelerated hard, overtaking a caravan that was struggling down the road, the driver's window down and a woman with masses of curly hair leaning her head half out into the wind like a golden retriever. At least she was doing something.

19

FOUND & LOST

THE LONG, STRAIGHT ROAD LED OUT THROUGH HAREWOOD and down toward Harrogate, where it sprouted roundabouts like cramps in the route. Adams navigated them impatiently until the signal from Scott's phone finally sent her peeling off into an altogether smaller, less travelled lane, bordered by rolling fields that spread out beyond the ubiquitous drystone walls. It wasn't the Dales here, not really, and it lacked the wild, barely-tamed feel of Toot Hansell, where the high fells sprouted rock faces and sheer cliffs and wind-scoured heather, and the peaks grabbed for the sky. Here civilisation had crept closer, the endless advance of humanity heralded by flashy car garages and outlet malls, organic food shops and smallholdings.

Not that it was unpleasant, amid the green fields and bands of trees and stone houses. No, it was just softer and quieter, an altogether gentler place to live than those further removed. But Adams couldn't help feeling it was a poorer place as well. It lacked both the raw, restive edges of the city and the entirely different rawness of the fells and moors with their endless skies and haunting winds, the hidden valleys and insular woods and twisting, hungry waterways.

But it was a rather lovely place to have an Airbnb, particularly the one she pulled up in front of. She knew it was an Airbnb because when she checked the map on her phone, it came up with an advert that said it was. But it wasn't any sort of Airbnb she'd have recognised without help. This was not a garden shed hastily outfitted with a broken-down sofa bed, or a caravan with a leaky roof stuck in the backyard, or a spare room with bunk beds and someone's gran's cross-stitch hanging on the walls. This was a full house behind big stone walls, a sweeping drive leading from the metal gates to the front door. The building was long rather than tall, and had wooden cartwheels and half-barrel planters at the entrance to give it some farmyard cred, although it both looked and smelled completely unlike any farmyard Adams had encountered. It was all very Hunter wellies and Barbour jackets, and not at all in the price range of a divorced small business owner who'd just had his car repossessed. Adams doubted she'd get any change from her monthly salary after a night in this place. Evidently Scott was relying on the necklace to smooth things over for him.

She climbed out of her car at the gates, spotting a keypad entry below the tasteful slate sign that proclaimed it *Endless Skies*, and a little video camera peering down from the top of the wall. She held her ID up to the camera and hit the intercom. Nobody answered, so she waved the ID more insistently at the camera, then pointed at herself and at the gates, which she hoped would be interpreted as, *I'm coming in whether you like it or not.* Although she didn't really fancy tackling the gates, seeing as they were both slippery-looking and quite high. She figured she'd manage if she really had to, though. She usually did.

She buzzed the intercom a third time, and this time someone answered.

"I'm a little bit indisposed," a male voice said, sounding as if its owner were trying to pitch it a bit deeper than was natural.

"You'll be more indisposed if you don't let me in," she replied.

"Sorry, who's this?"

"You know damn well who it is, and I know you're Scott Samuels. Let me in."

"I don't know any Scott—"

"Do *not* try it on with me. I know what you're bloody playing at. You've got the necklace, and you're the reason Meredith's been kidnapped. Now let me in so that we can sort this out before things get any more out of hand."

There was no response from the intercom, and Adams was wondering if she could get the car near enough to the wall to help her climb over when there was a buzz from the locks, and the gates began to swing slowly open. She hurried back to the car and jumped in, driving through quickly before Scott could change his mind.

The grounds were fairly flat, and she could see Scott waiting on the doorstep in front of a gravel turning circle, the farmhouse forming a long, low U shape behind him. A fountain sprouted in the middle of the circle, scattering water gently into a huge bowl, and more half-barrel planters and tastefully decrepit bits of farm equipment pocked the lawns and gave a bit of interest to the flowerbeds. No topiary in sight, though, thankfully. Adams didn't think she could stand any more topiary after the spring.

Scott was wearing a white dressing gown and a pair of matching slippers, and he gave her a nervous look, trying for a smile as she climbed out of the car.

"You found the necklace, then," he said. "That's what you said?"

She scowled at him, marching up the steps to meet him, one hand closed firmly around the duck keyring. She wasn't sure how any of this worked, but the duck had kept her safe once before. Maybe it would again. Scott took a step back, his eyes wide, as if he thought she might be about to take him by the lapels of his dressing gown and shake some sense into him. It was tempting, Adams had to admit.

"Hand it over," she said.

Scott hesitated, then plunged a hand into his pocket, snatching the necklace out and holding it toward her like a priest confronting a vampire with a crucifix. "You're not interested in the necklace," he said, his voice firm.

The sharp spike of a migraine flared momentarily behind Adams' eyes, and she could see reds and purples and deep blues and greens rolling in the necklace's stone like galaxies, luminous and distant and bewitching. The sun slid off the old, smooth gold, turning it lustrous, and she looked up at the sky, sighed, then looked back at Scott and said, "Give me the necklace."

Scott frowned and waved it more enthusiastically. "You're not interested in the necklace," he insisted. "You haven't even seen me. You're going to go back to Leeds and forget you ever saw me at all."

Adams made to grab the necklace, and he snatched it away with a yelp. "You need to give it to me," she said. "You don't know what you're playing with. The people who are after it are dangerous."

"Why isn't it working? What's wrong with you?"

"What's wrong with *you?*" she replied. "What did you honestly think? That you could just nick this sort of stuff and play about with it, and there wouldn't be any consequences?"

Scott shook the necklace as if he thought it might be malfunctioning and he could somehow jiggle it back into submission. "I was just borrowing it," he said.

"Give it here." Adams reached for it again and Scott lunged forward, shoving her hard enough that she staggered back down the stairs. She caught herself quickly, but he'd already turned and sprinted into the house, slamming the door behind him. Adams groaned as she heard the locks turn. "Scott!" she shouted. There was no response from inside.

She looked around, considering. A flashy sports car (not a Porsche, she noted) was parked in front of the garage, so she moved hers behind it, making sure he couldn't leave, then started around the house. She checked the windows as she went, but there was no sign of Scott or anyone else inside. Before long she'd made it onto a large, stone-flagged patio at the back of the house, overlooking the graceful blue curve of a pool. Big bifold doors displayed the vast stretch of an open plan kitchen and dining room, and she banged on them briskly.

"Scott," she shouted. "You have to let me in. This is *not* going to end well if you keep hold of that necklace."

Still no response from inside, and she turned to look out over the countryside beyond the property. The fields rolled away softly, dotted with the fat round sausages of hay bales, and birdsong washed over the garden around her along with the scents of warm earth and cut grass. She could see another little cluster of buildings a couple of fields over, barely close enough to call neighbours, and she wondered how far behind her the abductors were. Not far enough, she had a feeling. She turned to try banging on the door again, and as she did she caught the slam of a door from the front of the house. She didn't hesitate, just broke into a sprint, legging it around the irritatingly long sprawl of the building in time to see Scott bolting for the gates. He was slipping and sliding on the gravel in red trousers and fancy-looking loafers, and she charged after him, shouting as she went.

"This is resisting arrest!"

"I haven't done anything wrong," he shouted back, still running.

"Other than theft," she yelled back, veering toward her car as she realised she wasn't going to get to him before he reached the open gates. Then she spotted Dandy bounding easily across the lawn, dreadlocks flying, and she altered course back down the drive. Dandy slipped past Scott, barely touching him, but Scott gave a shout of alarm and pitched face-first into the gravel, his momentum sending his feet flying up and almost rolling him into a somersault. Adams winced, but didn't slow, only stopping when she was standing over him. He'd rolled onto his back, staring at his torn hands, and she glared down at him.

"Are you quite done?" she asked him.

"This is police harassment," he said, showing her his hands.

"You know I was nowhere near you. Tripped over your own silly shoes."

"Did not," he said sulkily, and examined his trousers. Both knees were torn, and Adams could see gravel embedded in the skin underneath. He pulled one leg up a little, frowning at his ankle. "Did something bite me?"

"Contrary to popular belief, cops do not go around biting people." She offered him a hand, but he waved it away. "I'm doing this for your own safety, Scott."

"I can look after myself," he said, reaching into a small bag he had strung around his waist. He brandished the necklace at her with rather less assurance than he had earlier.

"Evidently it doesn't work on me," Adams said. "And I'm

going to guess it won't work on most of the other people that are coming after you."

He frowned, tucking the necklace away again. "Who's coming after me?"

"The same people who took Meredith," she said. "Plus took the poor lad from the Apple Store, and the one from the Porsche garage. *And* they've bloody well got my constable."

He stared at her. "Really?"

"Yes. They'll be trying to find out who really has the necklace, and if they work out you've got it, and that Meredith's of any importance to you, they'll likely use her to make you hand it over."

He looked genuinely horrified. "I didn't know about any of that. I just knew you seemed to be getting a bit close, so I decided it was time to run for it."

"Even after Meredith had vanished?"

"I thought maybe she'd finally had a bit of a wild night or something. I keep telling her she needs to."

Adams shook her head. "Well, if I worked out you've got it, so will they."

"Who are *they?*"

"I don't know," she admitted, and held her hand out. "Give it here."

"I don't want to," Scott replied.

"You have to. It's not meant for what you're using it for." Not that she was really sure *what* it was meant for, but it definitely wasn't sports cars and red trousers.

"But Gladys wasn't looking after it properly. Not bringing it into the shop like that."

Adams nodded. "But it is hers." Although honestly she wasn't sure Gladys should have it either. Using magic to get good deals on virtual reality headsets and a flashy coffee machine was hardly abusing the privilege, but it didn't seem *safe*.

Scott sighed. "I just wanted a little bit of help," he said. "Between the divorce, and the child support payments, and the shop wasn't making enough money, and the rent's so high … You wouldn't believe how much it costs to have a shop in the middle of Leeds."

"I'm sure. But it doesn't mean you can go around nicking things, with or without persuasive necklaces."

"It was an accident to start," Scott said, and scratched the back of his neck. "I had it out in the office when some bloke came in getting all aggressive about a little loan I had, and wanting to take stock to settle up. And then he just seemed to forget about it."

Adams sighed. "And then you just kept it going."

"Yeah," Scott said. "I kind of settled up all my debts, the bank and everything. Do you think I'll be able to keep that?"

Adams beckoned to him. "Give it here."

Scott's shoulders slumped, but he unclipped his bag and handed the whole thing over. A chill washed over Adams' fingers as she took the bag by the strap. It was unnaturally heavy, and she shivered. There was something hungry about that cold, the way deep frosty nights are hungry. Indifferent, and full of a silent ancient power. She grimaced and stepped back, holding the bag away from her and nodding at the house. "Go on."

Scott looked at her warily. "I thought you were going to arrest me."

"I am. But I need to get you out of here first."

He stopped, looking from her to her car and back again. "You're just going to drive off with me? How do I know you're going to be able to keep me safe? You don't even have any backup!"

She scowled at him. "You seemed perfectly happy to run off on your own just now."

"That was before I knew there were all these people chasing me."

"And now you do. I'm going to take you to the nearest police station and hand you over."

"This is really unfair. I didn't hurt anyone. It was just a small redistribution of wealth."

Adams snorted. "You'd be surprised how often people use that excuse."

She thought Scott might protest more, but the fight seemed to have gone out of him, and he followed her docilely toward her car. Adams checked the gate, but she couldn't see anyone. Not that she could see anything at all through the high walls, but the way out was clear at least. For now. Someone would definitely be on the way, whether it was police or magic workers or both. Someone was probably pinging Scott's phone right now. She just hoped they weren't pinging hers. That could be a bit difficult to explain.

"I don't really want to go to the police station," Scott said as she opened the car.

"No," she replied. "I doubt you do. I also doubt you want to stay here and wait for whoever's going to turn up. Because if someone else finds you before the police do, you're going to be in some serious trouble."

He grimaced. "Do you know who else is after it?"

"Not exactly," Adams admitted.

"It's magic, isn't it?" Scott asked.

She tipped her head slightly, glad she wasn't the one who had to say it. It felt strange, the word being out in the open like that. *Magic.* "You didn't know that from the start?"

"Not really. But I figured it out. I used to watch David Copperfield and David Blaine all the time, so it made sense."

Adams resisted the urge to slap a hand to her forehead and said, "This isn't trickery, though. It's actual magic."

"Yeah, like David Copperfield."

Adams wondered if she could slap him instead. It was tempting, what with him running around pretending he was David bloody Copperfield when she could still feel the chill of the necklace laying wreaths of power over her hands. Aloud, she just said, "Do you need anything? Got your wallet, ID?"

"Yeah," he said, somewhat dejectedly.

"You can sit in the front," she said.

"Gee, thanks," he replied, but clambered in.

She got in herself, and stashed the necklace in the glove-box, locking it just in case he took it in his head to grab it at a traffic light and make a run for it. Then she got them moving, heading down the drive. Dandy stuck his head between the seats, panting at Adams.

"Why does it smell of dog in here?" Scott asked. "Do you have a dog?"

"Something like that," Adams replied. "Put your seat belt on."

The road beyond the gate was clear in both directions, and Adams pulled onto it smoothly, heading back the way she'd come. She kept checking her rear-view mirror, but they didn't seem to be being followed by anyone, and she allowed herself a moment to think that maybe she could get Scott back to Leeds and safely locked up, then deal with the necklace. That maybe she'd got away with it and there wouldn't be any wild clash of old magic over the quiet fields of Harrogate.

She was still tense, though, the high stone walls hiding the fields and curves of the road from view. But as the house fell behind them and they fled for the shelter of the main road, it seemed as if they'd got away with it.

Until something hit the car so hard and fast Adams had no time to react. She didn't even see it, wasn't even sure there *was* anything to see, but whatever it was slammed into the side of the Golf, shunting them sideways and forcing them off the road, pinning them to the stone wall. Scott was screaming in her ear and Dandy was barking frantically, but before she could shout at either of them to shut up something hit her head, or she hit her head on something, and then everything was darkness.

20

CARRY A VERY BIG STICK

DI ADAMS WOKE TO A SPLITTING PAIN IN HER HEAD, DAMPNESS on her neck, and teeth in her arm, which was by far her most immediate concern. She jerked her arm away with a yelp, her head full of images of hunched, toothy goblins sprinting over cold high fells. She rolled without thinking about it, managing to get halfway to her feet before the pain slapped her and she stumbled, dropping to one knee. She stayed there, waiting for the teeth to come back, and when they didn't she opened her eyes cautiously, blinking against the sunlight. Dandy looked back at her with his head tipped to one side and his ears twitching, so close that she could barely focus on him.

"What the hell happened?" she asked him, touching the back of her head gingerly. The blood was sticky and wet, but not as copious as she'd thought. Which told her two things: she wasn't about to bleed out, and she hadn't been unconscious long enough for anything to congeal. She looked at her arm, which was slightly slobbery and dimpled with toothmarks. "Did you *bite* me?"

Dandy huffed without any particular contriteness, and

she sat back on her heels, resting a hand on his back while he investigated her face with a snuffling nose. She was behind the wall, in the long grass of a field. The smell of crushed grass was warm and familiar, although the ground beneath it was still cool with the memory of more typical Yorkshire weather. There was a gate not far away that she could glimpse the road through, but it was still closed, and certainly far enough from her that she hadn't been thrown over it by the crash.

She turned her attention to Dandy, and scratched him behind the ears. "Did you do this?" she asked, and he huffed, warm breath washing over her face. She wrinkled her nose, but said, "Good boy. What about Scott? What happened to him?"

Dandy just whined, so she was going to have to work that one out for herself. She leaned on him as she got up, her legs a bit wobbly. Everything still seemed to be bending where it should and staying in one place where it should, though. She twisted experimentally, one side then the other, shook her arms out, and cricked her neck. Every part of her had a dull ache to it, and she had a feeling that by tonight it was going to be hurting a hell of a lot more. But she was standing, and the pain in her head was already retreating, so that was better than she could've hoped.

She headed for the gate, Dandy walking alongside her and her fingers still twined into his fur. He seemed to have grown a bit, and she shouldn't have been able to do this without leaning, but she put that off to one side. That was yet another thing she didn't need to think about right now. She was limping a little, but it seemed to be more from stiffness than injury, just the shock of the crash tightening everything up. She opened the gate and let herself through, wondering how Dandy had got her over it. Her car was pressed into the wall on the driver's side, as if it had snuggled in for a nap, and there was no sign of Scott, not that she'd really expected there to be. She stepped onto the road to check the passenger's side, but she couldn't see any damage. She frowned, remembering that double impact, the force that had shunted them off the road then slammed her head into something, hard enough to knock her out. She touched the sticky blood on the back of her head again, and wondered what she'd hit it on. Or what had hit her.

That was another thing to worry about later, though. She opened the passenger side door and looked at the open glovebox, sighing. The necklace was gone, which wasn't surprising, but she hadn't expected this degree of ruthlessness. She should have, she supposed, given what the stakes were, but she'd still been thinking of this case as somehow *different,* as if, because magic was such an impossible, intangible thing, that those who pursued it would be somehow softer and less dangerous than the criminals she was used to. She had a feeling she was going to have to rethink that, though.

She eased herself into the car gingerly, checking underneath the driver's seat and sliding her hands into the pockets of the doors, and eventually finding her phone where it had been thrown into the back. The crack on the screen had spread, but it was still working, and there was a message from a number she didn't recognise. She clicked on it, her stomach turning over. She already thought she knew what it was going to be.

And sure enough, James. He wasn't in a van this time. He was sitting in a straight-backed chair, and next to him, lined up like naughty kids outside the headmaster's office, were Meredith, Patrice, and Kelvin. They weren't restrained, but just sat there with hands loose in their laps, staring blankly at the floor in front of them. Adams wondered what it was doing to them, being held like that for so long, trapped by whatever force their captors were exerting. It couldn't be anything good.

She zoomed in on the photo, looking for details in the background, any clue as to where they might be. It seemed to be a large space, the walls looking like plywood or some similarly sturdy, industrial material, and the floor covered in the same. A pre-fab shed of some sort, perhaps? Although it could as well have been a storage unit, or a garage. It was impossible to be sure, but the message was clear enough. They had hostages, and they had the necklace. She needed to back off. Call Temper, tell him what had happened, and take the consequences.

She needed to do that, but she couldn't. Because there was a leak, and there was someone on the inside. What if Temper really was the one who'd been cancelling her requests? Sending her after the necklace in an attempt to find it for himself, or for whoever he worked with? It had been strange to pull her off more pressing cases to investigate nothing more than a harassment complaint, after all. Had he had an idea what was involved, and thought he'd just pull her off when he could step in and take the necklace? Just as he *had?*

And then there was Lindsay. Adams still didn't know what Lindsay's motives were, if she was maybe the one somehow tangled up with Folk, or simply an average colleague out to sabotage someone she saw as a rival. Either way, she couldn't be allowed to walk into the middle of this. Not her *or* Temper. Adams had to get ahead of them and deal with whatever magical bloody shenanigans the necklace was causing, and do it before a bunch of police officers on the hunt for James stumbled into it completely unprepared, with no idea what was really going on. Assuming anyone was after James, of course, and Temper hadn't vetoed the whole thing in order to cover his own tracks.

She rubbed her forehead. She was thinking in circles, and her head hurt far too much for it. And on top of that, she was *angry.* Someone had hit her car. Bumped her on the head. *Used* her to find the necklace, then taken it. And it was her fault James had been kidnapped, and her responsibility to get him back, so she may as well just get on with it, and never mind the details. She had to get him out before whatever they were doing to the captives had a permanent effect – or his captors decided to vanish him permanently, just to cover their tracks. It'd seem risky to release a police officer, after all. Even a drugged one.

But she did need a little help, and she was going to have to take a chance. She took a breath, poked her phone, and hit dial.

Isha answered almost immediately. "Adams? What's happening?"

"If I send you a message, do you think you can track down where it was sent from?"

"Should be able to," Isha said. "What's it about?"

Adams rubbed the tender spot at the back of her head again and said, "It's another photo." The silence told her she didn't have to clarify what it was of. "And you can't tell anyone, not even Temper. I have to deal with this."

There was a long pause before Isha said, "I get not telling Lindsay, but why not Temper?"

Adams tried to think of any excuse that didn't involve *oh, magic is real,* or (possibly worse) saying *this is personal* like she was in some '80s cop flick, neither of which were likely to go down well. Finally she said, "We still don't know who the leak is. This situation'll be common knowledge as soon as Temper makes a move, but they won't be expecting me. I can sort this before they even know anyone's coming at them."

Isha made a dubious noise. "Pretty thin, Adams."

"It makes sense, though. You know it does."

More silence, then, "Well, send it to me. It's not going to run on over by itself."

Adams did, then got out of the car again while she waited, listening to the tap of keys on the other end of the phone. As far as she could tell, the driver's side was lightly dented and heftily scraped, which her insurance was going to just *love,* but otherwise the damage seemed pretty minimal. It should be drivable. Which meant it hadn't actually been the crash that had knocked her out. She supposed if they had the means to render their captives as pliable as mannequins, it wouldn't take that much to do some sort of mental bop on the head.

She scrambled over the passenger seat to the driver's side, finding the keys still in the ignition, took a breath, and turned the key. The engine fired into life obediently, and she released her breath with a sigh and patted the dashboard.

"Good girl."

"I'm sorry?" Isha said.

"The car started."

"I'm starting to have serious concerns about you, Adams. It may be all that caffeine."

"Possibly."

"Anyway. I've got the general area of where the text was sent from."

Adams put the car into reverse and started to slowly back onto the lane, wincing at a couple of fresh squeals from the car's side as it parted company with the wall. "Where?"

"Not far from you."

"From me?" Adams asked, frowning. "How d'you know where I am?"

"Don't flatter yourself, I'm not stalking you. Just got your position now so I had a reference."

"Right." It still felt slightly on the creepy side. But she

wasn't going to upset Isha about it when she was the only help available. "Can you send me a pin drop or something?"

"Done," Isha said, as Adams' phone dinged. "Do you want me to send you backup?"

"No. Don't tell anyone. I'll call you when I'm sure what's going on."

"You're putting me right in the middle of things here. If it all goes tits up, I'm going to be at least partly responsible. So a reason would be good, at least."

"I don't have a decent one to give you," Adams replied. "But I do know what I'm doing. This case … it has similarities to something I dealt with in London."

There was a long pause, and she could feel Isha weighing her words. Finally she said, "You've got an hour, then I'm sending bloody everyone after you."

"Fair enough," Adams replied, and hung up. She tapped the pin drop Isha had sent her, put the car into gear, and got moving without anything falling off or exploding, and nothing sounding worse than a slight rattle at the front that suggested her bumper wasn't too happy about recent developments. An hour. She had an hour to get in, get James and the others out, and seize the necklace. If she could.

It was going to have to be enough.

SHE DROVE AS FAST as she dared along the narrow lanes, following the GPS as it pointed her deeper into the countryside, away from Leeds. An hour on Isha's side, but who knew how long she had on the other? How long until they got rid of the witnesses, now that they had the necklace? The GPS beeped at her, and she swung into a single-track lane that curled and twisted between the drystone walls, pocked with passing bays here and there. The country was riddled with these empty, unsigned roads, and each one seemed more remote and distant than the next. She didn't even understand how the place could hold so many. Sure, Yorkshire was the biggest county in England, but it wasn't *that* big. England itself wasn't even that big, and it was crammed with people. There shouldn't have still been room for all these hidden, mysterious places, and yet here they were, as if the physics of the land didn't obey the rules that she knew and understood. She thought of Charles and his pockets, the hidden leftovers of magical towns that persisted in the world, and wondered if that was the explanation for it.

She was almost convinced of it when she pulled into a little hamlet that wasn't even marked by a scrap of shading on her maps app. The houses pressed close to the road, imperious and hostile in grey stone, while around them gardens rioted with flowers. Ivy and climbing roses swamped garden walls, and a stream ran between the houses, capped by a little stone bridge that tugged at Adams' attention. There was no one around, but she could feel the car being noticed, and she was glad enough when the GPS led her through the hamlet and out the other side.

Not far from the scattering of buildings, she saw a big, two-storey house sitting on its own at the end of a long drive, gates blocking access from the road. The phone beeped, but she drove straight past, not even slowing until she reached the next passing bay, around a curve in the road where she couldn't be seen from the house.

She parked, and looked at Dandy. "That's it," she said. "There's nothing else out here."

He whined, and she nodded agreement, then got out and dug in the boot, which thankfully still opened. There was a backpack in there, and she loaded it with the Yorkie bars, her collapsible baton, and her torch (because it might be the middle of the afternoon, but one never knew when a torch might come in handy), then shouldered the bag and picked up Gladys's staff. The weight of it was reassuring, but she doubted it could do very much against whatever had been used to drive the car off the road, knock her out, and presumably imprison four people. Five, if she counted Scott. But it was what she had, and so it was what she was going in with.

She shut the boot, and with Dandy following her she found a low point in the drystone wall and clambered over, trying not to knock too many stones loose. A few cows looked at her without much interest as she dropped into the field beyond, and she started back in the direction of the house. There was a small stream here, making the ground soggy under her boots, and trees and shrubs sprouted along it, offering her a little shelter. She took out a Yorkie bar and ate it as she walked, wishing she had some coffee. The sugar helped, though, and by the time she'd finished it she'd threaded her way through the rough cover almost to the wall that encircled the property.

She found a decent-sized bush and crept into its shadow until she could peer straight over the wall into a rolling green garden, full of furiously tamed flowerbeds and regimented rockeries. The house sprouted out of it, all big windows and warm stone walls, pleasant without being exceptional, and, more importantly, there was a shed off to the side, a big boxy thing that looked like it had come in a kit, glaringly modern. It seemed to have stumbled out of a building site and taken a wrong turn.

"That's it," she whispered to Dandy. "It's got to be."

He didn't answer, just went up and over the wall, a shadow in the sunlight. She watched him go, wishing she could pass as unremarked as he did. But she couldn't, so all she could do was be fast, be sure, and carry a very big stick.

21

A BREAK-OUT & A BREAK-IN

ADAMS DIDN'T FOLLOW DANDY OVER THE WALL. THERE WASN'T enough cover for her in all the low-profile, manicured tidiness of the garden and its perfectly plotted flowerbeds. Instead, she stayed on the field side, keeping low and hoping no one was looking out the top floor windows, because if they were, they'd probably see her. The cover of the shrubs was patchy at best. She headed for where the shed crouched in a corner of the garden, popping up every now and then to check if she could see anyone.

There didn't appear to be anyone patrolling the garden or guarding the shed, but she supposed that with the captives unable to move they weren't too worried about escapees. And they were unlikely to be worried about her. She had an idea that if Dandy hadn't got her out of the car, she'd still be unconscious in it now. There was a migraine-like throb going on behind her eyes, an aftereffect of whatever she'd been hit with, but the Yorkie bar seemed to have done its job reasonably well. That, or the prospect of arresting someone.

The shed loomed up between her and the house, hiding her from view, and she straightened up to examine it. On this side, at least, it had no windows, not even shuttered ones, just a long, featureless flank, so she scrambled up and over the drystone wall, swinging herself down into the small gap between the shed and the boundary. A few weeds had reclaimed some territory from the manicured grounds, and she felt oddly encouraged by them.

She had to move slightly sideways in the narrow space, and she edged to the corner of the shed, peering carefully around it and ready to duck back into cover if necessary. At this end of the building, uncomfortably exposed to both the drive and the front door of the house, there was a set of double doors. She didn't fancy stepping out into the open to try them, but she hadn't seen any other way in, and she could feel time draining steadily away. She stayed where she was for a couple of minutes, looking for movement in the windows of the house, or for someone to come patrolling across the garden. There was nothing though, and finally she stepped around to the front of the shed and tried the handle. To her surprise, it turned easily. It wasn't locked, and she had a sudden stab of doubt. Maybe she'd got this wrong. Maybe no one was being held here at all.

She put her eye to the crack between the doors, unwilling to go charging in until she knew what was waiting inside. The interior was dimly lit, and after the brightness outside she couldn't see very much at all. She couldn't just wait here for her eyes to grow accustomed to it either, not with the house looming over her and the risk of someone spotting her at any moment. So she quickly pulled the door open, just enough for her to slip through, whipped around it and eased it shut again. She ducked away from the spill of light at the door's edges, dropping into a crouch as she waited for a shout, or for someone to rush her. But there was nothing, no movement at all.

As her eyes slowly adjusted to the dimness, she saw the

four chairs lined up in the middle of the floor. They were all facing the door, and James, Meredith, Patrice, and Kelvin were sitting in them, hands still loose on their laps just as they had appeared in the photo. None of them gave any sort of indication that they'd seen her arrive, even though they were all facing in her direction. There was no one else in here, but the four hardly looked like they needed guarding. Not with their vacant stares fixed on the floor in front of them.

The skin was crawling on the back of Adams' neck and setting chills down her spine. It wasn't just the sight of them all sitting there, strangely comatose, as if they were asleep with their eyes open. No, there was something else about the shed, something that prickled and stung, plucking at instincts that were older and deeper than even the ones that had kept her out of trouble in the dark streets and dens of London. Instincts as old as the ones that had kept her alive on the bridge. Her hand slipped into her pocket of its own accord, squeezing the hard brass form of the duck, and she let herself focus on the feel of it, the cold metal and the ridges of its wings. Then she let it go, putting both hands back on the staff, and walked slowly across the creaking panels of the floor, her eyes darting into the corners of the shed, looking for guards and attackers.

There was no one here, though. There was nowhere for them to hide. The whole place was empty other than the captives. There wasn't a single piece of equipment, not a lawnmower parked in a corner or a garden rake leaning against a wall, no shelving or bags of compost or stacked furniture being stored out of the way, nothing to justify the shed. Just bare walls and bare floors, giving slightly under her boots. She found herself looking for runes or summoning circles, not that she'd really know what one of those looked like if she saw it, but she couldn't help thinking there needed to be a *reason* for this place, and given the feel of it, that seemed like a likely one.

When she was sure she hadn't missed anything, she crossed to the chairs and crouched in front of James, clicking her fingers in front of his face. He didn't even flinch. She tapped his cheek with her fingers lightly, and that elicited a flicker of the eyelids.

"Come on," she said, trying it again. "James. *James!*" This time there was nothing, no twitch or shift, and he didn't seem to hear his name at all. She thought about it, then pulled back and slapped him hard enough to set her palm stinging.

His face whipped to the side with the force of the blow, and she had to grab his arms to stop him tumbling off the chair to the floor. He gasped, drawing in a huge, desperate gulp of air as if he'd been drowning, then coughed it out, one hand going to his cheek.

"*Ow.* Bloody hell, Adams, did you just *hit* me?"

"Yes," she said, letting go of him. "Are you alright?"

"You *hit* me!" he said, then looked around. "Wait – where are we?"

"You don't remember anything?"

"No. I was on the way to the GP … or at the GP, I don't know. What's happened?" His gaze was darting around, barely settling on anything before flitting off again, and he finally spotted the others next to him. "What the *hell*, Adams?"

"I think you were all drugged," she said, putting as much conviction into her voice as she could manage. He gave her a scowl that suggested she hadn't done as well with that as she'd hoped. "Can you stand?" she asked, before he could pursue the point.

He tried, then dropped back into the chair with a wince,

massaging his thighs. "My legs have gone to sleep. How long have I been here?"

"Long enough," she replied. "Get yourself sorted. I'm going to try and wake these three."

She went to Meredith next, giving her a little shake and trying to be somewhat gentler than she had with James. There was no response, though, and she was about to go for the slapping method again when she remembered something from some long ago first-aid course. She pinched Meredith's earlobe between her short-cropped fingernails, hard, and the young woman gave the same panicked gasp as James as she surfaced. Adams wondered just how deep they'd all been, if they'd even been breathing. She glanced at Patrice and Kelvin, but she couldn't actually see their chests moving. It was if they'd been cut out of time and set aside, Sleeping Beauties woken with some mild and judiciously applied violence.

Meredith was still panting, staring around wildly, and now she grabbed Adams' arm, peering at her short-sightedly. "What's happening? Why are you here? You weren't here!"

"Do you know where here is?"

"No. No, I was in bed, and then there was a knock at the window, and then ... and then ..." Meredith stared around, trying to make out details in the shed, and Adams caught her arms, gently unfastening the young woman's hands from her own.

"It's okay," she said. "We'll sort it all out later. For now, just get yourself woken up and make sure your legs are feeling okay. We're going to have to run, alright?"

Meredith gave her a wide-eyed look, not answering, but pushed herself up out of the chair. She promptly collapsed to the floor with a squeak.

Adams sighed and said, "It's okay. No rush." Even though

there was. But she didn't think they were going anywhere very quickly.

She woke Patrice and Kelvin with the same ear-pinching technique. Each was as bewildered as the other, unsure of where they were, and Patrice sat there massaging his thighs while Kelvin gave Adams an accusing look.

"You said I was safe," he said.

"Well, you were when I put you in there," she replied. "Just get yourself moving, all right?"

She went to the shed door before he could argue, peering out at the garden. She could only see the small section of the lawn heading down to the drive, the house out of sight from this angle, but there was no one there. There was also no Scott, and she'd rather hoped to find him with the others. But that was fine. If she could get James moving, he could get the rest of them out of here, and she'd deal with finding Scott.

She turned around to find James behind her, standing but still looking somewhat like a new-born giraffe who doesn't quite trust the control of his limbs yet. But he gave her a wonky sort of grin and said, "What next?"

"Now we've got to get out of here without being noticed."

He pointed at her head. "What happened there? You've got blood in your hair."

"Car accident," Adams replied. "It's still running, though. We just need to get to it."

"Did you come here without backup?" James asked.

Adams scowled at him. "*You're welcome.*"

"I don't know how they do things in London," he said. "But around here, we don't go anywhere without backup."

She pointed at him. "You're my backup."

"I wasn't exactly helpful when you arrived," he said.

She almost said that she'd had Dandy, who was proving to be excellent (if unpredictable) backup, but managed to swallow it. "Just make sure everyone can move, alright? We're going over the wall, then straight down the field to the road. We're going to need to be quick about it."

James shook his head, but he didn't argue further, just turned and went to help Kelvin, who seemed to be having even more trouble with his legs than anyone else, despite being captive for the shortest time.

Before long everyone was gathered at the door, Adams still keeping watch on the garden. Dandy *was* excellent backup when he showed up, but she hadn't seen him since they'd arrived. She wished he'd come back with some sort of message, like barking three times to tell her how many people were in the house. But it didn't seem to be his style, and there was no sign of him anyway. For all she knew, he was off seeing if there were any lamb chops in the kitchen.

She shifted the staff from one hand to the other, and James looked at it curiously. "Where did you get that?"

"Borrowed it from Gladys's house," she replied.

"Why were you there? Are they all right?"

"Don't know, I've lost track of them."

"What about Scott?"

"Lost Scott as well."

He stared at her. "How long was I out?"

She scowled, and eased the door open. "Come on," she said. "Quick." She moved fast, leading them into the gap between the wall and the shed, giving them some shelter from the house.

James and Adams helped the others over the wall, boosting them up unceremoniously. Patrice went over easily enough, and Meredith tumbled after him, squinting at the field with a bewildered look on her face. Kelvin was still having trouble getting his legs to behave, and Adams had a feeling he was one of those guys that would spend hours in the gym on his upper body and kind of forget that the lower half existed. But before long he was safely over the wall as well, and she looked at James.

"On you go."

"After you."

Adams shot a look at the wedge of garden visible beyond their little bit of shelter. "I have to find Scott. Get them to the car."

"I'm not going anywhere," he said, and turned to look over the wall at Meredith. "Run," he said. "Hide in the trees."

She looked around. "I can't really see—"

"We're going." Patrice grabbed her arm and broke into a jog, steering her toward the shelter of the stream and its foliage. Kelvin staggered after them, arms waving wildly as he tried to keep his balance. They seemed painfully obvious as they bounced across the fields, looking like extras from a folk music video, and Adams braced herself for a shout from the house, but there was nothing. Not yet.

"Tell me why we're not just calling it in now this lot are off?" James asked.

"I think Scott must be inside, and the necklace. We can't risk losing it."

"And you haven't called it in before because …?"

"I'm off the case," she admitted. "And it's compromised."

"Lindsay?"

She stared at him. "You think it could be?"

He held one hand out, seesawing it. "I mean, she's ruthless, but I don't *think* she's corrupt? About the last thing I remember, though, is her stopping me in the parking garage when I was heading to the doctor's."

Adams nodded slowly. "I think it has to be her or Temper."

James grimaced. "I suppose Temper's got the clout to do what he wants."

"And he did put us on this silly bloody case." Adams

peered around the end of the shed, back toward the house, then flattened herself to the wall. "There's someone there."

James didn't answer, and Adams stayed where she was, hoping she hadn't been seen. She could still see the front of the house, and a big, broad-shouldered man in a pale blue shirt who had emerged onto the front step. He scanned the garden, and she saw him frown as he looked at the shed. The door. She hadn't checked the door was shut behind them. She cursed to herself quietly, but didn't move as the man trotted down the steps and strode across the garden.

Adams glanced at James, shifting her grip on the staff. They couldn't let the alarm be raised. There hadn't been enough time for the others to make their escape. She waited, listening for the quiet creak of the door swinging open, and hoped that the man would have to step inside just as she had done, to make sure of what he was seeing.

The door whispered, so quiet she almost missed it under her own breath, and Adams came around the shed fast. The man had vanished inside, and she followed him over the threshold, not hesitating, just bringing the staff down in a swinging arc, smacking him on the back of the head and sending him to the floor. James pushed past her and pounced on him as he groaned, unable to resist. Adams grabbed her handcuffs from her bag while James pinned the man down, twisting his arms up behind his back, and a moment later they had him firmly trussed. He moaned softly, not quite forming words, and Adams hoped she hadn't hit him too hard.

"There's nothing to secure him to," James said, still with one knee on the man's back.

"Leave it," Adams said. "It'll have to do. Hopefully we can be in and out before he comes around and starts shouting the place down." She turned back to the door. "Let's do this."

"Right behind you," James replied, and they slipped out of

the shed and sprinted for the house, where the front door stood slightly ajar.

Adams clutched the staff as she ran, and from around the house Dandy came racing to join her, and the afternoon sun burned high and hot, baking the old bones of the Yorkshire Dales and raising a heat haze as rich and thick as the magic that surrounded the house, and just as suffocating.

22

STICK IT TO THE MAN

THE DOOR OPENED ONTO A HIGH-CEILINGED, BRIGHT FOYER, open stairs climbing up on the right to a landing above, and black and white tiles forming an intertwined pattern on the floor that ran off to join other rooms. This house didn't have the jumbled, lived-in feel of Gladys's, even though it was equally as old. This had the feel of the ghosts of servants still hiding in the shadows, unnoticed and all but unnamed. The old, ingrained sense of class, of layers of society, of strata which would have put Adams right at the bottom, underneath anyone whose skin was just a shade or so paler, soaked out of the smooth wood walls, making her mouth twist into an unconscious scowl. An elephant foot umbrella stand waited in one corner, holding a couple of incongruously cheery umbrellas, and a huge oil painting depicting some sort of safari featuring great white hunters directing noble savages glowered down from the wall.

Adams wrinkled her nose equally at the painting and the umbrella stand, but kept moving, ducking her head into the first doorway she found. It was a boot room, complete with an old-fashioned wooden bench, coat hooks, and shoe storage. No one in there. She moved to the next door, James following close behind her, armed with an umbrella he'd picked up from the stand. Adams slipped into a square, softly lit reception room, furnished with one small table and a chair. More old oil paintings, portraits this time, stared down at them with supercilious expressions, and she jumped as Dandy arrived at the door across the room from the one they'd entered by. He looked at her and tipped his head slightly.

Adams started to say, *there you are,* but caught herself in time and instead followed him silently, James trailing behind them. The next room was large and grand enough that Adams assumed it had been the dining room, but it was set up as if for an impending ceremony. Fresh-cut flowers in modern vases adorned the small corner tables and sideboards, and most of the space was taken up with rows of chairs, all facing the head of the room, where a little wooden podium stood. Each chair had a soft cushion and a flowing white covering with a big bow tied at the back, and looked very much as if they'd been borrowed from a wedding shop.

Adams paused just inside the door, staring at the scene, then looked at James. He shook his head, frowning, and Adams wondered if it actually was some sort of wedding venue. She supposed even Folk needed a place for such things. But it was empty in here as well, so she headed across the room for the next door, each room opening onto another like an endless maze.

"Look," James said softly, just as she reached the door.

She turned back to him, and he waved what looked almost like a small white table tennis racquet at her, the number *23* printed neatly on it in black. He'd discovered a box behind the chairs stuffed with them, and Adams nodded in sudden recognition.

"It's an auction," she said. "They're selling the necklace."

He nodded. "Looks like it. But we're in time. No one here yet."

It was a win, even if it was a small one.

There was yet another door off this room, this one closed, and she hurried across the old tiles to put her ear to it. She couldn't hear anything, so she turned the handle carefully, just enough that she could peer through the crack, the staff at the ready. All she could see were walls lined with books, and no one standing inside, but her field of view wasn't great.

She pushed the door open to reveal a library, the windows framed by heavy curtains, half-drawn to keep the sun off the books. Small lamps on side tables were the main source of illumination, lending everything a soft glow that added to the hush of stories lining the walls, books packed tightly into shelves that filled every bit of space. And in the middle of it all, firmly gaffer-taped to a chair and not looking in the slightest bit stunned, was Scott, his blond hair dishevelled and his shirt torn at the collar.

There was no one guarding him, and Adams strode across the room to pull the gaffer tape off his lips. He gave a little yelp of pain and stared up at her. "You're alive," he said. "I thought you were dead."

"Not so far," she replied. "Are you hurt?"

"No, I'm fine."

Adams was already working on the rest of the tape while James kept an eye on the door and she asked, "Have they got the necklace?"

"They took it from the car when they grabbed me," he replied. "I thought they were going to knock me off right there, but they dragged me into a van and took off."

"Alright. Let's get you out of here." She looked at James. "You need to take him and head after the others."

"Not happening," he replied. "I'm staying here with you. We can just send him across the field too."

"We can't," she said. "They've kept him in here separately for some reason. They obviously want him for something."

Scott gave her an alarmed look, massaging his wrists, and James shook his head. "All the more reason for us all to go. We'll send someone else back for the necklace."

"And leave it for … well, whoever's behind this? We'll never get it back." *And who knows what'll happen then. When someone has that power.*

"Well, we can't all stay here," he said, and even as he spoke, voices rose from the next room, accompanied by the sound of footsteps. James quickly pushed the door almost closed, crouching next to it so that he could peer through the crack, and Adams hurried to join him, holding the staff at the ready. Scott looked around in a panic and picked up the nearest lamp, unplugging it and coming to stand just behind Adams.

"Put that down," she hissed at him.

"I might need it," he whispered back.

"Put it *down*," she repeated, then stopped, because the voices were coming closer. She pushed James out of the way so she could peek into the auction room, where another large, pale-blue-shirted man was showing a group of three newcomers to the chairs and handing out paddles.

Adams blinked at them, closed her eyes for a moment, then opened them properly, feeling that change in her vision, uncomfortably easy to access now. The lingering traces of her post-crash headache dissipated, and she looked back at the trio. One had wings folded tight to her back, but they weren't pretty, gauzy things. They were big, the tips almost touching the ground despite the way they hulked over her head, and the fabric of them was leathery and tattered. Her teeth were sharp and long, and Adams could see calluses built up on her bottom lip. Even so, she was pretty, but in a hard, angular way. Pretty in the way a shark's pretty, or maybe a praying mantis.

Next to her, a man who looked human enough other than that strange sharpness, that extra hint of reality to him, was fussing with the creases in his pinstriped trousers as he sat down. His cravat and pocket handkerchief matched perfectly, and his hair was combed smoothly back from a high forehead. The third person was seating herself on the other side of the aisle. It seemed to be a complicated affair, because while Adams couldn't entirely make sense of it, her brain simply refusing to understand exactly what was happening, the woman seemed to have far too many limbs going on, and not all of them bent the right way. In fact, a lot of them didn't seem to bend at all. They seemed to coil, tentacular.

Adams stepped back from the door and examined the library, crossing to check the windows. They were big, old affairs, sash ones that would slide upward. They didn't appear to be painted shut, so they'd probably be able to get them open, but it was going to make a hell of a lot of noise. There was no way they were going to get through that unnoticed. She went back to join James at the door. "We're going to wait for a few more people to come in," she said in a low voice. "Then whenever that bloody great blue-shirted lump isn't around, we're going straight out through the front door."

Both James and Scott looked at her.

"You reckon we can pull that off?" James asked. "We don't exactly look like auction guests."

Adams pointed at the room beyond the door. "They don't really look like your average auction guests either," she said. "I reckon we can manage it." Although, to be honest, she wasn't entirely sure they could. At least two of them, as far as she could tell, lacked the sharp edges of the people in the room beyond. "We'll say we're staff," she added. "Just walk through like you're meant to be there, and if anyone says anything, we're setting up for the event."

"Alright," James said. "About the best thing we can do, I suppose. Hang about, there's another lot coming in." Adams put her eye to the door, just as James added, "They're a right weird bunch."

She thought he didn't know the half of it. More people were trickling in all the time. There were hooves and horns, extra limbs and extra eyes, wings and tails. There were people that looked entirely inhuman, and others that she'd have barely noticed outside this house, except for the stutter of power surrounding them, rising off their skin like auras. The necklace was in high demand, and she had no idea how they were going to get it back before it fell into the wrong hands. And she was entirely certain that anyone who was in that room wasn't after the necklace for the good of humanity, or for the good of Folk, for that matter. But she also wasn't getting rid of James that easily, so getting him and Scott out had to come first. Then she'd just have to start the necklace hunt all over again, if that's what it took.

She sighed, scanned the room again, then said, "He's gone. Let's do this."

"What can go wrong?" James asked, and Adams shot him a scowl, then opened the door.

She went out first, walking with her head up and her shoulders back, the staff firmly clasped in one hand, trying to look as if she belonged there and hoping no one noticed the blood in her hair or the grass stains on her trousers. Dandy walked next to her, his head just as high, and she had the absurd thought that she should start twirling the staff and doing a high kick or something.

She didn't, though, and they headed straight across the back of the room toward the door out. They'd almost made it, too, when a woman with a couple of extra eyes and heavily bejewelled fingers said, "Excuse me."

Adams paused and managed a smile. "Yes?"

"Are there refreshments? We were told there were going to be refreshments, and it was a very long drive. I'm parched." The woman's voice was cut crystal in both accent and volume, and the other visitors turned to look at them.

"We're organising that right now," Adams said. "We'll be back in just a moment. Please bear with us."

She started forward again, and a man with luxuriously long hair and a pointy nose said, "Honestly, I don't think this is very well set up at all. And in the country. I can't *stand* the country. Get bits of mud in your hooves."

The woman with too many tentacles tittered, folding a few of them over the smooth swell of her belly. "You should try having as many legs as me," she said. "Pick up all sorts of muck."

James gave Adams a look which very clearly said, *These people are all insane and this was a terrible idea.*

She ignored him, said, "We'll be right back with refreshments," and pulled the door open. She stepped through and bumped straight into the huge man with his blue shirt, who was escorting four more new arrivals. He started to apologise, stepping back, then swore and lunged at her instead.

Adams was already moving, jabbing the staff straight into his belly and shoving him away with it. He doubled over with a grunt of pain, and she yelled, "*Get back!*" even as she retreated herself, feeling James grab Scott and haul him out of her way. They ducked back into the auction room and Adams slammed the door shut in the big man's face as he charged forward. She and James threw themselves against it, barely keeping it closed as the man hit it with a rumbling growl, making the whole thing shudder.

"What in the realms is going on?" the winged woman asked, sounding only mildly interested.

Adams was still looking for an answer when Scott straightened his shirt and said in a smooth voice, "Employment dispute. I'm their lawyer. You wouldn't *believe* the conditions here. No sick pay, no overtime, and they're a month behind on wages as well."

"A *month* behind?" the faun with the supermodel hair said. "Honestly, does no one have standards anymore? That's insupportable."

"It's illegal, surely," the man with the cravat and pinstripes put in, and the winged woman waved vaguely.

"We do operate in a grey area, Laurence."

"You do right," the faun said to Adams. "Don't let them beat you down."

"Hell, yeah. Stick it to the man," a woman who looked mostly human said. She was wearing tie-dyed trousers, and she took a long-stemmed pipe from somewhere and lit it, releasing clouds of fragrant smoke. "Right on, sister," she added, holding her fist out to Adams.

Adams returned the fist bump with a sigh, as the door shuddered at her back under the assault of the big man. He was still growling, and Dandy bared his teeth at the door, eyes glinting.

"That's no way to negotiate," the tentacled woman said. "Unacceptable."

"We're holding out for maternity leave as well," Scott said, putting his hands in his pockets. "Got to have good maternity leave."

"Quite," Laurence said. "I make sure all my staff have maternity *and* paternity leave." He licked his lips, exposing a long, pointed purple tongue.

James blinked as if he'd seen *something*, but couldn't quite work out what. He looked at Adams. "How are we getting out of this?"

She adjusted her footing and braced herself as the door shook again. "I have no bloody idea," she replied.

Beyond the door, the man's growl deepened into a snarl, and Dandy barked a short, sharp warning that echoed in Adams' chest. There were more things than just necklaces to fear here.

23

THINGS FALL APART

IT WAS THE TENTACLED WOMAN WHO CAME TO THE RESCUE. She bounded up, a rotund form held aloft by rapidly shifting limbs, and shoved Adams and James away from the door, leaving James looking both confused and alarmed, and Adams with a vaguely slimy sensation on her arm.

The door flew open, the big man stumbling into the room as the resistance suddenly vanished, and the woman slapped him across the face, leaving sucker prints on his cheeks. He yelped and staggered back, clapping his hand to his face.

"This is no way to negotiate with your staff," the woman shouted.

"They're not—" he began.

"Absolutely unforgivable!" She flung a couple of tentacles (or maybe an arm, it was all a bit unclear how things worked) out toward Adams. "She wants maternity leave!"

"Well," Adams started, and the woman charged on regardless, pointing at James instead.

"Or he wants paternity leave or maternity leave or … Look, *one* of them wants maternity leave!"

"We *all* want maternity leave," Scott shouted, and everyone in the room cheered.

The blue-shirted man gave them a confused look. "No," he started, and the tentacled woman slapped him again.

"Don't you *dare* say no. These are your *staff.* You have to look after your staff. Have they got proper holiday time? Sick pay?"

"No!" Scott shouted, jabbing one finger at the big man from a safe distance. "No one's got sick pay. It's completely unregulated employment. It's like the Wild West in this place!"

The entire room gasped.

"Disgraceful," Laurence said, standing up and adjusting his cuffs. "I won't work with anyone who perpetrates this sort of workhouse environment."

"Oh, yah," the winged woman said, and yawned, exposing her sharp teeth. "It's very boring."

The big man started to say something, raising his hands in protest, and Adams grabbed James and Scott, hauling them around and pointing them toward the door that led to the library.

"Go, go," she hissed, hustling them away from the argument. With any luck they could get a window open while everyone was otherwise occupied.

The faun pointed one well-manicured finger at the big man and said, "People like you are the reason why we have employment laws."

"They're not staff," the blue-shirted man finally managed, but Adams was already slamming the library door. She grabbed one side of a big leather armchair as James grabbed the other, and between them they hefted it to the door, shoving it against the frame as someone tried to force it open from the other side.

Scott had run for the nearest window and was tugging at

it frantically. It creaked and groaned just as much as Adams had thought it would, but by the time they reached him he'd managed to force it up enough to get his fingers underneath. James joined him, and they wrenched the sash up until they had a gap big enough to squeeze through. Scott went first, sliding out with an easy athleticism, then James followed, and finally Adams, slightly less gracefully simply due to the fact she had a bigger scramble to get onto the sill than they had.

"Move it," she shouted at them as they hesitated, waiting for her. "Over the wall, go!"

James grabbed Scott's arm and they bolted as Adams swung out of the window, landing clumsily in the flowerbed and crushing some geraniums. Then she was up and legging it after them, hurdling flower beds and going straight for the nearest stretch of wall, all three of them in a flat sprint, James barely outpacing Scott and coming to a stop by the wall, beckoning the others on.

All the confusion of the days gone, the complicated layers and hidden movements of the case, it all vanished in the simplicity of the moment. *Run*. The day was drawn in clear lines and hard contrasts, and Adams could hear her breath over the birdsong and shouts from the front of the house, smell crushed grass and pastries cooking somewhere. She reached for another notch of speed, closing on the wall as Dandy came bounding around the house joyfully, half a baguette in his mouth. Two more men in blue shirts appeared, running to intercept James and Scott, and Dandy angled toward them. The third man, the one from inside, shouted from the library window, ordering them to stop, and Adams raised her voice to be heard over him.

"Get over that bloody wall!" she shouted, as if it were some sort of Home Free, and once they were over no one could touch them. Scott had reached it and grabbed for the top, James still waiting, waving urgently at Adams as if that would speed her up. Scott launched himself up, the movement a smooth, muscled flow that spoke of time spent on rings and bars in the gym. It should have swung him up and over rapidly despite the unsteady structure under his hands, turning into a vault to the ground on the other side, but instead he slammed to a stop with a yelp, as if he'd hit some unseen stretch of wall that extended far beyond the stone. His momentum meant he bounced back, tumbling to the grass and pressing both hands to his forehead with a groan, and James looked from him to the wall with a bewildered look on his face, as if hunting for an assailant.

Adams swore, skidding to a stop at the wall and jumping up to slam her hand into the air above it. Her palm smacked into an unseen obstacle, hard and smooth as glass, and James leaned past her to prod at it. They may as well have been surrounded by some sort of giant cake dome. There was no getting through it.

Adams spun to face the approaching blue-shirted men, who had slowed to a walk. Dandy was standing in the middle of the lawn watching them, still with his baguette in his mouth, and she couldn't help feeling he could be a *little* more useful.

"West Yorkshire Police," James shouted before Adams could say anything.

Unsurprisingly, the men weren't exactly stricken with either a sudden attack of conscience or terror. One of them (he was blond, which was about the only way she could tell him apart from the dark-haired man next to him, and the one still leaning out of the library window), just said, "Bloody overrun with you lot around here. And we can't get Carl out of the handcuffs."

"Bit rough, that," the dark-haired man agreed. "You were the ones trespassing, after all."

"Can you just sort this lot out?" the man in the window shouted. "Put them in the shed. We don't have time for this."

"Yes, *boss,*" Blondie said, rolling his eyes, and the dark-haired man snickered. James looked so offended by how lightly they were taking things that Adams almost laughed herself. But, then again, she doubted he could see the sharp edges to the blue-shirted men, the way they moved just a little bit *wrong,* as if these forms weren't the only ones they were used to, and perhaps weren't the most comfortable, either. She wasn't sure what they were, but it wasn't exactly human.

She was pulled out of her speculation regarding the relative human-ness of large, interchangeable men by the dark-haired one reaching out as if he expected her to docilely let him take her arm. She slapped his hands away with the staff, taking a step back.

"Where's the necklace?" she demanded.

"The necklace isn't your business," he said, inspecting his knuckles with a frown.

"It's not yours either," she said, and found she meant it. It really *wasn't* their business, not any of them. The necklace was old, *ancient* really, and drenched in the power of a dead sorcerer, and it wasn't meant for *anyone*. Not when it being loose resulted in this sort of carnage, thefts and kidnappings and threats. Verity had been wrong to give it to Gladys. It should've died with her.

"It'll be someone else's soon enough," the man said comfortably, and grinned at her. His canines were just a little too long, and she got a whiff of something hairy and feral off him. "Now are you two going to come along into the shed, or do we have to drag you in there?"

"You can give it a bloody go," Adams said, raising the staff and planting her feet a little more firmly, feeling James readying himself with his umbrella.

"Honestly, you're exhausting," a new voice said, and the man in front of Adams glanced over his shoulder, a casual, almost dismissive look, his teeth still showing.

The voice was familiar, and not even necessarily surprising, but it still took a moment to register.

"Lindsay?" Adams said.

"Evidently." She walked toward them with her hands in the pockets of her immaculate grey slacks, her hair up in a tidy bun, looking cool and unbothered. Even her pale pink blouse looked as if she'd just taken it off the ironing board.

"You!" Scott said. He'd made it as far as sitting up. "I knew you weren't proper police when you came in the other day."

"Of course I am," Lindsay said, her eyes still on Adams. "You, *Adams,* on the other hand, seem to have slipped up. Caught selling stolen goods and all that."

"Bloody poisonous—" James started, and Adams cut him off with a sharp shake of her head.

"I thought it was Temper," she said. "Setting me off on this case and all."

"Of course you did." Lindsay sounded indulgent, like Adams had found someone in a game of hide-n-seek for five-year-olds. "I'm *very* straight, after all, and he's a dinosaur. I mean, if he's not guilty of this, he'll be guilty of something. Should be able to nudge him into early retirement at the very least. Losing two officers isn't going to look good."

Adams found herself very much wanting to use the staff to knock the smug little smile off Lindsay's face, but instead she simply said, "So bump us off, sell the necklace, and then what?"

Lindsay laughed. "I'm not going to sit here and explain myself to you. I've got an auction to get started."

"You know about all this," Adams said, waving in a way that took in everything, the bulky men and the stern house and the auction attendees who were emerging into the garden, shading their eyes and muttering. "You know about all *this*, and you just use it to make some bloody *cash?*" She could feel James watching her, almost feel the weight of his bewilderment, but she'd have to deal with that later.

"It's not about cash. This world works just like ours. It's about having what others want, or being able to get it for them. That's where the power is."

"I really didn't want to think it was you."

"No," Lindsay agreed. "But there's no proof, if it makes you feel better. I'm a bit more careful than you at covering my tracks."

"I don't have any tracks to cover."

"Oh? No secret conversations with occult silversmiths and hedge witches?" Lindsay laughed, a short, disbelieving sound that stung more than it should have. "You don't even know what you've got yourself into, do you? You come up from London all full of ideas, thinking you're this place's next bloody saviour."

"I didn't come up from London full of anything," Adams said. "And I'm sure as hell not the one whose career plans are *let's kill everyone*, so I've got that going for me."

The blond man swallowed a hiccup of laughter, and his friend stretched, long limbs creaking as he looked around at the crowd gathering on the lawn. "Are you finished, Lin?" he asked. "'Cause we need to get this moving."

Lindsay ignored him, still looking at Adams. "Think you're so bloody clever, don't you? But *I'm* the one with the necklace, and you're the one about to go down for it, so …" She spread her hands, smiling.

Adams was wondering if the best comeback was simply to start laying into Lindsay with the staff when someone shouted, "*You!* Give me back my necklace!"

Adams spun around, Lindsay staring past her, and

spotted Gladys and Olly looking over the wall, Gladys with a cap pulled down over her thick hair.

"Thief!" Gladys shouted, and Olly reached up with what appeared to be a carving fork. He tapped lightly on the air above the wall, and there was a loud popping sound that made Adams wince, while the blue-shirted men gave a chorus of yelps that were echoed by Dandy.

Olly grinned. "Just had to get the frequency right."

"Well done," Gladys said, then glared at Lindsay again. "I heard all that. Now just sort yourself out and give me my necklace back."

"It's not yours. You're not even a sorcerer," Lindsay said. She looked more puzzled than angry, which Adams understood. Yorkshire women of a certain age had a similar effect on her.

"I'm not saying we're not enjoying the entertainment," someone said, drawing their attention back to the auction attendees, who were now assembled on the lawn, watching with a mix of impatience and fascination. "Only is it going to take long?" the faun continued, running his hands down the sleek lines of his shirt, "Some of us are a *little* busy for human domestic disputes."

The woman in the tie-dyed trousers lowered her pipe and said, "I'm feeling this isn't about employment."

The tentacled woman patted her arm. "Do keep up, love," she said. "I think we're talking about ownership of the necklace."

"I intend to take ownership of the necklace," Laurence said, his feet planted wide on the soft grass and his arms crossed. He looked around, as if daring anyone to contradict him.

The woman with the leathery wings snorted. "As if, Laurence. You have no idea how to handle something like that."

"It's not meant for faeries," he replied. "It's meant for magic workers."

"You're hardly a magic worker. I mean, you call yourself a wizard, but you haven't even got a pointy hat. And you still have that lizard tongue thing going on, which is *very* questionable."

"That was an accident," he muttered. "It was meant to be for one night only."

"Exactly."

The tentacled woman broke into chortling laughter, which faded as she looked at Lindsay. "So," she said. "What's going on with this necklace, then?"

"It's *mine*," Gladys said. She was trying to get over the wall, apparently being lifted by Olly, going by the grunts of effort coming from the other side. She was hefted upward suddenly, giving a squawk of alarm as her belly hit the top of the wall, knocking loose rocks into the garden. She pitched forward and tumbled over, accompanied by bits of the wall, while Olly bounced up, shouting her name. Scott, who had just got to his feet, caught Gladys as she fell, and they crashed to the ground together.

Gladys pulled herself up, looked at Scott, then slapped him sharply across the face. "You stole my necklace," she shouted, and went in for another slap.

He fended her off. "I'm sorry! I'm sorry! I only meant to borrow it. I was going to lose *everything*. I was desperate!"

She stopped, frowning at him, then lowered her hand. "You could've just asked."

He stared at her, hands still raised to protect his face. "I didn't even know you."

"I'm very approachable."

"Sorry," he mumbled again. "I never meant it to get out of hand. The whole thing was an accident."

Gladys sighed. "I suppose I forgive you. Silly man."

"Honestly, it's *fascinating*," the woman with extra eyes said. "Humans are so odd."

James had edged closer to Adams, and now he said, "What's happening?"

"Drugs?" Adams suggested. "The aftereffects of what they hit you with?"

"I don't think so," James said, and looked at Lindsay. "I don't understand half of what's going on. Other than the bit where she's just filth."

"Oh, bless. You really don't understand *anything*," Lindsay said, and turned to the blue-shirted men. "Secure the lot of them in the shed."

"Carl's in there," Blondie said.

"Well, get him out, then." She looked around at the auction attendees. "Please do return inside. We'll be commencing—"

"He's handcuffed," Blondie said. "Can we use your keys?"

Lindsay took a visibly deep breath. "In a moment. As I was saying, the auction—"

"This all feels very messy," the faun put in. "I'm not comfortable with it."

"Or me," the faery said. She pointed at Adams and James. "Those are police, if I'm understanding you right, and not of your dodgy sort." She waved vaguely at Lindsay, ignoring her affronted expression. "I'm not interested in getting caught up in any of that. I'm out." She turned and headed for the gate, her head high and her feet light on the grass, wings shifting softly against each other. The faun followed her, his hooves gleaming in the sunlight.

"Me too," the tentacled woman said. "All this, and not even any refreshments. Most disappointing."

"Wait," Lindsay said. "You're not really going to walk away from a sorcerer's necklace, are you?"

"Tempting as it is," Laurence said, "you promised us this

was a simple sale of artefacts that had been released by the previous owner, and have given us utter …" He waved, his mouth pinching in a little moue of distaste. "*This.* You are evidently overreaching on your abilities." He offered his arm to the tentacled woman, and they started for the gates, the rest of the attendees already moving away.

"*Stop,*" Lindsay said, and pointed at Scott. "The only person who has to release the necklace is this one, as the last keeper, and he barely has any grip on it. The transfer of power will take moments." She shifted her attention to Gladys. "And *she's* got the book."

Everyone stopped, and Adams grimaced. She'd really hoped that Gladys had hidden it, but Olly was clutching a bag to his chest, and she could feel the heat of it, like the sun come low to shine on her face.

Gladys put both hands on her hips. "Sod off the lot of you. That's *my* property."

The faery examined her. "Do you even know how to use it? I mean, you're not a sorcerer. You're not really anything, are you?"

"I was her best friend," Gladys snapped, a tremble in her voice. "I was her best friend, and one of you killed her."

Adams looked at the crowd, her eyebrows raised, and Laurence said, "That's quite the accusation. Besides, you can't actually kill a sorcerer. They don't really work like that."

"Fine, then, someone pushed her into another dimension. And maybe it wasn't one of you specifically, but it was a magic worker. And I lost her. But I've protected all her things, and I'm going to keep protecting them for as long as I need to, because they're all I have left of her." Gladys was almost crying, and Olly put a hand on her back.

"And I'm going to protect them after," he said. Everyone looked at him, and Adams could tell she wasn't the only one feeling the power of what was in the bag.

"Bollocks," she whispered, grabbed her phone out of her pocket, and hit dial.

"What the hell are you doing?" Lindsay demanded.

Adams ignored her as the call connected. "Isha, get Temple, *now*," she said, and Lindsay threw her hand out toward her.

Adams dropped her phone and ducked, swinging the staff up without thinking about it. The charm shattered against the inlaid wood, spilling down the staff and chilling her fingers, making her shudder.

"What," James started, then seemed to run out of words. Adams felt a bit the same.

"Ooh," Gladys said. "I always wondered what those things were for."

"Get them in the damn barn," Lindsay snapped at the men. "Get that book, and we're going to auction both it and the necklace *now*. We've got time."

"This is very unprofessional," the faery said. "I still don't like it."

"Fine then, leave," Lindsay said. "But that means I get to keep everything."

No one spoke for a moment, then Adams stepped forward. "I'm arresting you for possession and resale of stolen goods," she said to Lindsay. "Also kidnapping with intent to harm, and anything else I can think of."

Lindsay stared at her, then burst out laughing. "You'd be funny if you weren't so unbearable. *Oh, look at me, all up from London with my precious mental health, I don't even have milk in my coffee, don't anyone use my first name, let's arrest the magic beasties.* I can't stand you."

"Honestly, you're not my favourite person either," Adams said. And this time when the charm came, she was more than ready for it. She swung at it with the staff as if she were back playing cricket in the green spaces of London, sending it spinning straight toward Lindsay, who hissed and ducked out of the way. The charm exploded against a bearded man standing behind her among the auction attendees, and he crashed to the ground like a fallen tree.

James put his head down and ran at Blondie, dropping his shoulder low and taking him out in a rugby tackle that sent them both spilling to the ground. Scott started hauling decorative stones out of the garden beds, pelting the other two blue-shirted men with surprising accuracy.

Gladys shouted, "Olly, the book!" and as she did so all the auction attendees took an alarmed step back.

Adams was left facing Lindsay, the staff at the ready. The duck was hooked over her fingers, metal hot against her knuckles, and she didn't know how any of this worked or what she was doing, but she did know that no one was leaving here with the necklace *or* the book. Not if she had anything to do with it.

24

FRACTURED YET WHOLE

"*Dammit!*" Lindsay spat the word at the world in general, and Adams in particular. "*Enough!*" She reached into her satchel and took out the necklace, holding it aloft.

A little *ooh* rose from the crowd, and the faery said, "Huh. She did have it. I was starting to wonder."

Lindsay shot her a furious look, then looked back at Adams and said, "*Stop.*"

A pulse of power rolled off the stone like the pressure wave from a bomb. It was raw and uncontrolled, toothy and ragged at the edges, tearing at the world, and Adams knew with some unfaltering instinct that it couldn't keep being used like that. That things – the world, their minds, reality – would fracture. It wasn't meant to be used in such a manner, and it wasn't sustainable.

James had been tussling with Blondie and now he simply *stopped*, and the big man pushed him away. The constable collapsed to the ground, floppy and loose limbed, and lay there with his face turned toward her, eyes open but unseeing. Adams had the same sense she'd had earlier, that someone had hit pause on him, and he wouldn't so much as draw breath again until he was somehow reactivated.

The fusillade of flung rocks stopped. Scott crumpled, still holding one in his hand, and curled up on the grass without a murmur. That left Gladys and Olly. Olly was clutching the bag to himself desperately, his head down. Now he looked up, his blue eyes wide, then turned to Gladys. He was just in time to catch her as she collapsed, lowering her to the ground gently.

He gave a little moan. "Oh no. Oh, *no*, Gladys. Gladys!" He tried to push the book into her hands, but she was no more responsive than James and Scott. "I'm sorry! You should've had it!"

"Olly, it's alright," Adams said, her voice level. "She'll be fine. Just you keep hold of that book."

"You'll give it to me if you want any chance of getting out of here," Lindsay said, and waved Blondie and his dark-haired buddy forward. They were unaffected, and Adams looked at them curiously, spotting slim woven bracelets on their wrists.

"Don't you touch her!" Olly stepped in front of Gladys, still clinging to the bag. "I'll use it! I will!"

The men stopped, and looked back at Lindsay.

"Ignore him. He has no idea how to use it," she said, giving them an impatient little *hurry up* gesture.

"I do!"

"Leave him," Adams said. She moved to intercept the men, her grip on the staff tight.

"I'm not loving this," Blondie said. "This was meant to be an easy job. No bloody police and oldies."

"Back off," Adams said, standing in front of Olly with the staff at the ready.

Lindsay raised the necklace again. "Drop that thing," she said to Adams.

"I really don't think so."

"Drop it."

The surge of power was so strong this time that Adams staggered, and heard Olly cry out. One of the men – or possibly both, she felt like she were caught in surf and couldn't quite see or breathe properly – had hold of her, and then she was on her knees, both the staff and the surge gone. She winced, rubbing her wrists. The staff had been wrenched away with more force than was necessary. Olly was sprawled on the ground behind her when she looked around, and Blondie walked back to Lindsay, handing her the bag. He still looked unhappy.

"That was a bit off," Adams said, and Lindsay, who had been unzipping the bag, looked up at her with a frown.

"How're you still up?"

"The staff wasn't the issue," she said, and found a grin from somewhere, wondering how far off Temper was. How long since she'd called? She needed to get the necklace *and* the book before he got here. The rest he could handle, because she had an idea, from the scowls of the Folk and the big men's indifference, that Lindsay wasn't going to find herself with much support when he did arrive.

"Of course it was the staff," Lindsay replied. "It came from the sorcerer's house too. No wonder it's making you immune to the necklace."

"If you say so." Adams folded her fingers over the comforting chill of the duck in her pocket.

"Allow me to demonstrate, so I don't have to bloody listen to you anymore." Lindsay raised the necklace, and that terrible pulse came out of it again.

Without the staff it seemed for a moment that it'd flatten her, bear her to the ground under its weight and strip the sense from her brain, but she just squeezed the duck harder, concentrating on the pinch of the metal wings into her palm, and leaned forward a little, as if against a high wind, holding onto her grin even as it felt her cheeks were beginning to cramp.

Then it was gone, and she widened the rictus of her smile at Lindsay. "See?"

A ripple of interest went around the group. "Who is that?" the faun asked. "I like her."

"I saw her first," the tentacled lady said, and Laurence huffed.

"What're you going to do with a human, Doris? Leave her to me."

Adams looked at them. "You can stop that and all. How come you're all fine, then? And the"––she meant to say *big lads* but that wasn't what came out, and somehow the words that did seemed to fit better—"good boys here? Is it directional? Or doesn't work on Folk?"

"We were all given bracelets," Doris said. "It was a way of ensuring no one could get hold of the necklace and use it against the rest of us." She held her hand up, showing the same woven bracelet as the men had on. "I don't see you wearing one though."

"No," Adams said. "Apparently I don't need one. And I'd take yours off, if I were you."

"Why?" Laurence asked.

"Because she was never actually going to sell the necklace."

"Of course I am," Lindsay replied. "It's worth a lot of money."

"Sure. But you said it, didn't you? The power's worth more. Those bracelets are nothing but traps."

Lindsay shifted just slightly. It was the smallest movement, but the faun gasped, covering his mouth with one hand.

"Oh, you dirty little human," he said. "You were going to

do us over. Get them off, then protective charms, everyone!" He clapped his hands urgently, and the others looked at each other blankly. He rolled his eyes. "Did *no one* come with protective charms?"

"I did," the woman in the tie-dyed trousers said. She had sat down amid a flowerbed of petunias and was watching everything with interest.

"It was meant to be a business deal," Laurence protested, tugging frantically at his bracelet. "Why would we need protection for that? It's not the bloody Middle Ages!"

Lindsay scowled, the bag clutched in one hand and the necklace in the other. "Oh, for heaven's *sake*. Adams, why did you have to get in the middle of this? Why couldn't you just mind your own damn business?"

"I'm police," Adams said. "This was my case."

"Oh, you're police, *you're police*. Precious bloody …" Lindsay trailed off, looking at the Folk, who were rapidly divesting themselves of their bracelets, biting and ripping at them. "You can't believe her!"

"Was it going to be a house fire?" Adams asked, then looked at the shed. "No, you were going to use that, weren't you? Looks pretty flammable." Her heart was going too fast. She had to move quickly, while Lindsay was still off balance, but her limbs were weak from the assault, and she wasn't sure if anyone would actually help her. And she was going to need help. She couldn't do this alone, not against the power Lindsay was now holding.

Lindsay started to answer, then looked at the Folk as Laurence started forward, scowling heavily, Doris right behind him. Lindsay snatched the book from the bag and shoved her hands upward, raising both it and the necklace high above her head. She screamed, something wordless and furious, and the pulse of power rolled away from her in all directions, roaring out like a tidal wave and leaving her in the epicentre of a massive pulse of energy. People fell like driftwood, swept away with it. Laurence caught the pipe-smoking woman as she tumbled past him, then wound up tangled in Doris's tentacles, while the faery crashed into the faun and they went down together, her wings half-crushed beneath them. Even the good boys went down, helpless as puppies.

Adams dropped her hands to the earth, digging them into the grass as if that could pin her in place, her whole body shaking with the effort of holding onto consciousness. The duck was so cold it seemed to be scorching her palm, and she reached out with her free hand, clawing over the grass and managing to close it on the staff, hoping maybe it would give her back some little bit of resistance. There was nothing, though. Nothing that could withstand the combined assault of both necklace and book. Not just the assault, the *theft.* She could feel them pulling power out of the fallen Folk, out of their charms and innate magic in order to strengthen themselves, and she wondered for one moment if this might be how it ended, all of them hollowed out into shells that would be slurped into the book and the stone, followed by the grass and the trees and Yorkshire and the *world,* all feeding their endless hunger.

She was almost convinced that was actually going to happen when the wash of power started to ease. She gasped, struggling for breath, and managed to lift her head to look at Lindsay. Lindsay stared back at her, her eyes wide, and Adams could see her arms shaking.

"Stop it," Adams tried to shout, but the words came out a rasp. "*Stop!*"

For a moment she thought Lindsay was listening, that she'd suddenly realised that she'd caught not a tiger by the tail, but a bloody Category 97 hurricane, as the surge dropped to nothing and Lindsay staggered, lowering the book and the necklace. She bent forward, elbows on her knees, gasping for breath, her shoulders heaving.

"Put them down," Adams said, curling her fingers around the staff. "They're not for you."

Lindsay didn't answer straight away, then she looked up. She was still panting as she straightened up stiffly, then walked toward Adams, each step unsteady. "They are," she said, and Adams could see burns running from the book up her wrist. She didn't seem to feel them, though, or notice the way the leather of the cover was wrapping over her fingers with a hungry intimacy.

Adams didn't move from her knees, just gripped the staff a little bit harder and let herself sag, allowing herself to look broken. Not that it was hard to do. It felt as though every last reserve of energy was being drained out of her, worse than jet lag that time she'd gone to the States, worse than the long nights of raging insomnia and nightmare-torn sleep brought on by cases that showed her the worst of humanity, cases that made her think she should just let the book scour the world clean. She was *fractured*, but through it all she could taste the Thames, copper and salt and old, cold magic, frozen under stars that watched the worst and best of all of them, humans and Folk alike, turning through years and decades and aeons.

And maybe it was the thought of that, the fact that there were so many terrible things, that people of all kinds *did* so many terrible things, but that just meant the rest of them had to do better, had to *try*, had to scream in the face of the worst of humanity and Folk and their shared nightmares, to make sure that hope persisted, however dirty and complicated and fragile it was. Maybe it was that which anchored her to the world, anchored her to the duck, anchored her *here*, in the raw and magical Yorkshire sunshine, anchored her to dragons and dandies as well as to long winter nights and darkness under bridges, and the way the creatures had turned away from her. And she'd been sorry when they had. She hadn't wanted to be the monster. But sometimes in order to protect, that was exactly what one had to become, and there was so much to protect here, so much beyond bridges. Maybe that was what held her against the onslaught of the book's nothingness, or maybe it was simply that she was really, really tired of people lying to her, or telling her half-truths that just made things more complicated, and she really needed a sodding triple-shot coffee and to arrest someone *right now,* preferably with a bit of a scuffle involved.

All of that or none of it, and in the end it didn't matter what it was, just that it worked.

Lindsay loomed over Adams, her perfect hair dishevelled, looking as if she were about to press the book straight into Adams' forehead, to crush her with it like a stray beetle. Adams didn't try to talk, didn't warn her, didn't even let the small adjustment of her position give her away. She simply fell sideways, and as she did she swung the staff up as hard as she could, slamming it into Lindsay's hands. The book crashed away from her, pages fluttering and bleeding old ink, and the necklace arced into the air, spinning over and over, the light catching it and shattering into rainbows. Lindsay sprawled to the ground, crying out some wordless, wrenching sound of loss.

Adams tried to roll to her feet, but her legs were shaky and weak, still unwilling to obey her. Lindsay was already up, running for the book first, and Adams couldn't get herself moving quick enough to intercept her. She tried, launching herself after the other woman in a clumsy tackle, but all that happened was she ended up sprawled on the ground in a different position. She shouted, an unformed yelp of protest, as Lindsay stooped, hands outstretched to scoop up the book, and Dandy hurtled past Adams, quick and light-footed on the grass. In one more bound he overtook Lindsay, and he snatched the book in his jaws just as her fingers went to close on it.

Lindsay gave a bewildered cry, then spun back to Adams. "Where did it go?" she demanded. "What did you *do?*"

Adams didn't answer straight away, just watched Dandy trotting back to her, the necklace hanging from his neck and the book firmly caught in his teeth. His snout was wrinkled and his ears were back, but his tail wagged softly. Then she smiled and climbed slowly to her feet. "Lindsay Marks, I'm arresting you for—"

Lindsay spun away, sprinting toward the gate, and Adams groaned, forcing herself into a run.

"Lindsay!"

Adams wouldn't have caught her but for Doris's tentacles. The effects of the attack were wearing off, and although no one looked like they'd be walking around any time soon, people were beginning to twitch and moan. Including the tentacles, which were flopping around anxiously, as if looking for a reason behind what had just happened. A couple uncurled in front of Lindsay and she tried to leap them, but they snapped after her like they'd sensed prey, catching her ankle. She went down hard, with a snarl of fury, and Adams pounced on her, forcing her onto her belly before she could recover and twisting her hands up behind her back.

"Thanks," she said to the tentacles, then had to tighten her grip on Lindsay as they tried to pull her toward Doris. Adams tried not to think why Doris might have hungry tentacles, and instead patted her pockets, looking for her handcuffs. She groaned again when she realised they were still on Carl, then noticed Laurence lying next to her. She commandeered his cravat and used it to secure Lindsay, then rocked back onto her heels.

"Stay put," she said.

"You can't do this," Lindsay said. "You have no idea what you're messing with."

"Eh. Not the first corrupt cop I've seen. First one I've been able to actually tie up, though. I quite like it."

Lindsay growled, a little animal sound, and Adams checked the cravat. It just had to hold for long enough for her to get some cuffs off James, or find a secure room if he didn't have his. She got up and looked around at the fallen bodies, some of whom were starting to move a little more purposefully, even if no one had managed to stand up yet. Dandy was watching her, the book still in his mouth, a long stream of drool descending from it. She beckoned him over and he tried to give the book to her. She shook her head and said, "No, hold onto it for a moment." His tail drooped, and she scratched him behind the ears, then went to find her backpack where she'd dropped it in the shed.

She tipped the Yorkie bars out of the bag, then held it open in front of Dandy. He looked at her, then let the book go, and she delicately took the necklace from his neck and put it in as well, then closed the bag. It felt infected, hot and far too alive, singing with promises that she could make things *better* if she just borrowed a little bit of power, if she just did this one thing, if she simply relented and held the book, just for a moment.

She shuddered, a whole-body judder, and dropped the bag. She didn't want to touch it. She didn't want that temptation, that idea that she could use it to *help.* It was insidious. But she couldn't just leave it here, either. She stared at the bag dubiously, like a poisonous snake she didn't know how to handle, and Dandy huffed. She looked at him, and he stared back for a moment, then delicately took one strap in his mouth and sat back.

"Really?" she asked him. "You don't mind?"

He shivered, and she understood. He did mind, but he'd do it anyway.

"You really are the best dog," she said, rubbing his head. "I'll buy you a coffee when we get back."

Dandy's ears went up, and he stood, trotting out of the shed into the sun with the bag swinging securely from his jaws. Adams collected the Yorkie bars and followed. Nothing made sense and reality had been upturned, but the world was yet whole and luminous and full of hope.

And that was more than enough.

25

SOMEONE BECOMES THIS ONE

ADAMS WALKED AMONG THE FALLEN FOLK AND HUMANS, distributing chunky chocolate bars. Everyone was coming around slowly, in various states of dishevelment, and whether it was simply the sugar hit or some mysterious property of Yorkie bars that never got advertised, the whole situation was quite calm. Adams had the vague impression of being in the aftermath of a particularly debauched garden party, everyone sobering up and making a silent pact to never talk about what had happened on the croquet lawn. She did wonder if other chocolate might share such restorative properties, but decided she wasn't going to take that risk. She'd stock up on more Yorkies as soon as she got back to town. Just in case.

Olly was one of the first to come round, sitting up with his thick ginger hair standing in all directions and bits of grass stuck to his cheek. He checked on Gladys, then started working his way around the rest, dispensing far more comfort than Adams was doing. When he reached Lindsay, still trussed up with the cravat, he looked at her for a moment then dug in his pockets and wordlessly handed Adams a handful of zip ties.

Adams looked at them, then at him and said, "Should I ask?"

"You could," Olly said. "But then I'd have to tell you the truth and it'd probably be awkward for everyone involved."

Adams nodded. "Fair enough. I don't really want to arrest you."

"That's a change," James said. He was still lying on the ground, and hadn't got as far as sitting up yet. "You normally want to arrest everyone."

"I've got plenty," Adams said, pointing at the three blue-shirted men. They probably would've been up by now, but what she strongly suspected was an actual troll of the non-online, fairy tale sort was sitting next to them. She was wearing a pretty floral maxi dress and had a hand on Blondie, another on his buddy, and a foot on the third man. The troll looked highly put out, and seemed to be under the direction of the tie-dyed woman, who kept patting her on one massive, knobbly knee and saying, "I know you've moved away from the confines of traditional troll behaviour, Mabel, but sometimes we need to access the more primal aspects of our nature in order to truly be the best versions of ourselves."

The troll huffed. "You talk rubbish, Gabby. This no best version, this *bad* version. I no like the breaking heads anymore."

"That's good," Adams said. "I'd really appreciate it if we could refrain from breaking heads."

The troll scowled at her, scrunching her three eyes suspiciously and exposing quite an astonishing array of broken teeth. "I no break heads. *I* no do brutality."

"Nice one," Adams said. More humans could follow that example. "Shall I tie this lot up?"

"Please," the troll said, with great dignity.

James got to his knees and crawled over to join Adams as she secured the men with more cable ties. He looked a little pale and wild-eyed, and he whispered, "Is it me or is there something wrong with these people?"

"I told you. Aftereffects of the drugs."

"There *weren't* any drugs," James said. "I know she didn't use an aerosol on us. Or if she did, where is it, and why are you okay?"

Adams got up, scratching her jaw. She did know someone who could deal with this sort of thing, pluck away inconvenient Folk-based memories, but unfortunately that someone was a cat and therefore not particularly available just to pick up the phone and call in for help. Plus he was irritating as all hell. She had an idea she was more of a dog person.

"Maybe it was the knock on the head."

"I didn't get knocked on the head. My head's fine."

"It's all right, dear," Gladys said, coming over to join them with Olly in tow. "I've a little something that'll help."

"I don't want a little something that will help," James said. "I want to know what's happening. Why is that person calling herself a troll? Why does that person over there have horns and *why does that person have wings?*" His voice was getting steadily louder with every question, and Adams wondered if she was going to have to slap him again.

Gladys just patted him on the shoulder and handed him a little plastic cup, the sort that comes on the top of an old-fashioned thermos flask. "Have a little tea," she said.

"But I don't *want* tea!"

"Drink the tea," Adams said. "Then go and sort out Meredith and the others. Let them know they're safe."

"*Are* they, though?" James asked, swigging from the cup automatically. "That woman has *tentacles!*"

"Rude," Doris said, petting her offended limbs.

Olly helped James to his feet and manoeuvred him toward the gate, beckoning to Scott to join them. Scott did, his shirt grass-stained and his hair dishevelled. Adams could hear Olly saying as they went, "Scott and I can find Meredith and the others. I bet the rest of the police will be here soon, James, so you should probably meet them. Show them where to go and so on."

"There's only one house," James said, sounding distinctly bewildered. "Where else would they go?"

Adams looked at Gladys. "What's in that tea?"

"A little forget-me-not," she said. "Or, no, not forget-me-not. The other way around. Forget-me-now? I do get a bit confused. This is why I get Olly to do that sort of thing. I was never set up to be a magic worker. My head doesn't work the right way for it."

"But all those years with Verity?"

"I loved her very much," Gladys said quietly. "And she loved me. But I think she loved that I *wasn't* magic, and didn't want to be."

Adams nodded. "I doubt that was the only reason."

Gladys gave her a sudden, luminous smile, so full of beauty that for a moment Adams almost forgot to be angry at her for proving, once again, that one couldn't go five feet in Yorkshire without tripping over ladies of a certain age poking their noses into her cases.

Someone tapped her on the shoulder, and she looked around to see that Laurence was standing in front of what appeared to be a delegation of Folk, all looking at her quizzically. "Yes?" she said.

"What happened here?" Laurence said.

"Well, I believe Lindsay was trying to get you all in one place, take your money, keep the necklace *and* the book when that turned up"—she gave Gladys a disapproving look—"then burn the lot of you in the shed and become some sort of all-powerful … something. I'm not clear on that bit. Kind of a gap in my knowledge, to be honest."

"Not *that,*" Laurence said. "*That* was quite self-explanatory."

"Was it?" Adams said, and he poked her in the shoulder hard enough to make her step back. "*Hey*. Hands off. I'm perfectly up for arresting someone else."

"You're *human*. You're not a magic worker or anything," Laurence said, and a murmur of agreement went up.

Adams scowled at him. "I know that," she snapped.

"Who *are* you?" Doris asked.

"DI Adams, West Yorkshire Police," she said, turning her scowl on the group as a whole. "Now, I can haul you all in as witnesses and ask you loads of awkward questions, or you can all make my life a hell of a lot easier and get out of here before my boss arrives."

No one said anything for a moment, then the faun said. "She speaks a lot of sense." He turned and headed for the gate at a pace that was very nearly a trot, his hair flowing majestically with his gait. As if everyone had just been waiting for someone else to make the first move there was an instant exodus after him.

The last to go was the woman in the tie-dyed trousers, who gave Adams a friendly pat on the shoulder as she passed. "Nice work," she said. "Like your style." Then she was gone as well.

Adams rubbed her forehead and looked at the three fallen bodyguards and Lindsay, all trussed up next to each other on the ground. Then she beckoned to Gladys, leading her out of earshot before she said, "I can't give you the necklace back."

Gladys sighed. "And I suppose you have my book as well."

"I do. But I don't think it's safe to return them. You may be able to resist them, but at some point someone's going to come looking. And what if Olly gets caught by them?" She couldn't quite explain that siren song, the promise and whisper of power, but she thought Gladys knew. Thought she was quite aware that what had started with a coffee machine and a TV was unlikely to end that way.

Gladys examined her for a long, still moment, and Adams could feel herself being evaluated. Finally the older woman walked away, picked up the staff, and brought it back, handing it to Adams. She raised her eyebrows, the wood warm and comforting under her fingertips.

"It suits you," Gladys said. "And I really do have everything I need. Just make sure that whatever you do with the rest, it stays safe. Verity would hate to see them misused."

Adams nodded. "I have somewhere safe."

"Good," Gladys said, and smiled at Olly as he came to join them. "So I suppose we say that Lindsay was trying to ransom the necklace back to me, and that's why we were here."

"Oh, excellent," Olly said. "I like that, Gladys." He grinned at Adams. "She has the most amazing imagination. We're going to write some mysteries together."

"Great," Adams said, and looked toward the road as she heard the wail of sirens approaching. She hoped the auction attendees had got off all right, but she had a feeling that, even if the police passed them, all they'd see was a bunch of ramblers collected around their cars, completely nondescript and entirely innocent.

DCI Temple was the first out of the cars, jogging toward them and waving James off as he tried to say something. He stopped in front of Adams, a tall, slope-shouldered man with a furiously balding head, and looked from Gladys and Olly to Lindsay and the three men sprawled on the ground, and pinched the bridge of his nose. "I did tell you to go home," he said.

"Yes," Adams agreed. "But if I had, we wouldn't have caught Lindsay."

"She'd have got away with *everything*," Gladys said, her eyes wide and her hands clutched dramatically to her chest, which Adams thought was overplaying things a bit. "She had me bring money, and she was going to bury us in the shed, or burn us alive, or … I just don't know. It was *terrible!*"

Adams looked at Temper and shrugged. "I thought I sniffed some accelerants in the shed." It wasn't entirely a lie. The shed had certainly had a whiff of *something*, and it could well have been magical accelerants of some sort.

"This is an *outrage*," Lindsay said, into the ground. "I had *nothing* to do with this. I think Adams' mental health issues need revisiting—"

"Shut up, Lindsay," Temper said. "Isha took a dive into your cases *and* your accounts – don't ask me how she got those, I'm just glad she's on our side – and she's been updating me on the way here. Always bloody suspected someone was up to some mischief, but could never quite pin it down. Got you now, though, don't we?" Lindsay didn't answer, and Temper looked at Adams. "Go on, then. Say it."

"What?"

"*It.*"

"I don't—"

"You're nicked, sunshine," he said, and started laughing.

Adams grimaced. "I've never said that in my life. I'm not living in the '70s."

"Bloody Londoners," he said, and wandered off, still chuckling to himself.

Adams shook her head, and looked for Dandy. He was ambling around with the bag dangling from his mouth. No one had given the slightest sign of seeing it, which seemed to be the way with anything Dandy was holding. She still had a lot of questions about why *she* could see him, but for now she was simply grateful that he could keep the damn thing safe. Not forever, of course. She had a plan, but it was going to necessitate a drive out to the deeper, wilder parts of the Dales, to places she wasn't even sure she could find, and some hanging around waiting for dragons.

DUSK WAS DRAWING DOWN, the short summer night setting the last of the day on fire at the edges, when Adams found herself leaning against an oak tree which stood in the centre of a small clearing, as if the old, deep woods that surrounded it had stepped back to give it a little space. The grass in the clearing was long and scattered carelessly with wildflowers, and Adams was wondering if every bird in the bloody place had taken up residence in the tree. She almost needed ear protection.

It wasn't exactly easy to get hold of dragons when you wanted them, even if they fell far too easily into her investigations when she *didn't* want them. She'd had to ask a fellow detective to find a talking cat, a discussion which had made her question both of their grips on reality, then the cat had to find her (and demand payment in fresh herring, which he swore was standard practice, but she had her doubts), then the cat had to contact the dragons, but even a cat couldn't just walk through the protections that wreathed the dragons' mount uninvited, so he'd had to hang around until he could find a dragon in the village and have a quiet word, all without alerting the ever-present and *far* too involved force of nature that was the Toot Hansell Women's Institute. It had all been quite complicated, according to the cat, who hadn't hesitated to air his grievances and demand some cod, having overdosed on herring.

And all through this Adams had been able to feel the weight of the book and the necklace, wedged in the bottom of her wardrobe and seeping its influence out into the world, like something festering behind the walls. It wasn't the threat of it in itself that she disliked, because the power in such things was always in the way they were used. It wasn't going to jump out and bite her. But the temptation kept her awake at night, her mind going back to it again and again like a tongue to a rotting tooth. It'd be so easy to start. To think, *well, this evidence doesn't quite fit, but it should, so I'll make it.*

Or, *this jury's being taken in by this woman's act, and she's going to get away with stealing the savings of a dozen pensioners. They'll be destitute. I'll make sure she confesses.*

Or, *I can't prove what this man did to his family, but I know he did it, so I'll just ... sort it.*

Yes, she could see how it started, and how easy it'd be to continue. And that was what kept her awake at night.

Things had all come together after the house, in one way or another. Between James drinking Gladys's tea, and the enchantments that had been put on Meredith, Kelvin, and Patrice, no one remembered anything of importance. It was generally assumed they'd all been drugged, affecting their memories. Scott hadn't had any tea, but he had been more than happy to give evidence about Lindsay's attack on the car and threats at the house without mentioning anything Folk-related. With no way to prove he was behind the Apple Store or Porsche incidents, he was going to wind up with a slap on the wrist and nothing else, but Adams felt that wasn't a terrible outcome. Gladys had already ordered him into some sort of unofficial community service on her part, which sounded like it was going to consist of him taking her to the theatre and fashion shows when Olly wasn't available. It seemed fair, really.

The auction attendees had slipped away as unnoticed as Adams had suspected, and Lindsay, for her part, never brought up anything about Folk. Adams had an idea that it would have been even more dangerous for her to turn on them than it would have been for the average criminal to turn on the rest of their gang. Unfortunately, that also meant Adams hadn't been able to find out anything more, either, and she'd have liked to. Because surely Lindsay hadn't stumbled into the world of Folk by accident, into her network of contacts and knowledge of charms. All these things Adams on the one hand didn't want to know, because that would be admitting she was sunk so deeply into this world that there was no climbing out, but on the other hand, she had a feeling she *needed* to know it. After all, she had an invisible bloody dog, a cat contact, a magical duck keyring, and now an excessive fondness for a wooden staff. It was currently living in the boot of her newly-repaired car along with three bulk boxes of Yorkie's chocolate bars, which had entirely bewildered James when he stumbled on them. She'd had to claim she'd bought them in order to support a charity, which he seemed quite dubious about.

Unlike Temper, who'd leaned into his car as the scene at the house was tidied up and had come back with a lukewarm coffee and a chocolate bar. Not a Yorkie, but a Lion. He'd handed both to Adams, rubbed the back of his head, and said, "Need to keep your blood sugar up."

Adams had looked at the chocolate, thinking it might just answer her question about the effectiveness of different brands, and said, "Why give me this case?"

"Told you. It fit your skill set."

"What skill set?"

He sighed, looking at the sky. "Just eat your chocolate,

Adams. This sort of thing brings me out in bloody hives." And he'd stalked off, leaving her thinking that there may have been more than official case notes that followed her up from London. More than the memory of bridges and the importance of ducks.

So yes, given that this was apparently *her skill set* now, it would've been handy to get some information out of Lindsay, at least so Adams could keep an eye out for whoever would inevitably fill the vacuum her removal from the police had left behind. Because such gaps never lasted. Someone *always* stepped up to fill them. It'd take some doing, though. Lindsay had been crooked for so long Adams was amazed she could even walk straight. The stuff that Isha had dug up, both from Lindsay's bank accounts (the ones that were official and the ones that were held under other names and other places), and more immediate things, like the amount of security footage and records missing from the evidence room, had actually been impressive in their scale. Lindsay had been dealing in human corruption long before she'd started into Folk ones.

Adams had been listening for the rush of heavy wings above the birdsong, but it was a shadow flashing over the ground that startled her out of her thoughts and told her she wasn't alone. She looked up, the sky above the clearing deep blue and clear, and the next moment a dragon filled it, wings arched and wide, the sun running off his deep green scales and setting the gold edges on fire. Adams' breath caught in her throat, some mix of primal, instinctive fear, and awe at the sheer wonder of a world that could contain such things.

The dragon landed lightly in the clearing in front of her, shaking his wings out and regarding her with warm, burnt amber eyes. He wasn't huge, only about the size of a Shetland pony, but the bulk of him dwarfed Dandy, who wagged his tail in greeting.

"Inspector," the dragon said. "How wonderful to see you!"

"Hi Beaufort," she said. "Nobody else knows I'm here, do they?"

"I have completely sneaked away," he said, with evident pride. "I've even shaken off Mortimer."

"And the W.I.?"

"Some things even the Toot Hansell Women's Institute have no need to know."

"Don't tell them that," she said, and he gave a warm purr of laughter.

Adams didn't consider not trusting him, not really. He might be annoyingly *interested* in everything – including far too many of her cases – but Beaufort Scales, High Lord of the Cloverly dragons, had been around since the days of knights, and she had a feeling that their supposed code of honour was a pretty flimsy one compared to a dragon's. Besides, if she trusted him with what she was about to, it meant she trusted him with anything.

She clicked her fingers at Dandy, who trotted up to her, bag swinging from his jaws. "I've got something that needs to be kept very safe."

Beaufort nodded. "I see you don't even like carrying it."

Adams had forgotten the dragons could see Dandy. "It feels safer with him, and I don't want anyone to see me with it."

"And you want it hidden."

"I never want it to see the light of day again," she said. "It's dangerous. A sorcerer's book, plus their necklace."

"Those are indeed very dangerous," Beaufort said. "And what of the sorcerer's house?"

"That's in safe enough hands, I think. Can't exactly drag that up here, anyway."

"Indeed. It will eventually fade, but once the magic is in the land, it endures."

She smiled, thinking that he endured in this land pretty well himself, then took the bag from Dandy and held it out to Beaufort.

The old dragon took it gingerly in one heavy paw, wrinkling his snout. "Yes, I can smell it."

"Can you keep it safe?"

"Yes. Dragons have many ways of concealing their hoards, and such things don't tempt us. It will be safe."

"Thank you," she said, her shoulders slumping with a wave of unexpected exhaustion that made the trek out here seem suddenly insultingly long.

"Thank *you,*" Beaufort replied. "Such things can't be left out in the world. We need those who will protect both Folk and humans from them."

Adams shifted slightly. "Well, that's not me. I just got caught up in it. It started as a normal case."

"No one just gets caught up in these things. If you were an ordinary detective, you would never have solved it. You wouldn't have been able to see through the layers of illusion to the truth, or comprehend it when you did."

Adams shrugged. "I just did what I had to do."

Beaufort sat back on his hindquarters and reached out to rest one big paw on her shoulder. Her knees just about buckled with the weight of it, but she returned his gaze as he regarded her with those old, cracked gold eyes and said, "The world always needs guardians, DI Adams. And though you've always known you were a guardian of the human world, it seems you have other duties too."

"I didn't ask for this," she said.

"No one ever does," Beaufort replied. "I didn't ask to be High Lord, yet here I am, eight hundred years later. I can no more stand down from it than I can turn my back on it. And neither can you."

They looked at each other for a long moment, then he

broke into an enormous, toothy smile. "I believe Miriam has made lemon drizzle cake," he said. "If you were to pop round there. Very rejuvenating, is lemon drizzle cake."

Adams grimaced. "Oh, bloody hell, no. The W.I. is the last thing I need right now."

He tipped his head. "As you wish." Then he turned, taking two great lumbering strides before he swept off the ground, transformed into pure, liquid grace, the bag still clutched in one talon. The setting sun slid off his scales, outlining him in light, and for a moment Adams could only watch, her heart full of a terrible, aching wonder at both the beauty and horror of it. That this was her world now, and there was no going back.

Then Dandy shoved his head into her leg, making her stagger, and she scratched him behind the ears as he leaned against her. They looked at each other, then she turned and started the long walk back to the car, Dandy leading the way through the hidden paths and secret ways that threaded the forest, intricate as tapestry.

She was driving, halfway back to the main road through a network of single-track lanes, before she got phone signal and hit call on the number on the display. It was answered after only a couple of rings.

"What now?" Isha asked. "It's after hours."

"I need a favour."

"Do you know how many favours I've done for you, Adams? I don't even believe in favours. They're a bad habit."

"One last one."

Isha groaned, but didn't protest.

Adams hesitated for a moment, then decided that sometimes one needed more than lemon drizzle cake, no matter how rejuvenating. "Know anywhere that does buffalo cauliflower as well as wings?"

There was a pause, and Adams could hear Isha's smile when she replied. "I can dig somewhere up."

"See you in an hour or so."

Adams hung up and settled back into her seat, guiding the car through the deepening shadows and rolling, stone-wrought fields of the Dales, Dandy panting in the passenger seat with his dreadlocks hanging in his eyes. She put one hand on his back and thought that, just maybe, if she could manage to keep one foot in the human world and hold it close, then she could survive having the other in the Folk one. Survive, and maybe more. And also that while it seemed she had little choice in the matter, she wasn't at all sure she'd change things even if she did. For there was as much beauty in one world as the other, just as there was as much horror, and hurt, and loss, and joy, and love in all its broken, glorious forms. Because people are just people, Folk and humans alike, and someone had to help. Someone had to hold back the worst so that the best and the ordinary and the beautifully, wonderfully strange could survive and thrive and work the magic that would never heal the broken parts of the world, but which made life among its scars so utterly necessary and desperately worthy of protection.

And at some point, *someone* had to become *this one.*

So this one drove on, armed with a very big stick, while the world turned onward and the stars looked down, and lives rose and fell and loved and broke, large and small alike, and the sheer beauty of it was as impossible as any magic.

Life always is.

THANK YOU

Lovely people, thank you so much for joining me on this latest excursion into the less well-traveled parts of Yorkshire, and for being willing to accept that koi ponds are dangerous and no one should trust small dusty shops in the hidden corners of the city. Not entirely, anyway.

This is, of course, not the last we shall see of DI Adams and the sporadically helpful Dandy. Their next tale is already brewing up, and will be with you in the second half of the year (that year specifically being 2024, just to be clear). Things are never calm for long when it comes to the magical Folk of Yorkshire, and Adams isn't standing for any nonsense, no matter how many tentacles or eyes people are sporting. It's not like a couple of extra limbs can stop her arresting them, after all …

I hope so much you've enjoyed finding out a little about what Adams' life is like outside of Toot Hansell and the complications of the Toot Hansell Women's Institute, and that you'll join me for the next case.

And until then, I have a small request …

If you did enjoy this book, I'd very much appreciate you taking the time to pop a review up at your favourite retailer or on Goodreads (or both, if you're feeling particularly generous …).

Reviews are to authors what caffeine is to detective inspectors and invisible dogs. Highly motivating, slightly addictive, and vital for the successful execution of our work. Plus, they're duck-level magic. More reviews mean more people see our books in online stores, meaning more people buy them, so giving us the ability to write more stories and send them back out to you, lovely readers. Less vicious circle, more happy story circle.

Plus it allows us to keep our chocolate supplies well stocked, and we all know that's *vital.*

Thank you again so much for reading. If you'd like to send me a copy of your review, duck-related theories, or anything else, drop me a message at kim@kmwatt.com. I'd love to hear from you!

Until next time,

Read on!

Kim

PLEASE MIND THE POND

Never trust the waterlilies ...

Sure, the necklace is gone, and the book has been removed for safekeeping.

But there's still the house, and, more to the point, the garden.

And they're feeling a little *restive* …

Gladys and Olly have a small and potentially deadly landscaping issue in this free short story download. Grab yours by scanning the QR code below, or heading to:
https://readerlinks.com/l/4044187/rm

THE KING OF ALL HANGOVERS

This beer festival's going off with a bang ...

A call from an old colleague has DI Adams off her patch

and out of her depth, investigating a mysterious new beer with unexpected side effects.

Deadly brewers. Super-powered DJs. Raging florists. There's a lot more than a hangover at stake.

But she's got her invisible dog, her trusty duck, and her really big stick. Plus she's just *dying* to arrest someone …

Scan the QR code or use the link to join Adams and Dandy on their latest, slightly sudsy adventure now!
https://readerlinks.com/l/4358382

ABOUT THE AUTHOR

Hello lovely person. I'm Kim, and in addition to the DI Adams tales I also write other funny, magical books that offer a little escape from the serious stuff in the world and hopefully leave you a wee bit happier than you were when you started. Because happiness, like friendship, matters.

I write about baking-obsessed reapers setting up baby ghoul petting cafes, and ladies of a certain age joining the Apocalypse on their Vespas. I write about friendship, and loyalty, and lifting each other up, and the importance of tea and cake.

But mostly I write about how wonderful people (of all species) can really be.

If you'd like to find out the latest on new books, learn about giveaways, discover extra reading, and more, jump on over to www.kmwatt.com and check everything out there.

Read on!

amazon.com/Kim-M-Watt/e/B07JMHRBMC
goodreads.com/kimmwatt
bookbub.com/authors/kim-m-watt
facebook.com/KimMWatt
instagram.com/kimmwatt
x.com/kimmwatt

ACKNOWLEDGMENTS

Lovely people, if you have made it this far, thank you so much for sticking with me, and for being so invested in discovering the hidden wilds of Yorkshire (and the poor dietary choices of detective inspectors). I mean, thank you even if you haven't made it this far, because who really reads the acknowledgments, and the book is more than enough to ask of you. But if you haven't read this far you won't see this, so …

I've said more than once that books do not exist in a vacuum. The writer doesn't whip it out of their imagination and bestow it upon the world, all neat and tidy-like.

No, a book is a joint effort. It may start in my strange and slightly murky little mind (please watch the swamps. There are things with teeth in there), but it finishes in yours. Without you, lovely reader, there would be no stories. So thank you for your patience, your support, and your belief in the power of ducks and chocolate. You are *astonishing*.

And to all the incredible people who have helped this book get from vague idea to *hello world*, thank you. None of this would be possible without you, either. Which includes (but is definitely not limited to):

My wonderful friends, online and off, who remind me to eat, get off the computer, and occasionally talk to actual people in real life so I remember how to do it. I love you all, even if I do not always love that social thing you keep telling me about.

My wonderful friend and editor Lynda, who accommodates my erratic schedule, finds all the characters who I've given the same name to (not Barry this time), and sympathises in the nicest way when I declare, like some deranged Dr Seuss character, that *I do not like this grammar rule, what is this thing, it's bad and new?* As always, all good grammar praise goes to Lynda, while all mistakes are mine. Find her at www.easyreaderediting.com for fantastic blogs on editing, grammar, and other writer-y stuff.

The fabulously supportive community of The Ripping Scribblers, who are a ridiculously talented group of very funny writers, and the best thing I've fallen into in the last twelve months.

The very talented Monika at Ampersand book design, who produces magical covers for panicked writers who've left everything to the last moment. Find her at www.ampersandbookcovers.com

You are all the best sort of magic. Thank you for being here. Thank you for being you.

Until next time!

Kim x

ALSO BY KIM M. WATT

The Gobbelino London, PI series

"This series is a wonderful combination of humor and suspense that won't let you stop until you've finished the book. Fair warning, don't plan on doing anything else until you're done ..."

– Goodreads reviewer

The Beaufort Scales Series (cozy mysteries with dragons)

"The addition of covert dragons to a cozy mystery is perfect ... and the dragons are as quirky and entertaining as the rest of the slightly eccentric residents of Toot Hansell."

– Goodreads reviewer

Short Story Collections

Oddly Enough: Tales of the Unordinary, Volume One

"The stories are quirky, charming, hilarious, and some are all of the above without a dud amongst the bunch ..."

– Goodreads reviewer

The Cat Did It

Of course the cat did it. Sneaky, snarky, and up to no good – that's the cats in this feline collection, which you can grab free by signing up to the newsletter. Just remember – if the cat winks, always wink back ...

The Tales of Beaufort Scales

Modern dragons are a little different these days. There's the barbecue fixation, for starters ... You'll get these tales free once you've signed up for the newsletter!

Need more stories?

Join the Ko-fi membership site for monthly, member-exclusive short stories, behind-the scenes content, early access to ebooks, and more!

Printed in Great Britain
by Amazon

57686290R00182